# THE VIKINGS

# The Vikings
## *Culture and Conquest*

Martin Arnold

Hambledon Continuum is an imprint of Continuum Books
Continuum UK, The Tower Building, 11 York Road, London SE1 7NX
Continuum US, 80 Maiden Lane, Suite 704, New York, NY 10038

*www.continuumbooks.com*

First published 2006

British Library Cataloguing-in-Publication Data
A catalogue record for this book is available from the British Library.

ISBN 1 85285 476 6




Typeset by Egan Reid Ltd, Auckland, New Zealand
Printed and bound by MPG Books Ltd, Cornwall

# Contents

# Illustrations

## Plates

*Between Pages 124 and 125*

# Maps and Text Illustrations

# Introduction

The period into which the Viking Age falls has long been known as the Dark Ages. In the late eighth century, when the fury of the Northmen first troubled their European neighbours, the darkness can seem impenetrable. In recent times, however, this assessment of the Dark Ages has become something of an anachronism. Over the last forty years in particular, the lights have been gradually switched on. Painstaking archaeological investigations backed by huge investment from national governments, and the steady accumulation of scholarship on European languages, etymology, microbiology, numismatics, onomastics, and even the occasional emergence of a new manuscript, have all contributed to a lightening of the Dark Ages and a clearer picture of the Vikings themselves.

The Vikings ranged not only across three centuries but also across three continents. Individual sites – including York or Dublin or Kiev – have produced enough information to fill several books of this size. To begin to consider in detail all that is known about early medieval Iceland or Viking voyages to North America or Scandinavian contact with Byzantium and the Caliphate would fill many large volumes.

Despite this, I am far from being the first person to try to give a coherent outline of what is known in a single volume, and I am as indebted to those who have attempted to do so before me as I am to those who have laboured in carefully plotted trenches or over obscure manuscripts. I hope, however, to have helped focus some of the new light that has been shed on the life and times of these remarkable but often amoral adventurers, whose gods in the first place inspired their belligerence and then, in the passage of time, faded into memory, as the adventurers became settlers among those of a different faith.

In studying this transformation, one senses that there is much to be learnt from the history of the Vikings, besides their turbulent history of raiding and conquest in the latter part of the first millennium. Fearsome and strange though the Vikings seemed to those who suffered at their hands, it is clear that they were also, like their victims, trying to get the best for themselves and their dependants in what were precarious times. It was not through violent assault that the Vikings made their most lasting impact, but rather through their adoption of tolerance and their use of the politics of diplomacy. By these they eventually found what they most wanted: a measure of security.

For Mike Williams –
*Han var víkingr mikill.*

# Acknowledgements

I am indebted to the Faculty of Arts and Social Sciences at the University of Hull; the Keith Donaldson and Brynmor Jones Libraries of the University of Hull, the Library of University College London, the Brotherton Library of the University of Leeds, the Rasmuson Library of the University of Alaska Fairbanks, and the British Library, London. I also thank Professor Tom Shippey of the University of St Louis, Missouri, Professor Rory McTurk of the University of Leeds, Dr Philip Cardew of London South Bank University, and Professor David Crouch of the University of Hull for giving me the benefit of their expertise. Particular thanks are due to Martin Sheppard, whose expertise as an editor has rescued me from embarrassment on many occasions and whose guidance has been invaluable. Mike Williams has provided me with excellent advice on numerous occasions regarding maritime technicalities; Peter and Fiona Norton have been supportive and helpful throughout, particularly in my search for Viking Age artefacts in the north of England; and Leah Aronow-Brown was more helpful than she realized during my stay in Alaska. My thanks go out to numerous friends for their support and, at times I am sure, their patience. Finally, I am eternally grateful to my family for putting up with my Viking obsessions, and in particular my wife, Maria, whose help I rely on in all that I try to do.

# 1

## The Viking Age

Images of the Vikings are among the most enduring in European history: the sinuous, pagan warrior at the fore of his dragon-prowed longship, on the one hand; rapists, slavers and pillagers, on the other. These are images that have resonated from medieval to modern times and there is more than an element of truth in both representations. Yet, too often, the popular view of the Vikings is romantically glossed. A great deal of this is a consequence of nineteenth- and twentieth-century formulations of Viking deeds and character. The Romantic revival in Europe and America in the nineteenth century invested the Vikings with honour and courage fit to rival the heroes of classical Greece and Rome, finding in them the qualities to inspire national myth-makers and builders of empires. Much of the source of this inspiration came from new and widespread scholarly research into the lore, languages and literature of the early Germanic period. What amounted to a rediscovery of the 'Old North' rapidly influenced literary and visual artists and composers, most notably, in this instance, Richard Wagner's operatic formulation of Nordic myth and legend, *Der Ring des Nibelungen*. Twentieth-century Hollywood stereotypes of the Viking, as well as fascist ideas of Germanic racial purity and authority, are both, in part, derived from this period.

Romantic imagizers were, and still are, largely uninterested in evaluating the merits of written sources concerning the Vikings. A lot of this material was set down by medieval historians and Icelandic saga writers centuries after the end of the Viking Age. The colourful stories these authors bequeathed invariably served contemporary political or ethnic agendas. Where the writer was Scandinavian, the Viking forebear was often presented as a heroic model, usually at the expense of Viking forebears from neighbouring Scandinavian countries. Those discomfited by Viking war bands in the British Isles and continental Europe were largely disregarded. Where the writer was not Scandinavian, it was the ultimate triumph of Christianity over pagan brutishness or the legitimacy of a ruling dynasty that directed the narrative. While these sources should not be dismissed out of hand, neither should they be relied upon without question.

The matter of reliability is, of course, most critical in the case of source material contemporary to the Viking Age. Accounts of Viking attacks were more often than not the inevitable responses of outraged victims. Anglo-Saxon, Irish and Frankish annalists were, unsurprisingly, profoundly critical of Viking marauders. The fact that at the outset of the Viking Age, in the late eighth century, Scandinavian raiders and invaders were not Christian served to exacerbate the fear and loathing of Christian commentators. 'From the fury of the Northmen, O Lord deliver us', the unwritten litany of anxious congregations, expresses both the bewilderment and impotence of the victimized, and their lack of confidence in the ability of temporal rulers to defend them. This does not mean, however, that their views and assessments were necessarily embellishments and distortions in the same way that later authors selectively interpreted Viking deeds. Indeed, there are marked consistencies in the contemporary accounts of differing, wholly independent commentators.

Modern historians are obliged to tread warily in the journey back through time. For some, this has meant that all written sources are to be regarded as dubious, that medieval histories are fictions and that accounts contemporary with events are, more often than not, gross exaggerations. The pendulum of fashion has, in the last forty years, swung away from romantic credulity toward sceptical dismissal. One consequence of doubting source material to excess is that the Vikings have been rehabilitated. Many books have been written stressing their extraordinary maritime genius, their poetry and decorative art, and their invigorating effects on European commerce. In these it is noted, not entirely without justification, that the Vikings were no more or less brutal than many Christians, and that rival Christians, for example in Ireland, could be equally sacrilegious toward each other's holy places. It is rightly pointed out that Scandinavian colonists were just as able to deal with their neighbours peaceably and constructively as anyone else and that, in time, Viking powers established all the trappings of civilized international politics, with diplomatic missions, treaties and negotiations rather than intimidation. And it is argued that, because the Vikings were in the first place illiterate pagans who targeted religious communities, desecrated Christian shrines and saw no value in the learned books they tore apart for their ornaments and precious metals, Christian commentators dehumanized them. Yet the reconstituted image of the Vikings, now presented in politically correct form in many school textbooks, fails to acknowledge the essential character of the Viking Age.

No amount of scepticism can diminish the underlying truth of what took place in Europe between the late eighth and mid eleventh centuries. The Viking Age was without doubt a period of extreme political turbulence, even by the standards of the day. Without warning, from beyond the northern fringes of Christendom, there emerged a force without precedent on the political scene, undaunted by the vested interests of kings and popes, ruthless in its military tactics and equipped to take advantage of feeble seaward defences. A brief overview of the main developments of the Viking Age from 793 to 1070 provides an insight into the scale and scope of the Viking onslaught.

The size of Viking armies (*here* in Old English; *lið* in Old Norse) is never at any point absolutely certain. Nevertheless, it is apparent that relatively small raiding parties, perhaps involving no more than a hundred or so men, carried out the initial raids. The first recorded Viking attacks of major significance were Norwegian assaults on monasteries in northern Britain: Lindisfarne in 793, Jarrow and Wearmouth in 794, and Iona in 795. These were followed by further assaults on monasteries near Dublin in 795. By the end of the century, Norwegian Vikings had expanded their range of operation to include the coast of Aquitaine. In 810, after sporadic raids since the late eighth century on the Franks, the Danes under King Godfred ravaged Frisia, heedless of Emperor Charlemagne's new defences. By 834, the Danes and Norwegians having greatly increasing their manpower, the raiding parties had become sizeable forces, often involving thousands of men, capable of doing great damage, as was the case when the Danes sacked the trading centre of Dorestad on the Rhine. Exacting tribute as a price for peace, temporary though it might be, became a lucrative source of revenue for Viking armies. According to the *Annals of St-Bertin*, substantial Danish attacks in Frankia became an annual event for forty years after 836.

The audacity and ambition of Viking raiders continued to increase over time. Early in the ninth century Viking armies were confident and brazen enough to pass the winter on islands such as Noirmoutier at the mouth of the Loire and Sheppey at the mouth of the Thames, ready to attack in the spring. By the middle of the ninth century, Danes were ubiquitous in lowland Britain, while Norwegians had set up permanent bases north east of Scotland on Orkney and Shetland. Elsewhere, Danes hastened the demise of the Carolingian Empire and ventured as far south as Spain and the Mediterranean to confront Muslim forces. In Eastern Europe, the Swedish Vikings known as the Rus had penetrated as far as the Black Sea and were exploring eastwards into the Caspian. In Ireland, Vikings established themselves on the site of modern Dublin and expanded their influence across the Irish Sea. The escalation of Viking activity in this first sixty to seventy years of the Viking Age entailed a movement from raids to full-scale attacks, from permanent or semi-permanent bases to the colonization of fringe areas. The last half of the ninth century saw tentative Viking colonization turn to full-scale occupancy. Such was the case in 865 when the so-called Great Army seized York in the north of England, having perhaps exhausted for the time being the possibilities in Frankia. By 870, well over half of England was under Danish control in what later became known as the Danelaw. On the Continent, during the early decades of the tenth century, Viking warlords had become permanent rulers in the area that became known as Normandy and had occupied Brittany.

From 930 to 980, there was a period of assimilation and a lull in large-scale Viking aggression in Western Europe. The early Viking invaders had become established as settlers who integrated with the native populations, developed urban centres and farmed the land they had seized. In England, the resistance of Alfred the Great of Wessex and the campaigns of his successors had succeeded in restricting Danish-controlled areas to territories north of the River Humber and, by the middle decades of the tenth century, had incorporated Danish set-tlers into a unified England. In eastern and southern Europe, Greek and Muslim forces had put up enough resistance to Viking aggressors to incur their respect, and in the Baltic regions and the Slavic territories, Swedish integration with the indigenous population had led to a fusion of Scandinavian and native identities. Significantly, many of the Viking colonists of this period adopted the Christian faith and were largely content to trade peaceably with their neighbours.

So it was, with matters largely settled in mainland Western Europe, that the Scandinavians once again turned their attention to Britain. From 980 to the mid eleventh century, newly powerful Scandinavian kings, whose dominions came increasingly to resemble the modern Scandinavian nations, particularly in the case of Norway and Denmark, brought vast fleets and armies to bear on England. Viking ambitions were not now satisfied by extortion and parcels of land but looked toward setting the entire country under Scandinavian rule. Olaf Tryggvason, later king of Norway, exacted huge tribute from the hapless Anglo-Saxon king Æthelred the Unready. Encouraged by Æthelred's generosity, more Vikings followed. By the first decade of the eleventh century, Viking armies rivalled each other for domination of England, almost in contempt of Anglo-Saxon authority, and in 1016 Cnut of Denmark was able to call himself king of England, Denmark and Norway.

The Viking Age ended, in a general sense, with the integration of Viking settlers on foreign soil and ever-increasing internal conflicts in the Scandinavian homelands. Specifically, it ended with the death of Harald Hardrada at Stamford Bridge in his failed bid for the English throne in 1066, and with the strategic withdrawal of Svein of Denmark from England in 1070 under pressure from William of Normandy, England's new French king. Surprise attack and sheer violence were, at the outset, the key to Viking successes and often produced victories in the face of powerful opposition. Footholds were gained throughout Western Europe and the fearsome reputation of the Vikings was enhanced to such an extent that those threatened with attack frequently preferred to negotiate peace at any price. But the opportunism of the Vikings, their readiness to exploit local political strife, their disdain for any resistance, and their initial contempt for the values of Christian and Muslim alike, meant that Viking aggression resulted not only in territorial and material gains but also in the destruction of cultures.

A case in point is the devastation of Anglo-Saxon intellectual life during the Viking occupancy of England in the ninth and tenth centuries. At the centre of intellectual life was monastic scholarship. Richly stocked with valuables, often located by the coast and forever vulnerable to attack, the monasteries were an obvious target for Viking raiders. It is clear that monastic life was in poor shape in the late ninth and early tenth century when reformers set about rectifying matters, but to what extent can the Vikings be blamed? Seeming to exonerate the Vikings is the evidence of charters dating from the early ninth century forcefully indicating that monastic decline in England had been in train for some time, irrespective of Viking attacks. Alfred the Great, the king of Wessex and vanquisher of the Danish-led Great Army in the late ninth century, noted as much. But seeming to implicate the Vikings is the annal for 870 in the Peterborough recension of the *Anglo-Saxon Chronicle*, which claims that the Danes 'did for all the monasteries to which they came' and that at Peterborough they 'burned and demolished, killed the abbot and monks and all that they found there, brought it about so that what was earlier very rich was as it were nothing'.[1]

Which, then, was it: Viking greed or Anglo-Saxon apathy? Again seeming to favour the Vikings, it has been argued that there are grounds to doubt the Peterborough evidence for, after 835, this type of entry is unique in the *Anglo-Saxon Chronicle*. What is more, this particular entry is a twelfth-century interpolation. In effect, it has been claimed, the report of 870 on what allegedly took place at Peterborough was little more than retrospective dynastic propaganda.[2] Maybe so, but this is also querulous to the point of misleading and we would be quite wrong to assume that Vikings suddenly avoided English monasteries when it was the monasteries that attracted them in the first place, and when Irish and Frankish chronicles are replete with entries detailing Viking sacrilege in exactly the same period. To dismiss Peterborough and then dismiss the likelihood of any Viking attacks on monasteries is to generalize from a particular. A further comment from Alfred the Great gives us exactly the right perspective, for Alfred not only recognized that monastic decline was an internally induced problem but also recalled 'how – before everything was ransacked and burned – the churches throughout England stood filled with treasures and books'.[3]

If the Vikings cannot wholly be blamed for monastic decline in England, neither should their contribution be dismissed. Where matters were ailing, as seems to have been the case with the English monasteries, the Vikings put them beyond recovery. Even in the rare instances of Vikings showing respect to monastic buildings, the libraries and scriptoria received no such courtesy. In truth, the destructive force that the Vikings brought to bear on monastic centres meant that almost two centuries of Anglo-Saxon learning simply vanished in areas under Viking control. Where there was a will there was a way of building new monasteries, repopulating deserted ones and stimulating new learning along with religious rigour. But burnt books were lost forever.

For at least the first 150 years of the Viking Age, the Vikings were wholly outside the sanctions and controls that other European kingdoms had institutionalized in the relationship between church and king. This meant that they were unconstrained. Doubtless many in Viking-Age Europe felt that the incidental benefits Vikings brought to European commerce might have been better achieved at far less cost. That the Vikings were sophisticated is beyond doubt, but that their sophistication was channelled into calculated greed and violence is equally beyond doubt. If Viking aggression did little more than hasten rather than cause the decline or breakdown of existing European systems of secular and religious control, this does not mean that the Viking Age was a positive period in European history. On the contrary, it was the very fact that Viking aggression, for whatever reasons, was set against the Christian infrastructure of Europe that made the Viking Age such a turbulent and destructive one.

It is certainly the case that among the unintended outcomes of the Viking Age was the union of the disparate kingdoms of England and prospects for

Anglo-Scottish union. Equally, the Norman aristocracy, descended as they were from Vikings, ultimately had a massive impact on the futures of England, France and Italy. But for those tens of thousands beleaguered by Viking attacks, displaced from their homelands or sold into slavery, the political outcomes or benefits were not either apparent or, if they were, not of uppermost importance. Of course, the energy of the Vikings in opening up new trade routes and discovering and colonizing new land is to be admired, but this needs to be balanced against the incalculable damage to the social structures and intellectual life of Europe in the last quarter of the first millennium.[4]

What was a Viking? The term itself is generally accepted as meaning a Scandinavian pirate, whether Norwegian, Swedish, Danish or Icelandic. A more precise definition, however, is elusive. In Old Norse, the language common to all Scandinavians in the early medieval period, the nouns *víking* and *víkingr* were used extensively. The main evidence for this is found in the numerous Icelandic sagas of the thirteenth and fourteenth centuries, where Old Norse persisted very much in its original form, but the terms were clearly current in the early twelfth century, as is testified in the Icelandic *Book of Settlements* (*Landnámabók*). In these sources, *víking* signifies 'a pirate raid' (or 'pirate raiding') and *víkingr* signifies one who goes on such a raid, typically a young man seeking fame and fortune from plunder. Further evidence for the use of *víkingr* among Scandinavians in the Viking Age is restricted to certain eleventh-century Swedish inscriptions that employ the pre-alphabetic indigenous script form known as runes, where it is given as a personal name, presumably one that reflected the occupation of the owner. Some have argued that the earliest use of *víkingr* meant 'a pirate from Víken' in the Oslofjord district of Norway, whilst others have seen the first element *vík* as meaning 'bay', and so signifying a broader designation. The Old Norse noun *víg*, meaning 'battle', has also been considered an appropriate root for the *vík* element, whereas other arguments have been set forth suggesting that *vík* could be cognate the Old Norse verb *víkja* meaning 'to turn aside', thus 'one who has left his homeland'. Indeed, the blurred semantic line between ideas of trade and piracy in the terms *víking* and *víkingr* accords with the seemingly capricious decisions of the same Viking war bands to indulge both these activities in turn. 'One who sailed out of Scandinavia in order to gain wealth by all necessary and available means' is probably the best way of summarizing what it meant to be a Viking.

Whatever its origin, the term 'Viking' became a common medieval description of a Scandinavian sailor who had little regard for the laws of property. In the nineteenth century, however, when the word was revived, it came to signify not so much a uniquely Scandinavian vocation but an ethnic identity. This extension of the meaning has irritated professional historians, many of whom find such phrases as 'a Viking settlement', where the settlement is comprised solely of inland farmers, to be a contradiction in terms. The preferred description, where Scandinavians are identified in colonies or as land armies with particular regional ambitions, is that which assigns them to their country of origin.

Whilst archaeology is helpful to an extent on this issue, particularly where coin finds can be associated with specific trading activities or specific Viking warlords, the contemporary written sources are less helpful. Apart from recognizing that the earliest raiders were exclusively Norwegians (*Norðmenn*), entries in the *Anglo-Saxon Chronicle* tend to describe all Scandinavians on English soil as Danish (*Dene*). This tendency reflects the fact that the predominant problems in England were the result of Danish incursions, and also that the first chronicle entries were written down almost a hundred years after the first raids. The Frankish chronicles are even less discriminatory and are inclined to designate all Scandinavian invaders simply as Northmen. Irish records are clearer in that they distinguish two types of foreigner: White Foreigners were Norwegians (*Finn Gaill*); Black Foreigners were Danes (*Dubb Gaill*). The Swedes, operating largely down the rivers of the Slavic territories, were known only as Rus, possibly meaning 'oarsmen' or 'rowers'. For the main part, victims of the Vikings were more concerned with castigating them than puzzling over their places of birth. Perhaps the Arabs of Spain captured the true feelings of those recording Viking depredations in their description of them as *al-Madjus*, generally meaning 'pagans' but more specifically 'incestuous fire-worshippers'.

The culture of piracy signified by the terms *víking* and *víkingr* goes some way toward illustrating a general Scandinavian disposition toward violent excursions overseas. But this disposition was not solely a phenomenon of the Viking Age. Whilst the ninth-century residents of north Lincolnshire or the Loire valley would most certainly have felt conscious of being in an age that might rightly be called Viking, Scandinavian freebooters in Viking armies probably saw it as an extension and a refinement of what their ancestors had been doing for generations. The question is not so much why the Vikings brought havoc to Europe as why the Viking Age happened when it did.

Despite the fact that Scandinavia was geographically and culturally on the edge of Europe, there was significant pre-Viking Age precedence for Scandinavian forays into southern Europe. According to the fifth-century Spanish historian Orosius, two Germanic tribes from northern Jutland, the Teutones and the Cimbri, were harassing and occasionally defeating Roman armies in Gaul, Spain and Northern Italy as early as the first century BC. A general movement south, perhaps motivated by a worsening climate in the north, soon gave the Scandinavians, or the residents of 'the great island Scandza', as it was thought to be, a reputation for being warlike and implacable. The relocation of whole tribes into Central Europe, such as the originally Swedish Goths, rapidly drew the attention of Roman emperors including Augustus and Nero, who were enthusiastic about the trading opportunities with the north. In AD 100 the Roman historian and ethnographer Tacitus identified the Swedes of Uppland as masterful seafarers employing crafts with a prow at both ends. By AD 200 significant trade routes, perhaps brokered by the Goths, were operating north from the Rhine to the Black Sea through four main channels. Archaeological finds across southern Scandinavia and in Rome testify to the mutual benefits of new trading opportunities. Indeed, in certain areas, the traditional cremation practices of the Scandinavian tribes seem to have given way to the Roman practice of richly furnished inhumations. Throughout the Roman period, silver and gold found their way north, while skins, furs, amber, sea-ivory and, notably, slaves were transported south to the imperium.

What took place in Scandinavia between the second and sixth centuries is little known, but thereafter it is clear that Scandinavians were prospering and becoming increasingly mobile. The gradual diminution of Roman authority in Central Europe from the fourth century, and its eventual collapse in the sixth century, was marked by barbarian tribes flowing from all directions into the power vacuum, even as far south as Rome itself. The participation of Scandinavian tribes in this great reordering is undoubted. Known as the *Völkerwanderung*, or Age of Migrations, much of the legendary material that inspired Viking culture is drawn from this period, perhaps the most notable being the conflict between Burgundians and Huns across the Rhine symbolized in the Old Norse poems and sagas concerning the Rhinegold. But Roman departure and barbarian wars did not disrupt established trade for long, and the sixth-century historians Jordanes and Procopius both pay serious attention to identifying the distinguishing features of respective Scandinavian tribes, noting their wealth and, more worryingly, the savagery of their customs.

The Old English epic poem *Beowulf*, very possibly composed in the eighth century, supplies ample, historically attested, evidence of the bloody routine of internecine strife between Scandinavian tribes of the sixth century. It was in this period that the Danes first established themselves, displacing the Eruli, who, before returning to Scandinavian territories, had gained notoriety as the most brutal and warlike of the Germanic tribes. Procopius is uncompromising in his view of the Eruli, describing them as 'beastly and fanatical' and adding that 'no men in the world are less bound by convention or more unstable'.[5] By this time, also, the southern Scandinavian Angles and Jutes, in company with Saxons and Frisians, had headed west in large numbers across the North Sea to the English coast. Although these tribes first presented themselves as troublesome raiders in the late fourth and early fifth centuries, by the late sixth century they had established themselves as overlords in eastern and central England, leaving only the western fringes of the island under the rule of the Celtic Britons.

During the eighth century, Scandinavian exports were in such demand that flourishing trading centres across Western Europe became ever more devoted to the traffic back and forth from Scandinavia, perhaps the most notable of these being Dorestad on the western reaches of the Rhine. Archaeological finds at Dankirke in south Jutland and Helgö in Lake Mälar, Sweden, reveal an abundance of imported western goods, among which are many western European coins. Previously minor ports on the coastal fringes across southern Scandinavia rapidly evolved into fortified urban trading centres at such places as Birka, Hedeby, Ribe and Truso, and on the River Volkhov east of the Baltic there emerged the centre at Staraja Ladoga which serviced the eastward adventures of the Swedish Rus. Yet with trade and prosperity came criminal opportunism. For every merchant plying his trade through the dangerous waters of the Kattegat – the ingress to the Baltic Sea – there was a pirate prepared to make his fortune from the chances afforded him. Defensive fortifications against jealous neighbours – most extensively the so-called Danevirke which spans south Jutland – and careful control of the passages through to the Baltic became essential. A localized Viking Age was already underway by the mid eighth century.

Coupled with this increasingly dangerous trading environment was the need for longer sea voyages and faster ships. Ocean-going craft powered by sail were not an innovation of the Vikings; indeed the Scandinavians may be regarded as having been rather slow to develop sail power in comparison with their contemporaries elsewhere in Europe. But the adoption of sail, added to their expansionist and adventurous tendencies, and perhaps to their inherent aggressiveness, meant that the Vikings exploited the potential of sail far more effectively than anyone before them. When exactly the first Scandinavian designed a sail for his shallow-draught rowing craft to create a proto-longship, and whether it was a pirate or a merchant, is not known, but it was probably early in the eighth century. In any case, there was often no clear distinction between traders and pirates. Many Vikings were undoubtedly both.

Increased trade in the eighth century brought the Scandinavians into contact with new southern trading partners. Swedish traffic with the Slavs was soon to draw them towards Bulgar and Khazar markets on the River Volga and so towards the Arabs trading northwards from the Caspian Sea. The Arab silver dirhems that the Swedes received for their wares encouraged them to pursue the markets further and further east in search of the source of Arab custom. Meanwhile, in the west, Norwegian and Danish merchantmen became aware of the riches of Christendom in Frankia and England. The Anglo-Saxons of Northumbria, indeed, were so familiar with Scandinavian traders before the outbreak of Viking hostilities that they mimicked their fashions and styled their hair in the Scandinavian way. From these trading ventures unscrupulous Vikings must have learned of the lamentable lack of security that attended the ports and monasteries to the south.

An adventurous disposition, a warlike mien, a history of migration and expansion, a blind spot as to the difference between trade and theft, a familiarity with the riches and comforts of the south, and a ship that could master long distances at high speed, this was the situation on the eve of the first Viking attacks on Western Europe. It has often been argued that the clue to understanding the origins of the Viking Age lies precisely in the evolution of the longship, and that what then took place should be seen as continuation of Dark Age practices that were given wider range and increased profitability.[6] It is an argument that has much to recommend it, but there were several other contributing factors that brought the tensions in Scandinavia to critical mass.

Two conjectures have been made about the situation in eighth-century Scandinavia as trade ripened and expanded. One is that it became necessary to have greater, more centralized controls in order to police mercantile activity and encourage trading partners. Impressed, no doubt, by political models in the south, powerful aristocratic Scandinavian families in each of the main regions began to move toward a monarchical model of government with something resembling national boundaries. This happened in Denmark by around 800 under Godfred. Even before this, a fortification such as the Danevirke, now dated to 737, must have involved considerable centralized control. The route to monarchic authority, or at least a uniquely Scandinavian version of it, was probably underway much earlier. The encounter in Jutland in 725 between the first missionary to Scandinavia, the Anglo-Saxon Bishop Willibrord, and King Angantyr suggests that Jutland, at least, was under royal control at this time. It was not until the 880s that Norway was finally united under Harald Finehair, but petty kings had been in existence in the Vestfold district since the turn of the century. In Sweden, from at least the late ninth century, the Svear and Götar occupied realms in the north and south of the country respectively but, as far as is known, it was not until the late tenth century that Olof Skötkonung could claim that he held Sweden under something resembling a unified, if temporary, kingdom.

In accordance with the traditions of Scandinavian society, many chieftains must have felt dispossessed of their ancient rights by such developments. Even where it led to no more than the emergence of rival petty kingdoms they would either have resisted them or sought to exercise their autonomy elsewhere. It is known from the example of the settlement of Iceland in the mid ninth century that one of the factors motivating the settlers who set out from the fjords of western Norway was their dislike of monarchical rule. Inevitably, too, where ambitious aristocrats contended for power, there were those who were disappointed. The losers who survived the power struggles looked elsewhere to gain prestige and wealth. Western Europe offered not only the opportunities to maintain a loyal following, and perhaps to return home with the resources to mount a convincing claim to the throne, but also the chance to establish a power centre outside Scandinavia on newly confiscated land. As had always been the case among the North Germanic tribes, the impulse to migrate was never far from the surface.

The other conjecture, one that goes back to the historian Dudo of Normandy in the early eleventh century, is that increased prosperity coincided in some regions with increased population and that, by the eighth century, a pressure on land was being felt. This was the explanation given by Jordanes in the sixth century to account for the southern migration of Scandinavian tribes. In addition, some have argued, there may have been a gender imbalance in the population. If women were in short supply, the male impulse to stray from home would have been given increased urgency.

A precise link between this and the origins of the Viking Age cannot, however, fully be proven, even though dissent among the populace and rivalry among monarchic contenders was clearly widespread. As regards population pressures and imbalances, there is very little in the way of archaeological evidence to support the view that these were unprecedented problems; indeed matters were probably worse in the sixth century than in the eighth. Land shortage may have been a problem but, as a motivating factor for the start of the Viking Age, it is unconvincing on its own. It should be borne in mind that, with the possible exception of the Faroe Isles, Scandinavian settlement on foreign soil did not fully get underway until approximately fifty years after the first attacks.

While these tensions in Scandinavia can be judged as possible contributions to Viking expansion, a more dramatic development on the southern borders of Denmark may have supplied another ingredient to Viking mercenary ambitions. In 771 Charlemagne became sole ruler of the Franks. Less than thirty years later he became Holy Roman Emperor with authority over the greatest empire seen in Western Europe since the time of the Romans. The Carolingian Empire can be credited with bringing a measure of security and stability to western Christendom. In order to achieve this new order, one of Charlemagne's earliest priorities was the subjugation and Christianization of the pagan Saxons who occupied the lands between him and the southern Danes. His methods were brutal. In 782, when the Saxons rebelled against his perceived tyranny, he took prisoner and allegedly executed 4500 of them at Verden in Saxony, so winning to himself the epithet 'butcher of the Saxons'.[7] While three years later the Saxon leader Widukind, said to be the sole survivor of the Verden bloodbath, accepted baptism from Charlemagne and became his loyal vassal, further campaigns against dissident Saxons continued throughout the emperor's reign.

With the Frankish realm now abutting southern Denmark, the Danes were surely not unaware of the threat that Christian evangelism of Charlemagne's kind posed, not only to their independence of government but also to their beliefs. In the first decade of the ninth century King Godfred of Denmark sought both to exclude the emperor by reinforcing the Danevirke and to offend him by harrying his western shores and exacting tribute from the undefended residents. Could the origin of the Viking Age have had its prompting in a retaliatory religious war? This is unlikely to be more than part of the answer, but the violation of Christian centres, characteristic of the early Viking Age, may well have been undertaken with added enthusiasm in the light of Charlemagne's treatment of Germanic pagans. The fact that iron production in Scandinavia significantly increased in the last decades of the eighth century may not only be a matter of an increasing population requiring more tools to cultivate more land, it may also be related to a perceived need for more weaponry and a readiness for confrontation with Christendom.

A distinction between the means available to Scandinavians to harass their southern neighbours in the late eighth century and the moment at which those means were put to use cannot be made. To see the Viking expansion as a continuation of normal Dark Age activity interprets the transition from relatively localized Viking operations to ones that would engulf much of Europe and beyond too smoothly. Maritime developments certainly provided the means, but what followed is best seen in the light of what modern military analysts call 'catastrophe theory', a cluster of otherwise unremarkable circumstances that coalesced to produce a major crisis. Among these circumstances, the development of trade and the centralization of power structures in Scandinavia perhaps offers the most likely explanation for the origins of the Viking Age. Antipathy toward Christendom and land pressures may have been additional spurs, but the sudden outbreak of violence from Scandinavia is best seen in terms of Viking culture. Aggression was a traditional means to profit and one, at the end of the eighth century, which was without either regulation or inhibition.

So it was in the 790s that the region that Jordanes had called the 'womb of nations' gave issue to a child of violence whom Christian Europe would come to think of as a fulfilment of the prophecies of the Book of Revelation. Indeed, there is one further theory for the origins of the Viking Age. This is the view taken by the first victims who saw Viking sacrilege as 'the wrath of God' visited on them for their sinfulness. As Alcuin, the learned Northumbrian cleric and adviser to Charlemagne in Aachen, lamented in 793 after the Viking devastation of the monastery of Lindisfarne: 'A terrifying judgement has begun at the house of God where rest some of the brightest lights of all Britain. What must we think of other places, when divine judgement has not spared this most holy place?'[8]

Although this was without doubt a sincerely held belief, the church also saw the opportunity to exert greater influence over certain rulers and their subjects whose moral standards fell short of what the church prescribed.

While written sources, both those contemporary with the Viking Age and those cited by medieval historians, are vital to our understanding of the period, modern historical method requires painstaking analysis and cross-referencing of this material. It is important to recognize the context of the various commentaries and commentators and to evaluate them in the light of archaeological evidence.

Medieval and pre-medieval historians and chroniclers were not bound by the same scruples and principles of scepticism as modern historians. History, in the sense in which it was conceived a thousand or more years ago, often sought to represent the 'truth' of the matter morally or symbolically rather than by facts; indeed facts were sometimes negotiable, depending on the overarching purpose of the history in question. Portents derived from natural phenomena, folk superstition and religious doctrine could all be made to serve the truth of an event. Yet whilst objectivity and impartiality were neither the method nor the point, legitimacy was. Accounts of Viking activity were more often than not commissioned by secular dynasties or Christian authorities whose aim was to reinforce their right and might, both morally and territorially.

Scandinavian written sources for the Viking Age can be distinguished from all others in one key respect. With the exceptions of the highly wrought, encomiastic poetry known as skaldic verse, some of which survived intact from the ninth century in oral tradition, and runic inscriptions, no Scandinavian literature is contemporary with the Viking Age. The simple reason for this is that literacy did not arrive in the Scandinavian regions until Christianity took hold there. Once the benefits of the Latin alphabet had been appreciated in Scandinavia, however, the outpouring of historical comment on the Viking Age far exceeded all other historical writings on the period. The chief centre for the production of literature concerning the Viking past was Iceland.

The earliest surviving Icelandic history is Ari Thorgilsson's early twelfth-century *Book of the Icelanders* (*Íslendingabók*). Written in Old Norse and based on oral traditions, this gives a brief account of the first settlers of Iceland, starting in the last decades of the ninth century. It appears to have been the basis for the more comprehensive *Book of Settlements* (*Landnámabók*), composed shortly afterwards, and perhaps for the *History of the Ancient Kings of Norway* (*Historia de antiquitate regum Norwagiensium*), completed in the penultimate decade of the twelfth century by the Norwegian monk Theodoricus Monachus. The Icelandic histories give a brief account of the Viking activities of early settlers, their genealogies and the conversion to Christianity in 1000, but more importantly they provided a model for historical writing in the country. A great many saga histories concerning the individual careers of kings and bishops were produced throughout the twelfth and thirteenth centuries, but the widely acknowledged acme of Icelandic historical writing was the *Heimskringla* (literally meaning 'the world circle'). This history of the Norwegian kings, composed by Snorri Sturluson in about 1230, traces in considerable detail

Viking activity throughout Europe. Setting great store by skaldic verse and the reliability of 'men of excellent memory', Snorri's colourful account of Viking daring and their dramatic battles on sea and land was in many ways an attempt to construct a grandiose cultural heritage in which tradition rather than historical precision is the guide.

This revivification of the past took its literary form in the huge corpus of Icelandic sagas set down in the thirteenth and fourteenth centuries, in particular those known as the Icelandic Family Sagas. Written in a style that resembles modern realist fiction, but gradually giving way over time to medieval romance influences and an increasing element of fantasy, the Family Sagas focus mainly on the disputes of the early settlers, frequently setting these local problems against the background of wider European affairs, in particular the Viking exploits of Icelanders. Yet whilst the literary merit of the Icelandic sagas has rightly gained them a unique place in world literature, their historical interest is related more to the period in which they were written than the period they purport to record. Nevertheless, despite the fictionalizing tendencies of the sagas, much of the ethos of the Viking expansion can be gleaned from them. The domestic intrigues and political motives of Viking adventurers bound for Greenland and North America vividly bring to light the realities and hardships of long sea voyages and hostile terrain. Pagan ethics of loyalty, often coupled with the promise of profit, are also animated in sagas based around real historical personages, such as the adventures of the warrior poet Egil Skallagrimsson at the courts of King Eirik Bloodaxe in Norway and York during the mid tenth century. Similarly, dynastic sagas, such as those detailing the lives of the kings of Orkney, and sagas that concentrate on the careers of particular Viking war bands such as *The Saga of the Jomsvikings*, reveal something of the mentality and the motives of Viking colonists and raiders. If not all that the sagas relate can be relied upon, there is much that has a ring of authenticity.

Whilst Icelandic writings tended to concentrate on the bravura and intrigues of Icelanders, emphasizing the role of Icelanders in Norwegian history, but remaining ambivalent about Norway's long-standing ambitions to establish authority over Iceland, Danish histories were equally biased in favour of the Danes. The most comprehensive medieval history of Denmark is the *History of the Danes (Gesta Danorum)*, written in Latin by Saxo Grammaticus in approximately 1200, a work that either revises or wholly rejects previous efforts to locate the Danes in European history. Although a work of magnificent scope and contemporary learning, little store can be set by the exact details of Saxo's accounts of Danish royalty and their Viking exploits, and much of what Saxo has to say is chronologically confused or uncorroborated elsewhere. For example, Saxo's compelling account of the death of the fearsome, though historically questionable, Ragnar Hairy Breeches at the court of King Ælla in York, and the subsequent vengeance taken by his sons, is Saxo's explanation for the arrival of the Danish Great Army in England in 865. It is a splendid story but not history. Once again, it is oral tradition and chauvinist attitudes that are the chief sources.

Further insight into Scandinavia during the Viking Age comes inevitably from outsiders whose sympathy with Viking cultural traditions was understandably lacking. The earliest account is given in the largely hagiographic *Life of St Anskar* (*Vita Anskarii*). Written in the late ninth century by Rimbert, Anskar's successor as archbishop of Hamburg-Bremen, this tells of Anskar's two missions to Scandinavia earlier in the century and of his patronage by royal powers in both Denmark and Sweden. Although Anskar (d. 865) made little headway in converting the natives beyond building a church at Birka in southern Sweden, his biographer makes good use of Anskar's own writings, which unfortunately have not survived, and thus provides a valuable historical insight into Scandinavia at this time, particularly regarding trade. Underlying the *Life of St Anskar* are the wider politics of the northern church and the claims of Hamburg-Bremen in respect of the Scandinavians. Two hundred years later, at the end of the Viking Age, it was another archbishop of this powerful and ambitious see who turned his attention to the obstinate pagans of the north. Adam of Bremen's *Deeds of the Bishops of the Church of Hamburg* (*Gesta Hammaburgensis ecclesiae pontificum*) is a comprehensive account of Scandinavian and Baltic culture. It is enhanced by Adam's first-hand knowledge and the cooperation of the Danish king Svein Estrithson, whom Adam cites as his chief informant. Adam's disgust at, and disapproval of, Swedish paganism at the royal centre in Old Uppsala reveals as much about Christian ambitions in the region as it does about Swedish recidivism.

Two exceptional accounts of Scandinavia in the late ninth century are preserved alongside Alfred the Great's Old English translation of Orosius's fifth-century history of the decline of the Roman Empire. One, by Wulfstan, probably an Englishman, describes a sea voyage from the Danish trading centre of Hedeby to Truso in the Slavic regions, providing the earliest account of the customs of the Baltic peoples. The other is by Ohthere (Ottar in Old Norse), a merchant and farmer from Hálogaland in Norway who was welcomed at

Alfred's court. It is an account of his business trips gathering skins and ivory as tribute in Lapland and transporting them to the trading centres at Kaupang and Hedeby. As is often pointed out, Ohthere's unprejudiced account of far northern commerce is all the more remarkable in that it indicates that Anglo-Saxon rulers were quite able to distinguish a congenial Scandinavian merchant from a Viking marauder.

Although there is no body of Scandinavian literature contemporary with the Viking Age, the primitive script-form known as runes provides some valuable information about social structures and individuals, some of whom figure as heroes in Icelandic saga literature. Originally designed for carving on wood, perhaps for religious purposes involving ritual magic, early runic inscriptions make use of a twenty-four character alphabet, or *futhark*, which was reduced to a sixteen characters during the Viking Age. The extent to which runic literacy was widespread in Scandinavia is difficult to determine, as actual rune masters would have been few in number. It is probable that rune readers were chiefly people of status. Because of the limited number of phonemes that runes can express, and because each letter can carry conceptual as well as alphabetic significance, runes are notoriously difficult, and sometimes impossible, to decipher. Most runic inscriptions are extant as memorials on raised stones of which there are approximately 2500 scattered throughout the Viking world, chiefly in the homelands, or as marks of ownership decorating jewellery and other precious objects. Typical rune stones are little more than short statements saying who raised the stone, who it honours, and perhaps something about ancestry or surviving family. Sometimes the exploits of individuals from particular regions are added, such as those of Yngvar the Widefarer and his comrades on their journey from the Lake Mälar region of Sweden to the Arab caliphates, or *Serkland*, in the mid eleventh century:

> Tóla had this stone set up in memory of her son Haraldr, Yngvar's brother.

> Like men they went far to seek gold,
> And in the east they fed the eagle,
> Died in the south, in Serkland.

About thirty rune stones commemorate this event, giving us a fascinating insight into the sponsorship and constituency of a particular Viking war band. A few other rune stones are more fulsome, such as the Rök stone in Östergötland in Sweden on which a grieving father, Varin, has inscribed 750 individual characters commemorating the death of his son, Væmod. This tragedy is ennobled with poetic allusions to ancient legends. Inscriptions of this length and narrative quality are, however, extremely rare. For the main part, runes were the graffiti of the Viking Age, marking both the ephemeral concerns of the period and, by implication, something of its cultural values.

Further accounts contemporary with the Viking Age, or accounts reflecting, after the Viking Age, on the impact of Viking aggression, are all provided by victims or descendants of victims. In England, the chief source is the *Anglo-Saxon Chronicle*, which has survived in four recensions and seven manuscripts. The *Chronicle*, as we now have it, was originally compiled in Wessex at the behest of Alfred the Great in approximately 892. It mainly concerns events in the south of England, with a clear bias in favour of the Wessex kings. The *Chronicle* reconstructs English history from the fifth century and, except for certain lapses in the mid tenth century, was kept up to date from the late ninth century through to the Norman Conquest of 1066. Clearly, a degree of circumspection needs to be applied to entries for the reconstructed period, but entries from 865 onward are largely reliable and entries after 980, when the Viking onslaught was renewed, are of particular value.

A wholly different attitude to the Scandinavian invaders seems to have been taken by a chronicle composed in the north. Although this chronicle has not survived the passage of time, it was clearly a source of information for Simeon of Durham's twelfth-century history, and from Simeon's writings it is apparent that the common folk of northern England often favoured a Viking presence. This north–south divide in England explains something of the brutal attitude taken toward Scandophile northerners by William the Conqueror during the latter decades of the eleventh century. The irony, in this instance, is that William was a descendant of the infamous Viking chieftain Rollo, who founded the Norman dynasty in the early tenth century.

Supplementary commentary on England during the Viking Age can be gleaned from the letters of Alcuin at the outset of the violence in the late eighth and early ninth centuries, from Alfred the Great's biographer Asser during the latter half of the ninth century, and from Æthelweard's late tenth-century *Chronicle*. In all these, the respective religious and political convictions of the authors should be borne in mind. Two poems also shed some light on the English view of the Vikings. The *Chronicle* entry for 937 includes the poetic celebration the *Battle of Brunanburh*, which tells of King Athelstan's victory over a combined force of Vikings and Scots. Although clearly a landmark event

in the progress toward a unified England, it has not been possible to determine
exactly where this encounter took place. Transforming miserable military
defeat into heroic moral victory is the theme of the Old English poem *The
Battle of Maldon*, which movingly records the annihilation of English forces in
Essex in 991 by the invading 'wolves of war', possibly under the joint leadership
of a future king of Norway, Olaf Tryggvason, and the current Danish king,
Svein Forkbeard.[9]

Where the *Anglo-Saxon Chronicle* is either vague or doubtful for the
middle years of the ninth century, the Frankish annals supply many of the
missing details. The *Annals of St-Bertin*, a continuation of the *Frankish Royal
Annals*, are the best authority for the English situation between 844 and 861,
providing good quality information about events in wider Frankia from 835 to
882. Written by Prudentius, bishop of Troyes, up until 861, and thereafter by
Hincmar, bishop of Rheims, these annals are unlike the *Anglo-Saxon Chronicle*.
Ecclesiastical in character and as interested in the detailed affairs of state as
they are in troublesome Vikings, the *Annals of St-Bertin* have a worldly air
about them that the *Anglo-Saxon Chronicle*, almost exclusively concerned with
Viking enormities and the rise of the house of Wessex, lacks. There is even a
certain ironic detachment in, for example, the report given by Prudentius in
839 of a band of Swedish Vikings that arrived at the court of Frankish Emperor
Louis under the protection of the Byzantine Emperor Theophilus. Seemingly
these Swedes had found the homeward journey from Constantinople beset by
danger and had chosen to take the long way round in civilized company. One
can hardly help noting that this account is somewhat remote from the image
of the implacable Viking war band that is bewailed in English and Irish sources
and revered on Scandinavian monuments.

Numerous other Frankish annalists provide short regional accounts of
Viking raids on church property. Monks who fled before Viking raiders with
saint's bones were understandably aggrieved about Viking violence and offered
accounts of the country's suffering; for example, *The Life and Miracles of Saint
Philibert* (*Vie et miracles de Saint Philibert*), a mid ninth-century *translatio*
written by Ermentarius, a fugitive from the island monastery of Noirmoutier
at the mouth of the River Loire. There are also some poetic and high-flown
accounts of Viking ferocity, such as Abbo of Fleury's glorification of the
defenders of Paris in 885, but after the close of the *Annals of St-Bertin* reliable
sources are lacking. Among the most fanciful and dubious of the Frankish
sources is Dudo of St-Quentin's late tenth-century *On the Manners and Deeds*

of the First Norman Dukes (*De moribus et actis primorum Normanniae ducum*), which was revised and extended by the author in approximately 1030. Although a bewildering confusion of mythological traditions in its presentation of early Danish history, Dudo's account of the Viking foundation of the Norman dynasty and its succession is nevertheless unique and cannot wholly be ignored.

In Ireland, the *Annals of Ulster* provide the most reliable picture of the Viking Age's impact on the island. Although exclusively preserved in a fifteenth-century compilation of several independent sources, the *Annals of Ulster* are invaluable and can be proved to be authentic on linguistic grounds. They trace the complex politics of Viking Age Ireland, which entailed not only dissent between Viking factions but also numerous and often interminable internal quarrels. Additional information can be gleaned from the so-called *Annals of the Four Masters*, which draws on several different sources, including the *Annals of Ulster* and the *Three Fragments*. Unfortunately, the *Four Masters* is only extant in a seventeenth-century modernization of the sources, prohibiting a full evaluation of its authenticity. More help is gained from the *Annals of Innisfallen*, especially from 969, when the entries became more detailed.

In sharp contrast to the *Annals of Ulster* is the twelfth-century *The War of the Irish with the Foreigners* (*Cogadh Gaedhel re Gallaibh*). Written in the most excited and overwrought prose of the period, almost to the point of being comical to the modern ear, this propagandizing pseudo-history extrapolates from the *Annals of Ulster* and *Annals of Innisfallen* in order to lend prestige to the kings of Munster and their line from Brian Boru. Many wild distortions are admitted, including the story that Brian lost his life in gaining victory over the Vikings at the Battle of Clontarf in 1014. Whilst it is true that Brian died at Clontarf, and that Vikings were present at the battle, the reality was that this was a battle between Irish rivals with Vikings present on both sides as mercenaries. This caricature of the Vikings as oppressive colonialists vanquished by heroic native defiance has resurfaced in recent centuries to serve the cause of Irish nationalism.

Commentary on the exploits of Swedish Vikings, or Rus, in the south and east has three main sources of origin: Russia, Byzantium and the Arab world. The *Russian Primary Chronicle* is an early twelfth-century version of an eleventh-century compilation. Its chief preoccupation is with the ruling Kievan Ryurik dynasty, descendants of the semi-legendary ninth-century Viking Rurik. Much of what the chronicle has to say is fanciful or propaganda, and there is good reason to doubt its presentation of chronology. Some corroboration of the *Russian Primary Chronicle* is possible from Byzantine sources. These include the Rus–Byzantine treaty of 912, which mentions the Rus chieftain Oleg along with other names of Scandinavian origin, and a book on imperial administration written between 948 and 952 by the Byzantine Emperor Constantine Porphyrogenitus, in which the Scandinavian Rus are identified as key constituents of early Russian history. Further perspective is provided by Byzantine historians, whose accounts of encounters with the Rus often contrast sharply with the version of events given in the *Russian Primary Chronicle*.

The most useful commentary on the Rus is provided by the numerous Islamic writers of the period. Ibn Rusta's geographical survey (*c.* 903–13) benefits from the familiarity of the author with the Russo-Slav territories, and includes a detailed ethnographic study of the Rus from the Novgorod region, describing their appearance, their ferocity towards the Slavs, their trade and commerce, and their burial practices, including human sacrifice. The eyewitness observations of the Arab diplomat Ibn Fadlan in the early 920s, which happily have been preserved in the original, are just as valuable and certainly more dramatic. Confirming Ibn Rusta's information, Ibn Fadlan describes the ship-burial and cremation of a chieftain by a group of Rus merchants he encountered on the Volga, an event which involved ritual promiscuity and the eventual willing sacrifice of one of the chief's slave girls. Beyond this, Ibn Fadlan provides telling insights into the luxuries enjoyed by Rus royalty and into the particular fate of a band of Vikings in the Caspian in the early tenth century. Islamic writers are among the most readable and eloquent of all the sources for the Viking Age. Detached and intellectually curious, not unlike Roman commentators on the Germanic tribes in the second century AD, Islamic commentaries stand in sharp contrast to the anguished outbursts of their Christian contemporaries in the north.

Where written sources are doubtful or scant or late, as in Russia and Scandinavia, archaeological evidence is essential in building a more accurate picture of the Viking Age. The scientific study of the material remains of past human life and activities is, however, fraught with difficulties. For historians of the Viking Age one of the most valuable contributions modern archaeologists can make is in the determination of chronology. This is not always possible, of course, but when it is a distinction must be made between absolute chronology and relative chronology.

Absolute chronology is most reliable using dendrochronology or radio-carbon dating methods. While dendrochronology – the study of annual tree rings on surviving timber structures – can provide precise dates for timber constructions, as is the case with the Danevirke, radio-carbon dating operates within margins of error which may be as great as plus or minus a hundred years for the Viking Age. More often than not, using all available means, periodic dating rather than specific dating is the outcome of archaeological research. Relative chronology is commonly the case when contributory dating evidence, for example a dated coin, is not available. Some archaeological sites, such as urban centres, only reveal themselves in layers that indicate successive habitation over, perhaps, hundreds of years. Lower layers can, with confidence, be considered older than upper layers and, in respect of this stratigraphy, finds can be dated relative to each other. The same principle can be applied, for example, to the recovery of a brooch which bears similar stylistic features to another brooch found elsewhere. Comparisons of this kind can suggest that one style superseded another within a relative chronology. Where, however, a brooch is found with a datable coin in a burial chamber, dates can be suggested for its origins.

Added to the inherent difficulties and the need for caution in attaching firm dates to finds is the fact that treasure hunters and amateur enthusiasts have done irreparable damage to the study of chronology. A splendidly preserved and valuable artefact is always likely to attract widespread popular interest, but unless its exact location can be investigated it advances our understanding very little. Modern archaeological research is a rather less glamorous business than some of its finds might suggest and entails scrupulous attention to detail. An archaeologist is likely to be just as interested in the dark soil that surrounds what was once a posthole of a now vanished wooden dwelling as in objects of material value. Alongside the unscientific ransacking of sites is the all too common inhibition posed by subsequent building development. Here again, sites are invariably disturbed and, where there is current occupation, progress is inevitably stalled.

Among the most fertile sites for archaeologists are those of burials. Magnificent ship burial finds, such as the prestige longships, or *karves*, found at Oseberg and Gokstad, provide invaluable information about both Viking customs and technology, but grave chambers can be equally revealing. Inhumation had been a fashion among Scandinavian peoples during Roman times, but the tradition of cremation with grave goods had resumed long before the Viking Age. At the start of the Viking Age, perhaps as a result of cultural contacts with Christian communities to the south, inhumation was revived, along with the

non-Christian practice of interring valuables for the journey to the afterlife.
In such cases, the most richly furnished of which were the preserve of the
wealthy few and therefore not typical, grave goods can sometimes be located
within a fairly narrow span of time. Grave no. 581 from the grave field at Birka
in southern Sweden is a much-cited example of the way in which grave goods
can help clarify chronology. Along with the human remains are the remains
of two horses which, presumably, were slaughtered to accompany their master
into the afterlife, some weaponry and, significantly, a number of coins. Among
these is a silver Arab dirhem minted between 913 and 933, therefore providing
a *terminus a quo* for the inhumation. The fact that there are no English coins
from the last two decades of the tenth century, otherwise common in Swedish
finds, in either this grave or any of the numerous other grave and urban sites
at Birka, suggests that the *terminus ad quem* for the inhumation at grave no.
581 is 980. The burial also helps confirm that Birka was active by trading
with Arab regions during the tenth century and, given the absence of English
coinage, that the town was abandoned by 980, a date coinciding with the
exhaustion of silver in the Arab caliphate and the resumption of Viking attacks
on Britain.

Coin finds are particularly revealing in respect of Viking activities. As Viking
leaders did not start to issue their own coins until the late ninth century, the
practice of trading with weighted rings and ingots is one indicator of their
internal economic practices. Coins from the Arab regions, however, which
commonly carry a mint date, and from European kingdoms, had entered the
Scandinavian economies from trading activities that were current before the
start of the Viking Age proper. Coin hoards in graves and incidental stashes
range from a mere handful of coins to vast stockpiles. Outside Russia and the
nexus of trade with mineral-rich Muslim countries, the richest coin hoard
found to date is the 40 kilograms (80 lbs) of silver coin and bullion unearthed
at Cuerdale in Lancashire in 1840. Buried in a chest some time between 905 and
910, and perhaps intended to finance the reoccupation of Dublin, the 7000 coins
in the Cuerdale Hoard are predominantly issues from the Danish-controlled
areas of England and from Anglo-Saxon royal mints. The hoard also included,
however, about a thousand Frankish coins of various types, about fifty Kufic
dirhems, as well as some coins imitating this type, a few coins originating from
Scandinavia and a single Byzantine coin. Numismatists determined from this
and lesser finds throughout the Viking world a great deal about specific Viking
activities and even future intentions. The mere fact that the Cuerdale Hoard

existed also suggests a high level of military and economic organization among Viking war bands.

In effect, archaeological data can enhance, modify or even contradict what can be gleaned from written sources. Written sources can reveal something of the motivations of the Vikings and the changing reactions of their victims. Archaeology can provide evidence of a particular presence in a particular period and is also able to calculate successes, failures and shifts in custom among settlers and indigenous peoples. Both these resources, the manuscript and the artefact, should be regarded as complementary. Where archaeology and written sources are mutually corroborative it can be assumed that we have something approaching the truth of the matter.

# 2

# Society and Religion

Traditional Scandinavian society consisted of three, largely exclusive, classes: slaves, free farmers and the aristocracy. In Old Norse terminology the members of these three classes equated to the *þræll* (thrall), the *karl* (the common man) and the *jarl* (aristocrat or earl). Like much else in traditional Viking culture, this stratification is enshrined in the mythology of Norse paganism, notably, in this case, in 'The List of Rig' (*Rígsþula*). The date and origin of this poem are much debated but, given the poem's internal evidence, a reasonable conjecture is that it was composed in Denmark in the first half of the tenth century and has, therefore, a pre-Christian provenance. Whether or not this dating is accurate, the values it embodies are recognizably those of a world before, or at the outset of, the Viking expansion. The picture of Scandinavian society it presents is deeply conservative, in that it suggests a lack of, even the impossibility of, social mobility. This was, to a certain extent, an anachronism by the tenth century when many landowners and chieftains had acquired great wealth from piratical and mercantile activities or had prospered abroad as settlers. Although the poem reflects none of this, its presentation of a tripartite social structure provides us with an insight into the customs and moral assumptions of Scandinavian society.

The lay describes a journey through the land of humans by the Norse god Heimdall who, calling himself Rig ('king' in Old Irish), visits three homesteads and sires a son at each visit. These sons are the earliest ancestors of each of the three social classes; in this sense, Rig is the progenitor of the class system. The overall purpose of the poem is to endorse the actions and ambitions of kings and in so doing to confer upon them the authority of the gods. Both of the subordinate classes are seen as being fixed in their social positions, along with their tasks, their expectations and their lot in life. Rig's first visit is to the rude dwelling of Great-Grandfather and Great-Grandmother, who feed him 'coarse loaf' and 'boiled calf-meat' before taking him to their bed. In due course, Great-Grandmother gives birth to a baby 'dark as flax' whom they name Thrall.

> He began to grow and to thrive well;
> on his hands there was wrinkled skin,
> crooked knuckles,
> thick fingers, he had an ugly face,
> a crooked back, long heels.[1]

Thrall's work is 'to weave bast ropes to make baskets. Brushwood he carried home the whole day long'. Thrall takes to his bed the 'bandy-legged' Slavegirl and they produce a brood. Their sons are 'Weatherbeaten and Stableboy, Stout and Sticky, Rough, Badbreath, Stumpy, Fatty, Sluggard and Greyish, Lout and Longlegs', who 'put dung on fields, worked with swine, looked after goats, dug the turf'. Their daughters are 'Stumpina and Podgy, Bulgy-Calves and Bellows-Nose, Noisy and Bondwoman, Great-gabbler, Raggedy-Hips and Crane-Legs'.

Rig's next visit is to the busy farmstead of Grandfather and Grandmother. Following the same pattern as before, Grandmother duly gives birth to a boy 'red and rosy, with lively eyes; they called it Farmer'. The boy grows and 'tamed the oxen, worked the harrow, he built houses and threw up barns, made carts and drove the plough'. Farmer's bride is Daughter-in-Law and cheerfully they raise their children. Their boys are 'Man and Soldier, Lad, Thane and Smith, Broad, Yeoman, Boundbeard, Dweller, Boddi, Smoothbeard and Fellow', and their girls are 'Lady, Bride, Sensible, Wise, Speaker, Dame, Fanny, Wife, Shy, Sparky'.

Finally, Rig visits Father and Mother in their fine hall where the hospitality is lavish. The offspring this time is Lord: 'blond was his hair, bright his cheeks, piercing were his eyes like a young snake'. Lord's work is hunting with spear, lance and arrow, riding to hounds, swimming and swordplay. Rig takes Lord under his personal tuition and schools him in the esoteric art of rune-craft and in the ways of war 'and told him … to get ancestral property, a long-established settlement'. Lord prospers and soon takes as his bride the high-born maiden Erna,[2] 'the slender-fingered girl, radiant and wise'. They 'loved one another, raised a clan'.

> Son was the eldest and Child the second,
> Baby and Noble, Heir and Offspring,
> Descendant and Kinsman – they played together –
> Sonny and Lad – at swimming and chequers –
> Lineage one was called, Kon[3] was the youngest.

It is Kon the Young, whose name is a pun on the Old Norse word *konungr* meaning 'king', who is the favoured one. Only he can carve runes, perform magic and master the language of birds. The poem ends with Kon being urged by a wise crow to conquer the lands of Denmark.

With the exception of Kon the Young, who has to be educated to the highest level before he can appreciate either his potential or the expectations that are made of him, all others are defined in their social positions, as typified by their names. Slaves are perceived as physically and morally degenerate, farmers as industrious and robust, and aristocrats as athletic, warlike and, one notices, exclusively male. Noticeable, too, in the poem's hierarchical power structures, are the sharply defined gender roles and the essentially patriarchal nature of each of the three classes. None of this is surprising, for the poem speaks from the point of view of the male establishment. Even so, while the poem expresses only what might be expected of a ruling order, much of its detail about social conditions is supported by literary and archaeological evidence, particularly in respect of slavery.

Slavery was fundamental to the economy of the Viking Age. As 'The List of Rig' indicates, slaves functioned to bolster the security and comforts of the land-owning classes. Slaves were a vital aspect of agricultural and household work but they also served as mass labour on building projects, such as bridges and fortifications, and in shipbuilding. Yet the private ownership of slaves, who all had to be fed and housed, presupposes a degree of prosperity. An important source of the wealth that underpinned Scandinavian society during the Viking Age was the Vikings' exploitation of the seemingly insatiable appetite of foreign markets for slaves. One of the chief customers for slaves was the Arabs. The vast profits that could be made from this market allowed Viking traders in the Slavic regions to enjoy a sybaritic life with all the attendant moral turpitude. Ibn Fadlan, an Arab diplomat who witnessed the Viking Rus during his visit to the Bulgars on the Volga in 921–22, described the scene at the court of the Rus king:

> Each has a female slave who serves him, washes his head, and prepares all that he eats and drinks, and he also has another female slave with whom he sleeps. These four hundred men sit about the king's throne, which is immense and encrusted with fine precious stones. With him on the throne sit forty female slaves destined for his bed. Occasionally he has intercourse with one of them in the presence of the companions of whom we have spoken, without coming down from the throne.[4]

Merchant slavers were similarly prone to gratify their lust in front of clients, and slave girls were commonly used as 'comforts' by Vikings on long voyages.

Although Ibn Fadlan was shocked over the public sexual abuse of the slaves, as a devout Muslim, accustomed to cleansing himself five times a day before prayer, he was also appalled by the lack of hygiene among Vikings: 'They are the filthiest of God's creatures. They have no modesty in defecation and urination, nor do they wash after pollution from orgasm, nor do they wash their hands after eating. They are thus like wild asses.'[5]

By law, slaves were defined as property with which the owner could do as he or she wished; until Christian law prevailed, this included killing them. Aside from deaths resulting from the petulance and habitual cruelty of some owners, which are amply described in the Icelandic sagas, evidence for slave killings is to be found in pagan funerary rites. Male and female slaves, most commonly female, were often murdered ritualistically to accompany their masters or mistresses to the afterlife. A number of owner–slave burials have been unearthed, including same-sex burials, such as in the tenth-century grave from Stengarde, Langeland, Denmark, which contained two male figures, one of whom has had his feet tied together and has been decapitated. Ibn Fadlan provides a grimly detailed account of a Viking ship cremation among the Rus that entailed the suttee of one of the chieftain's slave girls.

> When a great person dies, the people of his family ask his young women and men slaves, 'Who among you will die with him?' One answers, 'I'. Once he or she has said that, the thing is obligatory; there is no backing out of it. Usually it is the girl slaves who do this [volunteer].[6]

As the cremation drew near, the slave girl 'went here and there into each of their tents, and the master of each tent had sexual intercourse with her and said, "Tell your lord I have done this out of love for him"'. Then followed a ritual in which a hen was killed and the girl was raised three times above a wooden frame, declaring on each occasion her vision of her ancestors and her dead master in the afterlife.

> Then men came with shields and sticks. She was given a cup of *nabid* [an intoxicant]; she sang at taking it and drank. The interpreter told me that she in this fashion bade farewell to all her girl companions. Then she was given another cup; she took it and sang for a long time while the old woman incited her to drink up and go into the pavilion where her master lay. I saw that she was distracted; she wanted to enter the pavilion but put her head between it and the boat. Then the old woman seized her head and made her enter the pavilion and entered with her. Thereupon the men

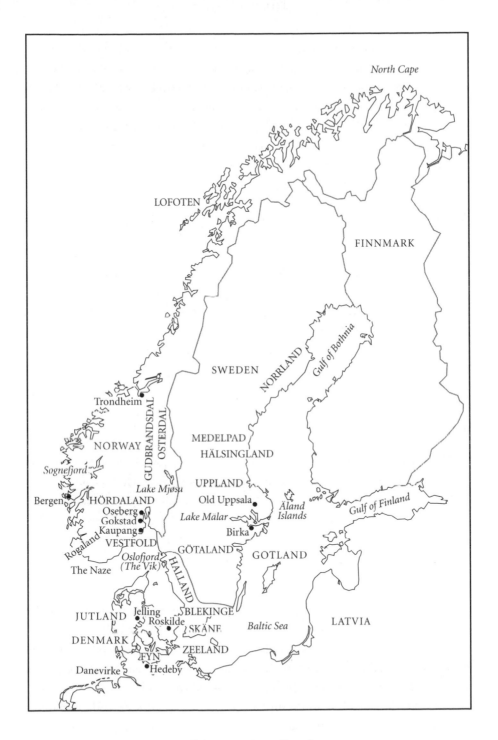

North Cape

LOFOTEN

FINNMARK

SWEDEN

NORRLAND

Gulf of Bothnia

Trondheim

GUDBRANDSDAL

OSTERDAL

MEDELPAD

HÄLSINGLAND

NORWAY

Sognefjord

Lake Mjøsa

UPPLAND

Bergen

HÖRDALAND

Old Uppsala

Åland
Islands

Gulf of Finland

Oseberg

Lake Mälar

Gokstad

Kaupang

Birka

Rogaland

VESTFOLD

GÖTALAND

GOTLAND

The Naze

Oslofjord
(The Vik)

HALLAND

JUTLAND

Jelling

BLEKINGE

Baltic Sea

LATVIA

Roskilde

SKÅNE

DENMARK

ZEELAND

FYN

Danevirke

Hedeby

Viking-age Scandinavia

began to strike with sticks on the shields so that her cries should not be heard and the
other slave girls would not be frightened and seek to escape death with their masters.
Then six men went into the pavilion and each had intercourse with the girl. Then
they laid her at the side of her master; two held her feet and two her hands; the old
woman known as the Angel of Death re-entered and looped a cord around her neck
and gave the crossed ends to the two men for them to pull. Then she approached
her with a broad-bladed dagger, which she plunged between her ribs repeatedly, and
the men strangled her with the cord until she was dead.[7]

The girl's body was then laid beside that of her master on the ship and
cremated.

Whilst it may well be wrong to extrapolate from Ibn Fadlan's account of the
Rus a common practice among Vikings, there is no doubt that slaves were a
stock currency of Viking traders and raiders. The more fortunate slaves, those,
for instance, who had particular skills or desirable attributes, were treated with
a degree of respect. Others who could command an immediate price by virtue
of their status in their home countries were sometimes ransomed. Vikings
would deliberately target monasteries for abductions, knowing that the church
would wish to redeem its own. Scandinavians themselves might to be forced
into thraldom, either because of debt or, as Adam of Bremen noted in 1075, by
ungovernable Viking raiders in the Baltic.

These pirates, called Vikings by the people of Zealand … pay tribute to the Danish
king for leave to plunder the barbarians who live around this sea in great numbers.
Hence it also happens that the licence granted them with respect to enemies is
frequently misused against their own people. So true is this that they have no faith
in one another, and as soon as one of them catches another, he mercilessly sells him
into slavery either to one of his fellows or to a barbarian.[8]

A degree of information about the Viking slave trade in Normandy can be
gleaned from an obscene Latin poem composed near the beginning of the
eleventh century by Warner of Rouen. It is a spiteful biography concerning
the enslavement of a misshapen Irishman named Moriuht, who on gaining his
freedom achieved minor celebrity as a grammarian and teacher at the courts
and monastic schools in Rouen, clearly provoking Warner's envy and contempt.
According to Warner, Moriuht's initial captivity involved rape and all manner
of sexual humiliation at the hands of Viking sailors who, having ruined him
for any other purpose, eventually sold him to the nunnery in Corbridge in

Northumbria for a mere three pence. Moriuht's bizarre sexual adventures continued among the nuns and led to his expulsion and thence his recapture by Vikings, whereupon he was again sold for a pittance to a widow in Saxony who required him as a sex slave. His indiscriminate sexual incontinence brought fear to the neighbourhood and, in order to be rid of him, he was granted his freedom. He traced his wife to Rouen where a countess helped him to buy her and his child. Thereafter, he set himself up as a poet and *grammaticus.*[9]

This crude, fictional invective in high classical style is intended more to ridicule Moriuht than to expose the horrors of the Viking slave trade, but the hard facts of slavery, including the contempt in which slaves were held by their captors and the traffic of human cargo across the Viking world, all have the ring of truth about them. The poem is equally interesting in its presentation of the culture of late tenth-century Normandy, where the aristocracy was keen to distance itself from its Viking pagan past and model itself on the more courtly ways of the Christian Franks. Yet the tradition of sexual insult poetry that Warner draws upon was also deeply embedded in Scandinavian tradition and would have been recognized and appreciated as such. Nor had the Viking slave trade become a thing of the past in Normandy, its ports remaining uncomfortably busy with slavers en route from Britain and Ireland to slave markets across Europe. Amid this ambivalence, Warner of Rouen, himself a Norman *grammaticus* attached to a monastic centre, seems to have absorbed as much of the culture of the barbaric north as the Norman aristocrats had of the Christian south.

Not all slaves were treated as inhumanely as Moriuht or the Rus chieftain's slave girl. Scandinavian law allowed for slave owners to set their slaves free or to declare their children by female slaves to be free. In some cases slaves worked to buy their own freedom or were emancipated after several generations of enslavement. At Hørning in North Jutland a runic monument from the year 1000 declares that Toki the Smith carved this stone for Thorkil Guthmundsson 'who gave him gold and freedom'. Toki's gracious monument is, however, unique and his good fortune almost certainly very rare.

The Christian conversion of Scandinavia in the tenth and eleventh centuries set some limitation on the Viking slave trade. While the church did not explicitly ban slavery, and indeed as late as the early thirteenth century the bishop of Lund owned slaves, it disapproved of the enslavement of Christians, particularly to pagans, and regarded manumission generally as charitable and godly. Other factors, apart from church disapproval, also began to have an impact on slaving from the eleventh century. Rising population levels in Scandinavia meant that paid labour was cheaper and more plentiful, therefore reducing the profit margins that slavery provided. The slave trade with the Arab caliphate also rapidly declined toward the end of the tenth century once its silver mines were exhausted. Added to this, slave taxes and legal responsibilities in respect of slaves came into force that proved burdensome for owners. By the twelfth century, slavery had been abolished in all Scandinavian countries except Sweden, which did not finally enact abolition until the fourteenth century.

Slaves were the static class of the Viking Age, but many farmers extended their influence among the aristocracy during the Viking Age and transcended traditional feudal constraints. This led to a concentration of power in the upper echelons of society that ran parallel with the centralization of political authority among the aristocracy and the move toward monarchical government and nation states. For those, such as tenant farmers and leaseholders, unable to benefit from upward mobility, the key distinction between themselves and slaves was their rights under law as freemen. The free were primarily denoted by their entitlement to representation at the local Thing, the legislative assembly. The free included landowners both great and small, tenants and leaseholders, servants and labourers, and members of the professional classes such as warriors, and, of course, the chieftain aristocracy whose role at assemblies was as the judiciary. All these were able to express their opinions at the Thing, albeit that good sense and judgement were necessary to avoid offending powerful families whose antipathy could be damaging and not necessarily conducted legally.

While the Vikings brought devastation abroad, at home they invested considerable effort in establishing justice in their own communities. Scandinavian law was not codified until after the Viking Age, the simple reason being that literacy did not arrive in Scandinavia until after the conversion in the tenth and eleventh centuries. Nonetheless, codified laws of the early middle ages were based on well-established principles. In Denmark the law codes were mainly derived from royal decrees, for example those of Cnut the Great (d. 1035) for the regulation of his armies, and Cnut II who was killed in an uprising in 1086, when his army rejected his legislative authority. In Norway, most of which had been temporarily unified in the late ninth century during the reign of Harald Finehair (d. c. 930), and, later, in Iceland, where the law was modelled on Norwegian principles but where no king was tolerated, the law was centred on the interests and problems of differing communities. Individual regions, such as the four provinces of Norway, each had their own legal assemblies

case precedent. In Iceland, a national
and received cases that had not been
. The situation in Sweden was rather
bally divided. Regional assemblies in
ratify or even dismiss the laws of kings.
n municipal laws, for example the busy
Bjarkey which introduced the *Bjarkeyar*
imitated by a number of towns across

the highest ideals. Icelandic law, about
agas and which was republican in spirit,
had established the principle of equality before the law as early as 930, slaves
excepted. One major shortcoming in Iceland was the absence of any independent
law enforcement, whereas the spread of royal power in other Scandinavian
countries involved greater enforcement. But without royal judgement, which
would have been impossible to enact in all cases, and without any 'police force',
the responsibility for enforcement often fell to the litigants. As a result, the more
powerful were able to behave contemptuously in respect of any judgement that
favoured someone of lesser influence than themselves. In order to avoid such
an outcome, plaintiffs of inferior status needed to ensure the patronage of a
chieftain beforehand.

Punishments for crimes varied between the different legal assemblies and in
mainland Scandinavia high status could, in itself, be regarded as a mitigating
factor. In general terms, many cases were resolved by the payment of compensation to the victim or his family. Compensation could be made for crimes
ranging from trespass to unlawful killing, and it is telling about Scandinavian
cultural values that it was usually only theft that incurred the ultimate sanction
of the death penalty, typically by hanging, although no such provision existed
in Iceland. Refusal to accept judgement or pay compensation was regarded as
extremely serious and resulted in a second judgement, where outlawry was
pronounced. According to the Icelandic law codes Grey Goose (*Grágás*), two
types of outlawry were imposed. A 'lesser' outlaw might be expelled from the
community for three years and obliged to find passage out of the country,
but the more serious form of 'full' outlawry entailed complete and lifelong
ostracism, and any attempt to assist such a man could itself result in outlawry.
All outlaws were subject to having their property confiscated and any man was
entitled to kill a full outlaw on sight without legal redress.

Women had little say in the operation of the law, save that of lobbying. Female roles were, by and large, predictable. For the main part, women conducted the domestic business of the farms, such as weaving, spinning, cooking, baking and making dairy products. They also carried the main responsibility for the raising of children and for nursing the sick. When men were away on voyages or at war, it fell to women to maintain the home front, including all aspects of animal husbandry and tillage. Women of high status were responsible for the running of estates, dealing with servants and supervising the rounds of feast days. Rune stones testify to the gratitude of some husbands to their wives; for example, this obituary inscription from Västmanland, Sweden:

The good farmer Holmgaut had this raised in memory of his wife Odindis.

A better housewife
will never come
to Hassmyra
to run the farm.
Red Balli carved
these runes.
She was a good sister
to Sigmund.

As wives, such women started out with both their dowries and their 'bride-price', a sum of money paid by their husbands, and had as a consequence a degree of independence. Wives also had the right to divorce their husbands, and simply by asserting their intention in front of witnesses they would automatically receive a share of their joint property. Grounds for divorce were numerous and included the right of a woman to disassociate herself from her spouse for wearing a low-cut shirt and therefore appearing effeminate.

There were, however, fundamental inequalities and men seem to have been able to take mistresses with impunity despite laws, for example in Denmark, which punished adultery by death. Doubtless unofficial male polygamy simply had to be tolerated. If not necessarily approved of, it was seen as inevitable. Male exploitation of female slaves was evidently common, but it is doubtful whether women were permitted the same licence with male slaves. Any comparable female promiscuity appears to have been so incredible an idea that it is scarcely even mentioned outside the context of tales about witches, troll women and succubae. There are no records of women operating as merchants or as members of a property-owning fellowship, or *félag*. Tales of amazonian female warriors, apart from those recorded in myth and legend, are unverifiable and unlikely, although women did sometimes accompany Viking armies and were present with their male relatives as migrants to new lands. There are, on the other hand, well-documented cases of women as heads of large and influential clans and as landowners. Aud the Deep-Minded was one such matriarch. Aud was accorded her own substantial entry in the Icelandic *Book of Settlements* and is lauded in the sagas as one of the noblest settlers in the west of Iceland. As a result of her shrewd judgement in marrying off her daughters and granddaughters, and her steadfastness in promoting the careers of her sons, Aud's descendants constituted one of the most powerful families in the country.

The ambivalent regard in which women were held can be measured to some extent by pagan burials. Inhumations of males with grave goods are three times more numerous than those of females, yet it is also apparent from the quality of the goods and the lavishness of the latter ceremonies that women's status increased with age, whereas men's declined. No doubt this applied only to women of high status, who enjoyed a greater life expectancy than did women of the servant classes. Ambivalence over the exercise of women's power can be seen in the Icelandic sagas. The 'strong' woman, who insisted on her rights of ownership, was fiercely loyal to her husband and kinfolk (although not always both) and disdained exploitative patronage, was much admired in the sagas. Yet women were also portrayed as wreckers of male solidarity through their wilfulness and sexual allure, sometimes shaming their husbands into impetuous acts of vengeance. In general, Scandinavian women's position in the Viking Age was better than most of their European counterparts, but their progress through life was rarely self-determined and was typically dependent on the success or otherwise of their menfolk, whether husband, father, brother or son.

The family was at the centre of Scandinavian society. Familial relations extended horizontally and vertically, across marriage ties and down through the generations. Loyalties and obligations were immediately due to the nearest kin, that is to say, spouses, parents, siblings and children. Wider family loyalties could be called upon in times of trouble, for example where a blood feud was in progress or when compensation for a crime had to be paid. Matters of family honour became more demanding the higher up the social scale one was, for pedigree and noble lineage counted almost as much as material assets. Crucial to the prosperity and cohesion of families, whether they were free farmer landowners or royal dynasties, was the matter of inheritance. The established principle was the *óðal* law, which effectively meant that the lion's

share of the inheritance went to the first-born male. This ensured that any
accrued wealth and property did not dissipate over the generations. It also
encouraged younger sons toward new enterprises. The chief beneficiary of
any inheritance was nonetheless obliged to pay compensation to his or her
siblings and to offer assistance to them in times of need. Needless to say, the
network of loyalties and the laws of inheritance could lead to deadly disputes.
Where disputes arose among royal families, whole regions could be plunged
into civil war, with brother against brother and father against son. Many of
the key figures in Viking adventures overseas were either from the ranks of the
dispossessed, fugitives or younger sons. The flow of money through inheritance
could also lead to extraordinary complexities. The following inscription carved
in serpentine swirls on a runic monument at Hillersjö, Sweden, describes
the unhappy convolutions that led to a woman named Geirlaug achieving a
measure of independent financial security as a result of inheriting from her
own daughter:

> Read these runes! Geirmund married Geirlaug, then a maiden. Later they had a son,
> before Geirmund was drowned; afterwards, the son died. Then she had Gudrik as
> husband … They then had children; of these only a girl lived; she was called Inga,
> and Rognvald of Snottsa had her to wife. Afterwards he died, and their son too, and
> the mother [Inga] inherited from her son. Inga afterwards had Eirik as husband.
> Then she died. Then Geirlaug came into this inheritance after her daughter Inga.
> The poet Thorbjorn carved these runes.

Extended family units living on farms might sometimes be as much as thirty
miles away from the nearest neighbour, but cooperation over land clearance
and animal husbandry, the ties that arose through marriage contracts and,
when and where necessary, the need for a collective approach to security gave
these disparate farmsteads a definite sense of belonging to a community. More
concentrated farming communities developed during the Viking Age in villages
and hamlets, and many established clusters of farms prospered and grew. The
fully excavated village of Vorbasse in Denmark has a history ranging from
the Iron Age through to the early middle ages. During this long period, the
village was relocated eight times within the same half square mile, probably to
exploit the land more effectively and certainly to upgrade the habitation. The
move which took place during the Viking Age, and which involved six separate
farmsteads, shows a marked and general improvement in resources. Steads

became halls, cattle byres were expanded and the largest farm supported twelve other buildings. The enhancement of Vorbasse, and many other villages like it, was directly related to Viking expansion. In all likelihood, young males of the village took whatever opportunities were on offer to join Viking raiding and trading parties; indeed those who declined an adventurous term abroad were known as *heimskr*, literally meaning 'homish' but actually signifying 'idiot'. As well as this, Vorbasse benefited greatly from its location, thirty miles equidistant from the trading centre of Ribe to the south and the royal town of Jelling to the north. As urban centres flourished, new markets for produce from the land and the sea opened up all across Scandinavia.

The economic boom that accompanied the Viking expansion was most evident in Scandinavia in the rise of urban centres. The port towns of Ribe and Hedeby in Denmark and Birka in Sweden had been established in the eighth century and all came under royal control in the ninth century. Falling sea levels led to the abandonment of Birka in favour of Sigtuna and Hedeby in favour of Schleswig, in the late tenth and eleventh centuries respectively, as they were no longer viable as harbours. Århus emerged in the tenth century as a manufacturing centre and during the late tenth century Trondheim, Oslo, Viborg, Odense, Roskilde and Lund all came to prominence as emporia with royal protection and subject to royal taxes. By the end of the eleventh century, Denmark had fifteen towns, Norway eight and Sweden four.

A great deal is known about the largest of these towns, Hedeby, which is located on the north-western edge of the Danevirke defensive fortification spanning Jutland. The relocation there of merchants from the Slav township of Reric in 808 by King Godfred established the town as an international trading centre. Hedeby's population was between 1000 and 1500 and the town consisted of approximately 200 buildings, including living quarters and workshops. Hedeby was strongly fortified from both land and sea, but this did not prevent it being overrun several times. Commercial life was typical of the trading centres across Scandinavia. Ship repair was one of its main functions, as was the offloading of trade goods, including slaves, from across the Viking world and the barter of supply goods for silver and other precious metals. The remains of a mint have been found as well as the debris of manufacturing activities that included workings in metal, bone, amber and glass, and the production of pottery. Hedeby also attracted merchants from far-flung places. The Arab merchant Al-Tartushi, having travelled from the Spanish town of Cordoba in the mid tenth century, was not favourably impressed:

Slesvig [Hedeby] is a large town at the farthest end of the world ocean. Within it
there are wells of fresh water. Its inhabitants worship Sirius,[10] apart from a few who
are Christians and have a church there ... The town is poorly off for goods and
wealth. The people's chief food is fish, for there is so much of it. If a child is born
there it is thrown into the sea to save bringing it up ... women have the right to
declare themselves divorced: they part with their husbands whenever they like. They
also have there an artificial make-up for the eyes; when they use it their beauty never
fades, but increases in both man and woman ... I have never heard more horrible
singing than from these people – it is like a growl coming out of their throats, like
the barking of dogs, only much more beastly.[11]

Al-Tartushi was obviously prejudiced by cultural differences, but his description
of the town, with its public pagan rites and scattered Christian worship, its
self-willed and fashionably accoutred women, and the exposure of unwanted
children, entirely accords with what we know from other written sources and
from archaeological investigations.

Apart from the commercial energies that towns like Hedeby stimulated,
their social significance lay in their importance to the aspirations of kings.
Royal administrative centres and, where Christian missions had been effective,
ecclesiastical centres, were established. Merchants were taxed and tolls were
paid. Along with the king's share of church revenue, all this helped to swell
the royal coffers. The strengthening of royal power was massively enhanced by
the control of trade, extending the influence of kings beyond Scandinavia to
the major markets of Europe and around the Mediterranean. Security at their
trading centres was critical to the safeguarding of royal revenue. According
to the *Annals of Fulda*, the Danish king entered into an agreement with King
Louis the German in 873 at the Frankish royal villa of Bürstadt near Worms
that aimed to protect mutual interests:

The envoys of Sigifrid, the king of the Danes, also came there, seeking to make peace
over the border disputes between themselves and the Saxons and so that merchants
of each kingdom might come and go in peace to the other, bringing merchandise to
buy and sell; the king promised that for his part these terms would be kept.[12]

Market towns also signified a new social stratum in Scandinavian society, in
which agrarian activities played little more than a service role. Some towns, such
as Kaupang in Norway, appear to have been entirely seasonal in their operations
and without any stable population. Farmers and fishermen in the surrounding

district of Kaupang could double as merchantmen in the harvest of North Sea goods moving south. Urban centres meant the commercial professionalization of certain sectors of Scandinavian society. The outlook of these few was cosmopolitan and open to influences that had little do with traditional attitudes. Urban traders saw Europe as not only a source of goods that did not necessarily have to be bought but also as a market that needed regulation. Only once the Vikings had come to understand the wider culture of Europe could these two perceptions be properly reconciled.

Scandinavian society in the Viking Age was dynamic in some aspects and static in others. The majority in the lower classes may not have noticed much change from the social conditions described in 'The List of Rig'. The slave population was constant in its position and may even have increased in number during the early and mid Viking Age. Dependent farmers remained dependent and probably also increased in number. Yet, among the more privileged, new markets and mercantile activities, as well as the spoils of war, enabled landowners and merchants to occupy much more powerful positions than previously. The ascendancy of the aristocracy, or rather those who were fit enough to survive the competition, led to a more regulated class structure, entailing a mutual dependency between the newly wealthy and the ruling orders. Population increase also resulted in a greater density of land occupation in many regions and so, on the one hand, in communal enterprises and a more effective exploitation of natural resources, but, on the other, in increased competition. Elsewhere, migration to new lands led to significant depopulation, for instance in the western fjords of Norway during the mass exodus to Iceland in the late ninth and early tenth centuries.

These changes in demographic and economic conditions were almost entirely due to the Viking expansion and are inseparable from pressures for change at a cultural level. At the outset of the Viking Age, in the late eighth century, Scandinavia was unique in northern and much of southern Europe as its only non-Christian community. By the end of the eleventh century few Scandinavians would have professed anything other than the Christian faith. As Vikings and their kings came to understand, Christianity offered much more than spiritual insight: it also offered commercial and political respectability. The extent to which the conversion of the Vikings effaced pagan sensibilities is debatable, but what is sure is that the Viking expansion was wholly consistent with the aggression inherent in a pagan view of life.

Our knowledge of the mythology of Norse paganism is almost entirely due to the antiquarian fascinations of thirteenth-century Icelanders. The two chief sources, both of which are known by the obscure word *edda*, are the *Poetic Edda* and the *Prose Edda*. The *Poetic Edda* is a single manuscript (*c*. 1280) preserved in an anonymous hand in the *King's Book* (*Codex Regius*), which contains thirty-four alliterative poems on mythological and legendary subjects. Although it is only possible to date the genesis of these poems in relative terms, it is generally agreed that the compositions span the tenth to the thirteenth centuries. In many cases, the underpinning subject matter predated the extant compositions by many centuries and elements of the poetry are traceable to shamanic practices in the early part of the first millennium. Despite the likelihood that Christian influences and interpolations affected certain of the older poems in the centuries following the conversion to Christianity, and the fact that many more were composed after the conversion, the mythology of Norse paganism is powerfully present in this collection.

Among the most notable of the older poems is 'The Seeress's Prophecy' (*Völuspá*). Although cryptic in a number of its allusions, this poem renders a compelling account of Norse mythology, ranging from the genesis of the gods to their eventual doom. The tribulations of the gods, their febrile interrelations, their ceaseless but often ambivalent strife with giants and other monstrous beings intent on their extinction, and their codes of honour and store of wisdom are related in such poems as 'Skirnir's Journey' (*Skírnismál*), 'Loki's Quarrel' (*Lokasenna*) and 'Sayings of the High One' (*Hávamál*). Among the legendary poems, which focus chiefly on human heroics, is the cycle of poems concerning the cursed Rhinegold treasure and the tragically intertwined fates of Sigurd the Dragon Slayer, Brynhild the Valkyrie, the Burgundian prince Gunnar and his sister, Gudrun. While the mythological material of the *Poetic Edda* is almost exclusively conveyed in Old Norse sources, the dramatic fates of the protagonists in the Rhinegold saga became common currency in the literature of the Germanic peoples and was most notably developed outside Iceland in the medieval German epic *The Nibelungenlied*.

The *Prose Edda* (*c*. 1220) is the work of Iceland's greatest medieval man of letters, Snorri Sturluson. Drawing explicitly upon many of the myths preserved in the *Poetic Edda*, which he systematized, as well as upon sources that have not survived, Snorri's apparent intention was to provide his contemporaries with an encyclopaedia of traditional techniques and themes for the composition of the indigenous Scandinavian verse form, skaldic poetry. The *Prose Edda* falls into four parts. The first, the 'Prologue', gives a euhemerized account of the origins of Norse paganism – that is to say, an account which explains myth as a misguided abstraction of real human history – and so, indirectly, indicates the unenlightened nature of those who practised its beliefs. The second, 'The Fooling of Gylfi' (*Gylfaginning*), is chiefly a dialogue between the bemused Swedish king Gylfi and three figures of great erudition who proclaim themselves to be the chief gods of the Norse pantheon. As a result of Gylfi's interrogations, the mythological cycle from the creation of the world to the twilight of the gods at Ragnarök, the Norse equivalent of the apocalypse, is revealed to him. The third, 'The Language of Poetry' (*Skáldskaparmál*), exemplifies the art of prosody and is copiously illustrated with mythological and legendary material, much of which elaborates on verses from the *Poetic Edda*. The fourth, 'list of verse forms' (*Háttatal*), explains the techniques of encomiastic verse, and catalogues in rigmaroles, or *þular*, the proper names and epithets of mythico legendary origin.

Five other areas or instances of literary activity supplement our understanding of Norse paganism. First, there are a number of eddic verses not included in the *Poetic* or *Prose Eddas*. These include 'The Lay of Eirik' (*Eiríksmál*) and 'The Lay of Hakon' (*Hákonarmál*), which commemorate respectively the deaths of Eirik Bloodaxe (d. 954), one time king of Norway and the last king of Viking Age York, and Hakon the Good Haraldsson (d. 960), whose rivalry with Eirik Bloodaxe, his half-brother, led to his own succession as king of Norway. Both men were remembered as obstinate pagans and defenders of the old faith, ironically in Hakon's case for he was one of the first Norwegian kings to attempt to bring his subjects round to a Christian point of view. Second, there is a sizeable assortment of skaldic verses exalting the achievements of royal personages. These encomia include a number of shield poems that elaborate on the mythological scenes which sometimes adorned the quarters of the shields of eminent Viking leaders. In so doing, these verses provide invaluable information unrecorded elsewhere. Third, there is the *Saga of the Ynglings,* the opening section of Snorri Sturluson's history of the Norwegian kings, *Heimskringla*, which further emphasizes the gullibility of Scandinavian pagans. It was the Swedes in the first place, alleges Snorri, who were awe-struck by migrant conquerors from Hellenic Greece and so assumed them to be gods. Fourth, there is Saxo Grammaticus's early thirteenth-century *History of the Danes* (*Gesta Danorum*), which, as in the writings of Snorri, gives an historical explanation for the origins of Norse paganism but, unlike Snorri, views the old gods and human credulity with complete contempt. Fifth, from the thirteenth and fourteenth centuries, there are hundreds of Icelandic sagas, ranging from novel-length fictionalized histories to short episodes or *þættir*, and from the realist Family Sagas to extravagant fantasies and adventures in which Viking heroes contest with monsters and supernatural events. Twelfth-century written histories, as well as the claimed fidelities of oral tradition, are the chief sources for the more realistic sagas. This group tends to concentrate on individuals, and their religious convictions are often integral to the development of the plot. For example, the dedication of the horse of the eponymous hero of *The Saga of Hrafnkel the Priest of Frey* to the fertility god he reveres leads to his degradation, while his abandonment of this folly leads ultimately to his recovery. The sagas, many of whose stories span the period of Iceland's conversion to Christianity in the year 1000, are mostly sympathetically critical of pagan ways, regarding them merely as anachronistic.

Whatever the value of the later sources, it is the *Poetic* and *Prose Eddas* together that provide by far the most detailed picture of the myths of Norse paganism as they developed during the Viking Age. Further elaboration toward a fully systematized explanation of the mysteries of the world, its natural phenomena and the purpose of human life was, however, cut short by the supervention of Christianity. Even so, the system was clearly at an advanced stage when the tide of conversion swept across Scandinavia in the tenth and eleventh centuries and what has survived gives a compelling insight into the mentality of pre-Christian Vikings.

The cosmos of Norse mythology was comprised of nine worlds divided tricentrically. Encompassing and unifying them were the roots of the sacred tree Yggdrasil, the Guardian Tree, whose branches were home to a riot of animals. Around the tree sat the three Norns, mysterious female agencies who wove the fates of all living things. In the upper tier were Asgard (the home of the warrior gods, the Aesir), Vanaheim (the home of the fertility gods, the Vanir) and Alfheim (the land of the Light Elves). Also within this tier was Valhalla, the hall of those warriors slain in battle who, through daily warfare, were readying themselves for the last great battle of Ragnarök as the chosen army of the Odin, chief of the gods.

In the middle tier were Jotunheim (the home of the giants), Nidavellir (the land of the dwarfs), Svartalfheim (the land of the Dark Elves) and Midgard (Middle-Earth, the land of humans). Round the circumference of this tier circled the gigantic venomous snake Jormungand, otherwise known as the

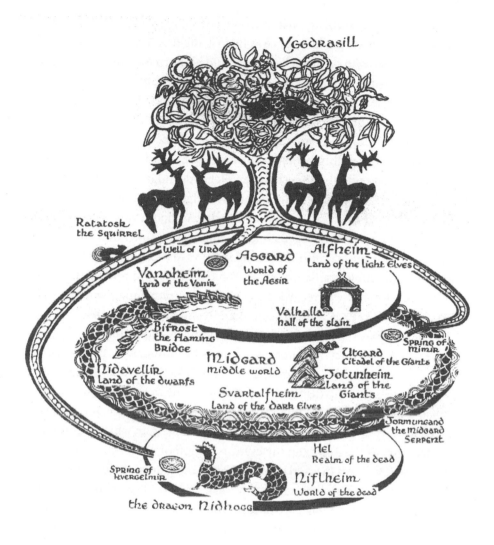

The Norse Cosmos.

Kevin Crossley-Holland, *The Norse Myths. Gods of the Vikings* (André Deutsch, 1980; Pantheon, New York, 1980). ©Kevin Crossley-Holland.

Midgard Serpent, which bit upon its own tale, so binding Midgard together. Connecting the upper and middle tiers was Bifrost, the flaming bridge, guarded by the god Heimdall, who sat in readiness to sound his horn warning of the coming of monstrous armies intent on the destruction of the gods and the world.

In the lower tier, at the remotest roots of Yggdrasil, were the dreadful goddess Hel, who presided over the region that bore her name, and Niflheim, the realm of those dead excluded from Valhalla. The fearsome dragon Nidhogg, the 'corpse-tearer', stalked this realm devouring the dead and gnawing at the roots of Yggdrasil. Spanning the abyss between Hel and Midgard was the Gjallabru, 'the echoing bridge', guarded by the giantess Modgud, who was set on deterring those who wished to cross to or from the frozen gloom of Hel. Imprecisely located to the south was Muspelheim, the land of fire, ruled over by the giant Surt, who would eventually bring his conflagration to bear at Ragnarök. Though gods and giants could traffic freely between the upper and middle tiers, none but the god Hermod was recorded as visiting and returning from Hel in his failed quest to recover Baldur, the son of Odin and pride of Asgard.

As the seeress of 'The Seeress's Prophecy' relates to Odin, this intricate cosmos was the product of evolutionary forces beginning with the creation of the world from the body of the frost giant, Ymir, and the gradual emergence of the various races from his dismembered corpse. As the world was materially evil, its inhabitants were fated to conflict and chaos. In the first place, it was the war between fertility and warrior gods, the Vanir and the Aesir, which was resolved in the triumph of the Aesir and the eventual union of all the gods under their aegis. Thereafter, it was the cold enmity of gods and giants which turns to open hostility when the giants were cheated of their price of the sun, the moon and the goddess Freyja for their part in fortifying Asgard. At the end, the seeress reveals the future in her grim vision of Ragnarök, followed by the renewal of the gods and a seeming return to the pattern of conflict and destruction. The cunning calculations of Odin, god of poetry and battle, the crude violence of the folk hero Thor, the thunder god, and the rejuvenating magic of the fertility gods and goddesses, significantly Frey and his sister Freyja, can ultimately do nothing to deflect inexorable fate and their doom. Chief agent in the undoing of the Aesir was Loki, the trickster god and, paradoxically, a descendant of giants. It was Loki's indiscriminate sexuality and perverted intelligence that led to the spawning of his monstrous brood – the Midgard Serpent, the apocalyptic wolf Fenrir, and Hel. It was Loki's malice that brought about the death of Baldur, the most beloved among the gods and their prospective saviour. And it was

Loki's vengeance after his Promethean-like punishment by his fellow deities that precipitated Ragnarök.

The characterizing features of Norse myth, then, were ubiquitous violence and the ravelling of fate. In their abstractions and personifications, these myths reflect the dynamics of a warrior society. In the struggles between gods and giants, Scandinavian pagans expressed their own struggle for survival and, in this respect, their moral ambivalence. The gods, as projections of human fears and imperfections, were presented as amoral pragmatists and, as such, exemplify human weaknesses. They might be superbeings but they were not idealized, indeed their actions were often guides as to what not to do and how not to behave. Scheming, acquisitive, licentious and reckless, the gods were actors in an ill-fated drama. As eddic poems such as 'Loki's Quarrel' and 'Thrym's Poem' (*Þrymskviða*) testify, scurrilous satires aimed at members of the pantheon recounting their sexual improprieties and weaknesses of character were just as much a part of pagan devotions as were invocations in times of need.

Norse paganism was not, however, a religious organization in the same sense as Christianity. There was no orthodoxy of belief and no figurehead determining religious policy, although there were for certain periods of time official cults sanctioned by rulers, such as Odin cults in Denmark and in Götaland in Sweden. Nor was there any evangelical mission or urge to convert disbelievers. Individuals or tribes were mostly free to decide which of the deities was best placed to bring advantage. For some, mainly the nobility, it was Odin's patronage that was sought for success in battle. This was the case with the leaders of the Danish Great Army that invaded England in 865 who, it is alleged, sacrificed their eminent captives to Odin in the grisly ritual of the 'blood-eagle'. For others, it was the hammer-wielding, thunder god Thor who inspired allegiance, as was the case when devotees set Thor against the Christian missionaries who sought to convert Iceland in the last decade of the tenth century. Neck pendants representing Thor's hammer, Mjöllnir, have been found all over the Viking world indicating Thor's popularity among the ordinary sailors and foot soldiers of Viking war bands. For those tilling the land or about to be married it was the priapic incontinence of the fertility god Frey that was essential for productivity. Freyja, Frey's sister, who was perceived as being the head of the *dísir*, a female fertility cult, also attracted a significant following. Some mythographers have suggested that Freyja was one of the oldest of the gods whose religious standing was diminished over time as a consequence of the masculinization of Norse myth.

Although neighbours rarely troubled themselves over each other's devotions, in matters of legal dispute, presided over by the tribal chieftain, dedications to a god or gods lent an essential authority to the proceedings. Norse paganism may not have demanded orthodoxy of practice and belief, and was, in this respect, religiously tolerant, but its character, its rituals and its habits of mind were deeply impressed on pre-Christian Scandinavian society. Given that the conversion of Scandinavia was relatively late in wider European terms as well as protracted, pre-Christian beliefs could not easily be eradicated. As the Icelandic sagas and Scandinavian folktales testify, as time went on the old superstitions soon diluted the Christian message with their lore of trolls, giants, dwarves and elves. It is also clear from the numerous accounts of individual Viking conversions during the latter years of the Viking Age that these often had more to do with opportunities for increased commerce and practical advantage than with any kind of spiritual revelation. While Norse paganism was a mix of beliefs and practices, with differing regional and other emphases, it was nonetheless a deeply rooted aspect of Scandinavian identity.

Scandinavian cultic practices evolved over a long period of time, dating back to beyond the Iron Age. In its earliest forms, members of a priestly cast used chant and dance, and perhaps psychotropic stimulants, to gain access to the spirit world and to higher knowledge. When, for example, Odin achieves linguistic mastery by drinking the blood (the 'mead of poetry') of the slain sage Kvasir, or forfeits his eye for the oracular insights uttered by the decapitated head of the god Mimir, or hangs from the world tree Yggdrasil for nine nights to gain the secrets of rune magic, the eddic myths are probably echoing ancient shamanic rituals. Hundreds of bracteates with religious inscriptions, and amulets, often in the form of small metal 'pocket' gods, have been found, suggesting continuity between primitive shamanism and Viking Age paganism.

As social interaction became more extensive during the eighth century, a religious geography emerged. The last element of many Scandinavian place-names, including *hof* (temple), *sallr* (sacrificial altar), *hörgr* (an altar with an idol) and *stafr* (staff or idol), indicated sites at which religious observances took place. The Old Norse adjective *heilagr* (holy), the noun *vé* (temple or sacred ground), and the verb *vígja* (to consecrate), were used to denote larger sacred localities; for example, Odinsvé, meaning 'Odin's sanctuary', now the town of Odense in Denmark. In Lejre in Denmark and Uppsala in Sweden, royal power was responsible for developing large cult centres furnished with great wooden temples. Tapestries from the early ninth-century Oseberg burial ship depict a vast procession of devotees of the type that took place at these centres. Some of the adherents are shown wearing religious paraphernalia, such as animal masks and horned headgear, which probably indicate forms of totemic veneration. In the rural hinterlands the natural landscape also provided the setting for ceremonials; and, according to early sources, fields or mountains were often dedicated to pagan worship. What gruesome rites sometimes took place at such holy sites have been revealed in nearby bogs and fens in Denmark, southern Sweden and north Germany, where weighted or bound human remains have been preserved.

Propitiatory human sacrifice, by hanging, stabbing, drowning or by breaking the backbone, is known to have been a common element of major rituals, such as those organized for the commemoration of the death of the god Baldur or the creation of the world from the dismembered body of the giant Ymir. The inhumation of high-status individuals, one of the richest sources of our knowledge about religious practices, was also attended by a blood offering or *blót*. Farm beasts were the most usual victims of the more convivial and festive form of *blot*, but evidence for ritual cannibalism has also been unearthed at some of the earlier sacrificial sites. At the more solemn *blót*, the bodies of human victims were cut open and the bones split in order to take auguries known as *hlaut*, a word that has its equivalent in modern English as 'lot', 'one's lot' or fate, relating to this process of casting lots to interpret the future.

Two accounts, similar in what they have to report, indicate the dismay of Christians at the barbarity of pagan religious customs among Scandinavians. A German, Thietmar of Merseberg, writing in 1016, some fifty years after the conversion of Denmark, says that at Lejre in Sjaelland major cultic ceremonies took place every nine years during January. At these, ninety-nine humans and a similar number of horses, dogs and cocks were sacrificed. Lejre was a place of great importance both before and during the Viking Age and was renowned throughout medieval Scandinavia as a seat of royal power. A large hall, over 46 m (150 ft) long and 13 m (45 ft) wide, has been excavated, but it is not certain whether this was for religious purposes. It is possible that the 80 m long (260 ft) stone settings outlining a ship was the open-air location for the festivities at Lejre.

Adam of Bremen's report (*c.* 1075) on the practices of the Swedes at Old Uppsala has a degree of archaeological corroboration in its favour. Adam's displeasure is obvious:

That folk has a very famous temple called Uppsala, situated not far from the city of
Sigtuna and Björkö. In this temple, entirely decked out in gold, the people worship
the statues of three gods in such wise that the mightiest of them, Thor, occupies a
throne in the middle of the chamber; Wotan [Odin] and Frikko [Frey] have places
on either side … It is customary also to solemnize in Uppsala, at nine-year intervals,
a general feast of all the provinces of Sweden. From attendance at this festival no
one is exempted. Kings and people all and singly send their gifts to Uppsala and,
what is more distressing than any kind of punishment, those who have already
adopted Christianity redeem themselves through these ceremonies. The sacrifice
is of this nature: of every living thing that is male, they offer nine heads, with the
blood of which it is customary to placate gods of this sort. The bodies they hang
in a sacred grove that adjoins the temple. Now this grove is so sacred in the eyes of
the heathen that each and every tree in it is believed divine because of the death or
putrefaction of the victims. Even dogs and horses hang there with men. A Christian
seventy-two years old told me told me that he had seen their bodies suspended
promiscuously. Furthermore, the incantations customarily chanted in the ritual of a
sacrifice of this kind are manifold and unseemly; therefore, it is better to keep silence
about them.[13]

Three large mounds dating from the fifth century are still prominent in Old
Uppsala and are clearly those that were dedicated to Thor, Odin and Frey.
Hundreds of smaller burial mounds surround them. As for the pagan temple, it
is likely that it was purged by Christians who built their church on the same site
in the twelfth century. In the early thirteenth century, both Saxo Grammaticus
the Dane and Snorri Sturluson the Icelander provide detailed and explicit
accounts of the Uppsala rites. The Anglo-Danish monk Ailnoth writing in
1130 remarked that they 'seem to honour Christian faith only when things go
according to their wishes and luck is on their side, [but when] storm winds
are against them … then they persecute the Christian faith that they claim to
honour'.[14]

Such religious beliefs and practices did not encourage respect for human life
or support any conventional notion of morality, such as that recognized, if not
always observed, by Christians. Exactly how this pagan view of life translated
into ideals of behaviour in the Viking Age is best viewed in terms of what
can broadly be described as the Heroic Code. The essence of this is expressed
in verses 76 and 77 of 'Sayings of the High One', in which Odin imparts his
wisdom:

> Cattle die, kinsmen die,
> the self must also die,
> but glory never dies,
> for the man who is able to achieve it.
>
> Cattle die, kinsmen die,
> the self must also die,
> I know one thing which never dies,
> the reputation of each dead man.[15]

Good reputation, the fame and glory won in the course of a life, was central. As in Christian-inspired poetry of the period, there was a full recognition of the transitory nature of existence, yet unlike Christian meditations on transience, there was no suggestion of consolation in the next life for the suffering in this and no spiritual transcendence. What counted instead was the judgement of others, whether one's life had deserved their praise and admiration and whether a man's social esteem would outlive his mortality. The issue was honour and, specifically, the onus was on the individual, typically the male, to lead a life of heroic fortitude, never flinching from an opponent, never breaking a vow, ever ready to avenge offences against kith and kin and, above all, eager for renown. The legacy of honour-driven heroics was twofold: on the one hand, lasting glory; on the other, the blood feud, for it was the explicit duty of succeeding generations to seek redress against any offence given to their forebears. Quite clearly, this was the ethic of a society for which conflict was routine. The expression and illustration of it is one of the chief themes of the myths, legends and sagas of Viking literary culture. It no doubt encouraged ferocity in times of battle.

But to what extent did the Christianization of Scandinavia help subdue the violent impulses of the Vikings? In one sense, the answer is ironic, as the overall effect of Christianization was to lend an air of divinely ordained legitimacy to Viking kings, enabling them to make even grander designs on the sovereignty of foreign powers. The Christian conversion of Scandinavia only became significant during the last hundred years of the Viking Age and was coincident with, and contingent upon, the centralization of power in the three main Scandinavian countries. In respect of Scandinavian rulers, the ameliorating effects of Christianity were as much political as they were personal, in many ways more so. There is no doubt that conversion for many ordinary Scandinavians meant a revision in their attitudes and perceptions to the point of enduring persecution for their beliefs. Some testimony to this is the 2000 or more runic monuments bearing Christian sentiments that were erected in Scandinavia between 975 and the early twelfth century. Yet for Viking rulers it was almost certainly more a matter of being incorporated into a wider European community, motivated more by the pragmatics of power than by spiritual considerations.

It is from the conversion of kings, or conversion 'moments', that we date the conversion of nations, for such kings that saw to it that their populations followed their lead. The Scandinavian kings most often achieved this by using methods of persuasion that were far from orthodox. There was an urgency about the conversion of their subjects that signified an understanding of exactly what was to be gained from a wider European identity. Becoming part of Christian Europe meant not only an accommodation with other European powers but also a streamlined mode of government. This had the significant advantage to kings of undermining the power of local chieftains, as religious authority was removed from the chieftains to the church and legal authority fell to the king's appointed representatives. A chieftain could only occupy a position of power with the king's blessing. With Christianity also came Latinate literacy for the privileged few and, as a consequence, the authority that only the written word could confer.

Missionary efforts at conversion can be dated from 725, when Scandinavia was still a relatively unknown and inoffensive backwater. Yet as an English cleric, Archbishop Willibrord of Utrecht (d. 739), discovered, the Scandinavians were not ready to see the benefits of transferring their allegiance away from the old gods, and his mission to Jutland made no headway, save that he was allowed to purchase thirty boys out of slavery. It was to be a hundred years before an effort was made again. In the 820s, Archbishop Ebo of Rheims (d. 851) succeeded in baptizing King Harald Klak of Denmark, almost certainly helped by the support that Harald was receiving from Louis the Pious, the Frankish emperor. The Frankish missionary Anskar (d. 865), later to become archbishop of the united episcopal sees of Hamburg and Bremen, tried to follow Ebo's work, but his efforts in Denmark were curtailed when Harald was sent into exile in 827 as a result of a pagan backlash. Anskar then turned his attention to Sweden where, with the permission of the regional Swedish king Bjorn, he founded a church at Birka. Anskar's success proved temporary and Ebo's appointee at Birka, his kinsman Gauzbert, was sent packing after only a few years in office.

Danish disrespect for the church came to a head in 845 when Hamburg and Paris became a target for Viking raiders. Curiously, this worked in Anskar's favour, for the Vikings who attacked Paris were smitten by a deadly affliction which they attributed to the vengeance of St Germain, whose monastery they had despoiled. King Horik of the Danes reacted by returning all property and captives to both Hamburg and Paris. Anskar subsequently exploited Danish superstition by gaining permission to build churches in Hedeby and Ribe, thereafter returning to Sweden to reconstitute the church at Birka. Within a generation, however, the Christians of southern Denmark and southern Sweden were relapsing into the old ways and behaving, as one Frankish archbishop put it, 'like typical Northmen'.

Missionary efforts were stalled during the latter half of the ninth century, but in the first half of the tenth century Archbishop Unni of Hamburg-Bremen personally encouraged the spreading of the mission from Birka. By the mid point of the century, missionaries were active in Denmark at Hedeby, Ribe and Århus. Christianity was spreading slowly both north and east. The major turning points in Denmark and Norway were both in the latter half of the tenth century. In Denmark the key moment was the conversion of Harald Bluetooth. The story goes that the missionary Poppo persuaded Harald of the power of the Christian god by holding a piece of red-hot metal in his hand without getting burnt. Although Harald was impressed, his decision had more to do with his desire to placate the Germans and to raise his own standing as a progressive king among Scandinavians. Poppo's 'miracle' gave him a sensational narrative to help in the conversion of his own people. Harald went about the business of abolishing pagan traditions by adapting them to Christian traditions. His father had been a die-hard pagan king, Gorm, who had raised a spectacular monument to his queen, Thyre, at Jelling. Harald developed and consecrated the site as a manifest assertion of his new faith and interred his father's body there in a Christian-inspired burial mound.

Harald's astute conversion did not convince everyone of the sense of relinquishing autonomy to the church. Among those unconvinced was his son, Svein Forkbeard, who in 986 raised an army against his father and killed him. According to Adam of Bremen, the patricide briefly returned Denmark to paganism. Svein, however, appears to have continued his father's work and in 990 a church was built at Lund, something that could not have happened without Svein's consent. There is no doubt that Svein was a Christian when he conquered England in 1013. It was Svein's son Cnut, the greatest of the Viking kings, who went on to rule England, Denmark, Norway and much of Sweden, and there is no disputing the sincerity of Cnut's faith and his conviction that kings needed papal sanction, even if after the fact. Nor could Cnut have ever hoped to gain the allegiance of the Anglo-Saxon hierarchy of England as a non-Christian.

In Norway, the move toward Christianity was abetted by the accession of Hakon the Good in 936. Hakon had been fostered out to the English king Athelstan and was imbued with the influences of a Christian court. On his return to Norway, and following his enthronement, Hakon imported many Christian missionaries from England, but his efforts lacked commitment and he took the middle way of religious toleration rather than imposing his will. His funeral lay, *Hákonarmál*, describes his entry into Valhalla and the warm greetings of Odin, but this is probably an indication of Hakon's refusal to persecute his pagan countrymen and women rather than any deathbed apostasy. Two generations later, in the last decade of the tenth century, Hakon's great-nephew Olaf Tryggvason proved to be less easygoing about religious affairs. Olaf had been baptized in England as part of a pact with the English king Æthelred the Unready, who made Olaf a huge payment of Danegeld on the condition that he accepted baptism and never again worried Æthelred's shores. Olaf realized that the road to success lay in other European kings recognizing his Christian credentials. When he became king of the Norwegians in 995, Olaf immediately set about converting his reluctant subjects. As an evangelizing force, he was ruthless: death and dispossession was the price of failure to accept the Christian message. Iceland, too, acceded to his wishes in 1000 when, as their sole trading partner and most powerful sponsor, Olaf convinced the Icelanders of the merits of Christianity. His missionaries there had brought the same 'convert or die' message that he had delivered round the coastal districts of Norway. According to the twelfth-century *Book of the Icelanders*, what Christianity meant there in the first place was a ban on eating horseflesh and on the practice of exposing unwanted children at birth. Pagan devotions were allowed to continue discreetly for a further fifty years. What it meant in the longer term was a radical realignment of internal power structures that would, over the next 250 years, lead to civil war and finally to annexation by Norway.

The completion of the conversion of Norway fell to Olaf Haraldsson, who ascended the throne in 1016. In company with Bishop Grimkell, Olaf, like his earlier namesake, was ruthless. Olaf's laws enforced Christianity, the old sanctuaries were purged and baptism was offered as the only alternative to mutilation or blinding. As with all other Scandinavian kings, the scarcely hidden agenda was the unification of the country and endorsement by non-Scandinavian powers. Olaf's violent reign ended in his dispossession by Cnut. Cnut, although Danish and a Christian, was preferable to many Norwegians, for he was preoccupied by the business of governing England and an absentee Danish king seemed a better prospect that an all too present Norwegian one. Olaf was killed in 1030 in his efforts to regain the throne. Miracles were reported in Trondheim where Olaf was buried and within a year his old accomplice Bishop Grimkell had pronounced him a saint, conferring on him his doubtful reputation as a model of justice and Christian piety. St Olaf's grave became a popular destination for pilgrims throughout the early middle ages.

In Sweden matters were less clear cut. Jämtland in the north west was converted, at least in part, during the eleventh century, a missionary outpost being established in Skara in Västergötland in 1020. But the Swedes were particularly resistant to Christianity and probably less inhibited by the opinions of western European powers. Christian pockets existed, however, alongside widespread paganism, often unhappily. The pro-Danish Swedish king Olof Skötkonung (d. 1022) followed the example of his Scandinavian contemporaries and is said to have converted in 1008, but coins picturing him with Christian symbols were in circulation from the beginning of his reign in 995. It was specifically as a Christian king that Olof succeeded in governing the Svear and Götar tribes in the north and south as one people in one realm. Although all the kings who followed Olof during the eleventh century were Christian, the unity he had achieved did not last and neither did his efforts at conversion. In 1060 bishops Adalward of Sigtuna and Egino of Skåne were dissuaded from their plans to desecrate the pagan temple at Old Uppsala by the sympathetic King Stankil, on the grounds that it would lead to an uprising; but they successfully broke up many idols worshipped by the Götar without reprisal. Twenty years later little further progress had been made; indeed a revival of paganism occurred under the leadership of Blót Svein, or Svein the Sacrificer. Overall, the situation in Sweden remained unclear until the early twelfth century, when a truly unified Sweden came into effect, whereupon Sweden could properly claim to be a Christian country.

In one way, the conversion of Scandinavia licensed kings to even greater acts of war, for the Christian standard carried with it the imprimatur of respectability. Many Viking travellers had long ago seen the sense of gaining such respectability. Clearly aware that trade with Christians was eased by adopting their religion, there are many instances of Vikings being baptized in order to further their own causes. Some were prime signed (*prima signatio*) as a compromise between the old and new faiths and only received baptism arrayed in white robes on their deathbeds; some received baptism on numerous occasions and enjoyed both the feasting and the finery that went along with it; some accepted Christianity as a sign of their future peaceful intent, as was the case when the Viking leader Guthrum bowed to the will of Alfred the Great in 878; and some merely saw Christ as another god to add to the pantheon and made sacrifices accordingly. Many others, in particular the colonists of the English Danelaw, Normandy and the Slavic territories, were largely content to set aside violence for the sake of good relations with their neighbours and were incorporated into Christian culture with surprising speed.

The conversion of Scandinavian kings reflected what had been taking place across the Viking world since the mid ninth century, only the impact was different. Unlike the colonists, the Viking kings of Denmark and Norway still sought to expand their power, whether over their own areas of control in Scandinavia or new ones in Western Europe. Territories that Vikings had once regarded as sources of plunder were now viewed by kings as targets for undisputed possession. This was the case with England: first ransacked, then effectively partitioned, then a site of violently contested monarchic legitimacy. During the eleventh century, Christian Vikings took their place amongst the rulers of Europe. As pagans they had only ever been perceived as fearsome gangsters; as Christians they were as legitimate as any other ruler.

# 3

# Battle on Land and at Sea

To speak of a Viking 'army' before the great royal armies of the late tenth century is misleading. Certainly, sea kings and warrior chieftains surrounded themselves with select bodyguards, but an army, or *lið*, in the sense of a large body of professional regular soldiers whose sole function is military, did not exist among the raiders and invaders that issued forth from Scandinavia during the ninth and most of the tenth centuries. Whilst a levy system was operated where there were threats to home territory, foreign offensives were, for the main part, optional. The incentive for being in a Viking army was more often to do with personal gain than national or regional causes. The code of honour which bound Vikings together in do or die enterprises should not, however, be underestimated in its capacity to meld an army in common cause. An army might be comprised of tribal militias, freeborn yeoman farmers and fishermen, merchant adventurers, otherwise aimless and landless mercenaries, royal, or at least powerful, family retinues, or, indeed, anyone looking for quick profit. Some element of an army may have been pressed, such as slaves or other degraded individuals beholden to a chieftain, but as their hearts were not in the job, they proved to be all but useless on the battlefield and would desert at the earliest opportunity. The composition of Viking armies reflected the general tactics of harassment, intimidation and surprise attack, for the Vikings were opportunists.

The size of an army could range from anything from a longship of thirty raiders to a vast array of warriors numbering thousands. Commanders were decided according to status, ranging from national kings and local kings to landless self-proclaimed sea kings and pirate leaders. The constituency of Viking armies was likely to change according to events, even during protracted campaigns. For some, for instance farmers, going on Viking raids was a seasonal activity fitted in between crop sowing and harvest; for others, it involved years of service with attachments to different Viking armies in differing theatres of activity. This was not necessarily a disadvantage, as part of the military success of the Vikings was the ability of their armies to coalesce and disband as suited. Wherever the action proved most rewarding, that was where an army recruited most effectively.

Despite this fluidity of manpower, armies large and small required a high degree of organization, with all the attendant logistical concerns and discipline. Foraging parties were critical to the maintenance of a large body of men on a protracted campaign where it was necessary to live off the land. Each man had to understand his particular role, whether as part of a unit detailed for scouting and relaying intelligence about the enemy's movements and vulnerabilities, for building makeshift and sometimes permanent defensive fortifications, or for more routine tasks such as smithying, ship repair and stabling. Field hospitals and catering were commonly the lot of women.

Although writers of Icelandic histories and sagas looked back nostalgically on their forebears' daring and belligerence, in reality Viking warfare was less glamorous. The Vikings were no more advanced in battlefield tactics and weaponry than those whom they fought, indeed much less so than the Byzantine and Muslim armies of south and Eastern Europe and the Middle East, who were skilled in the art of incendiaries, notably 'Greek Fire'. A tally of Viking successes against non-Scandinavian opposition, as calculated from written sources, suggests that it was persistence rather than any particular mastery on the battlefield that gained them their peculiar advantage. Sieges and short, often devastating, assaults were preferred to full-scale land battles. When it came to fighting each other, as often became the case when the stakes grew larger, as in Ireland in the mid ninth century and England during the late tenth and eleventh centuries, prudent evasion of massed opposition was not, however, so easily accomplished, nor so desirable. As far as foreign opposition was concerned, hit and run, guaranteed numerical advantage and a mixture of brawn and cunning, of Thor and Odin, were the standard tactics. This mercurial, almost guerrilla-style, approach to hostilities made counter-attack extremely difficult, all the more so given that many Vikings were far from home and without immediately accessible borders. Pursuing a raiding party to its homeland would have been largely pointless.

Reliable source material for the details of Viking battles is scarce but the often austere and prosaic accounts given in sources such as the *Anglo-Saxon Chronicle* and the *Annals of Ulster* can, nonetheless, be revealing. The Icelandic sagas are informative on the general atmosphere of battle and excellent for the pithy dialogue of Viking leaders, but anachronisms and improbabilities need to be filtered out. Snorri Sturluson's early thirteenth-century history of the Norwegian kings, *Heimskringla*, deals with the personalities behind major historical events and gives graphic details of battle scenes. One encouraging aspect of Snorri's historiography is that it is full of citations from skaldic poetry, which has some claim to being contemporary with events.

Archaeological finds of weaponry are plentiful. The most prized among weapons during the later Viking Age was the double-edged, but usually blunt-pointed, sword; a slashing rather than fencing weapon of, on average, 90 cms (35 in) in length. The single-edged sax-type sword had all but disappeared by 900, but knives of the short sax type were common and clearly essential for a number of reasons apart from violent attack. In battle such implements would have been a last resort: 'he who has a little knife needs a long arm', as was said in the Old Icelandic proverb. Full-size, carbon-steel swords were prestige weapons and carried with them significance that might almost be described as magical. Many good-quality swords with elaborately decorated hilts have been recovered, sometimes in excellent states of preservation. Approximately two thousand have been found in graves and in bogs and rivers throughout Scandinavia, and many more throughout the Viking world. It is, nonetheless, very doubtful whether all Vikings were fortunate enough to be owners of such weapons. The finest swords were imported from the workshops of master-smiths in Frankia, an arms trade that Charlemagne unsuccessfully tried to ban. Swords were valuable heirlooms, in some cases hundreds of years old, and carried their own history. Scandinavian writers, and Germanic sources generally, record the practice of giving swords names, such as Magnus Barefoot's 'Leg-Biter' and Olaf Tryggvason's 'Quern-Biter', investing them with anthropomorphic and even supernatural qualities. Poets found numerous euphemisms, or kennings, to express the potency and mystique of the sword: 'War Snake', 'Widow Maker', 'Odin's Flame', 'Torch of the Blood', 'Battle Flasher' and so on. According to Icelandic saga evidence, a sword was an aspect of its owner's identity.

Iron was in plentiful supply in Scandinavia, so decent hacking weapons and missiles were abundant. Common personal arms included throwing and thrusting spears, and axes. The single-head, bearded or broad-blade, axe was, like the spear, a cheaper weapon than the sword, although examples of axes superbly decorated in the Mammen style were in the possession of a few. In the last century of the Viking Age, the axe became the Viking weapon of choice, perhaps perforce, given the supply shortage of new swords. The effectiveness of an axe depended on the muscle-power invested in a great arching swing. Failure to connect would inevitably lead to the attacker losing balance or, worse still, embedding his axe in the ground and leaving him vulnerable.

The shield was critical to defence and no Viking would have contemplated entering the fray without one. Shields were circular and slightly less than a metre (approx. 3 ft) in diameter, typically made of softwood from conifers, and with a central raised iron boss intended as a deflector and a protection for the hand grip. Reinforcement consisted of iron struts at the back and leather or iron at the rim. The kite shield, longer and tapered to a point at the bottom, was clearly in use by warriors on horseback at the battle of Hastings in 1066, as is shown on the Bayeux Tapestry (c. 1080). There are many references in the *Anglo-Saxon Chronicle* to Viking raiding parties acquiring horses by hook or by crook from the locals and riding to battle during the Danish Great Army's campaigns after the invasion of 865, and King Alfred's biographer Bishop Asser refers to the Vikings becoming 'a mounted force' in Frankia in 881.[1] Horses were also transported by ship to battle sites, and Vikings certainly used horses for transport, but it is unlikely that there was such a thing as a Viking cavalry in the strict sense of their being drilled for, and permanently mounted during, battle. Vikings were able horsemen and used horses when circumstances permitted for fight or flight. Perhaps those who had horses used the kite shield, but it was not favoured by the infantry, who preferred the freedom of movement allowed by the circular shield rather than greater protection. Longships might carry as many as two circular shields per oarsman, mounted and overlapping along both sides of the ship. Shields were, of course, vital for defence during missile attacks, at which point a shield mountain, or *shieldburg*, was formed to shelter the leader. Some royal personages are recorded as having insisted that their court poets join them in their *shieldburg* to act as war correspondents and propagandists.

Armour, for the average soldier, can have consisted of little more than a leather jerkin and leather helmet. Plate-mail armour was unknown during the Viking Age and the few metal helmets (horn-free, contrary to the popular image) that have been recovered are of such excellent quality that they would have been out of the reach of the ordinary Viking soldier. The same is true for the chain-mail shirt – the byrnie – and headgear. The intricacy of the metalwork meant that only the most exalted can have had access to them. For body mail to be fully effective it needed to cover the upper legs, which, as the sword name 'Leg-Biter' suggests, were targets. Harald Hardrada (d. 1066) is said to have worn a mail shirt that 'reached almost to his middle leg and so strong that no weapon ever pierced it'. As it somewhat resembled a dress, it was nicknamed 'Emma', perhaps by Harald's less well protected men.[2] Unhappily for Harald, 'Emma' had been left on board ship when he met his doom at the battle of Stamford Bridge.

Some elite soldiers disdained protection entirely. These were the *berserkir* and *úlfheðnar*, the 'bearshirts' and 'wolfcoats', so-named because of what they wore and because of their strength and savagery. Legend accumulated around such individuals. Snorri Sturluson's *Saga of the Ynglings*, in recounting the extraordinary skills of the 'historical' Odin when he first arrived in Sweden, also describes his retinue of berserkers:

> His own men went to battle without coats of mail and acted like mad dogs or wolves. They bit their shields and were as strong as bears or bulls. They killed people, and neither fire nor iron affected them. This is called the berserker rage.[3]

At the battle of Hafrsfjord (*c.* 885), Harald Finehair's fleet was confronted by a crew of berserkers and wolfcoats who 'bellowed' and 'shrieked' and 'shook their weapons' as battle was joined. The turning-point of the battle came when Haklang, the berserk leader, was killed, leading to the fulfilment of Harald's ambition to unite Norway.[4] Berserkers were men who in the heat of battle became frenzied and were uninhibited by pain. Such men took the forward and exposed positions in the 'swine wedge' (O.N. *svínfylkja*), where as many as thirty men took up a triangular formation, thus resembling the shape of a pig's snout. Their aim was to advance in close quarter against an enemy shield wall with the intention of shattering it. Few chose to stand against a raging berserk. Away from battle, berserkers were renowned as misfits and bullies, and as men who would quarrel over a straw, but any army would have considered itself fortunate to have them in its ranks.

Close-quarter fighting was not an elegant business and the shortcomings of both weaponry and armour, even when it was good quality, were exposed in the grim choreography of a mêlée. This description from *The Saga of Hrolf the Walker* is convincingly realistic:

> Hrolf struck at Orn, but, as he tried to ward off the blow with his shield, the sword sliced through, and the point ripped open the whole of his belly so that his guts poured out. Next Hrolf ran Herkir through and cut both legs off Lifolf. Stefnir stabbed at Ulf with a spear; and, as Ulf thrust his shield against it, the spear pierced through into his thigh, wounding him badly. Ulf cut the spearhead off the shaft. Har pounced on Hrolf and struck him on the helm with a nail-studded club, knocking him almost unconscious: yet still Hrolf managed to turn on Ulf and thrust at him with the sword. The mailcoat failed, and the sword went right through him. Lodmund lunged at Stefnir and hit him in the calf, piercing it through. Just at that

moment, Hrolf came up and, making a two-handed stroke at Lodmund's head, sliced him through, so that the sword stuck in the ground. Then Sorli and Tjorfi set on Hrolf, and Har let fly at his back with the club. That would have been his death had the cloak and armour not protected him; even so, he was still beaten down on both knees. He sprang to his feet quickly and struck at Har, slicing through his leg at the knee. Hrolf took a swing with the sword at Tjorfi's side and cut him clean through at the waist.[5]

Broader battle strategies assigned particular tasks to detachments of men. One element of a large army consisted of shortbow and longbow archers, and the first phase of any battle, for both sides, entailed missile attacks. Beyond this, success in engaging the enemy depended largely on making the first blow effective. In 1030, the ousted Norwegian king Olaf Haraldsson, posthumously known as St Olaf for his Christian missionary zeal, mustered an army of roughly four thousand men in an attempt to reclaim his throne from Cnut of Denmark. Olaf's cause was not popular and the Norwegian chieftains raised an army of free farmers numbering 14,000 against him. They met at Stiklestad, north east of Trondheim, and on the eve of battle Olaf set out his plans to overcome the odds.

'We have a large army and one well equipped. And now I will tell you what our battle formation is to be. I shall have my standard advanced in the middle of our force, and with it are to go my bodyguards and retainers, and also the men who joined us from the Uppland districts, then too the troops that joined us from the Trondheim district. To the right of my standard is to stand Dag Hringsson, together with all the men he had with him to follow us. He is to bear another standard. To the left of my detachment is to be placed all that force which the king of Sweden furnished us and all those who joined our ranks from Sweden. They are to carry the third standard. I shall request all men to arrange themselves in groups so that kinsmen and acquaintances stand together, because everyone will best shield his comrade if they know one another. We shall put a mark on all our host and set a war token on all our helmets and shields by drawing on them with chalk the holy cross. And when we enter battle we shall all of us have one battle cry, "Forward, forward, Christ's men, cross men, king's men!" Having smaller forces we shall have to thin out our ranks, for I do not propose to let them surround us with their [superior] numbers. Let men now arrange themselves in detachments and then let these form ranks, so that everyone may know his station and watch whether he is [too] far from the standard under which he is to fight. Let us now maintain our rank and file and let the men

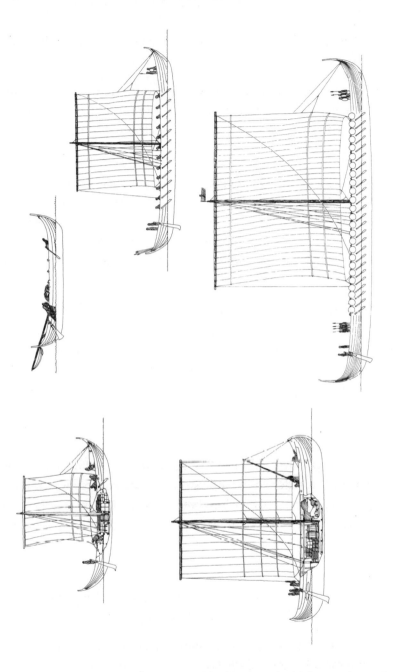

Scale drawings of five of the eleventh-century Skuldelev craft. To the
right are two warships (wrecks 5 and 2). To the left are two cargo ships
(wrecks 3 and 1). Centre at the top is an onboard rowing boat or *færing*.
Drawing by Morten Gøthche. ©Viking Ship Museum, Roskilde, Denmark.

have their weapons about them day and night until we know where the battle is to be between the farmers and us.'[6]

Despite having placed his men in good order, and according to where loyalties were best preserved, Olaf's strategy seems more hopeful than realistic. As battle was about to commence, Olaf made his plans clear to his men:

> 'Let us attack most briskly at the very start, because there will be a quick decision if the odds are against us. Victory will be ours if we rush at them swiftly, but fortune will not be with us if we fight till we are tired so that we are unstrung because of weariness. We are likely to have fewer reserves than they for pushing forward while the others merely defend themselves or rest. But if we rush at them so hard that those in the front ranks turn, then one will tumble on top of the other, and their defeat will be greater the more there are of them.'[7]

There is good reason to believe that the headlong charge was the basic offensive battle strategy among Viking armies, although this was rarely against superior numbers. As things turned out, Olaf's strategy at Stiklestad gained initial success from a downhill charge and was helped by the free farmer army turning on each other by mistake in a confusion over battle cries. In the end, sheer force of numbers won the day and Olaf was hacked down in the front ranks of his overstretched troops. Soon after his death, the remnant of his dispirited army was put to flight.

Olaf's decision to divide his men into battalions, according to their loyalties and nationalities, is reflected in battle strategies where there was a confluence of Vikings under different leaderships but with shared intentions. In 871, when Æthelred, king of Wessex, fought against a Viking assembly at Ashdown, the *Anglo-Saxon Chronicle* reports that

> they were in two bands: in one were Bagsegc and Halfdan, the heathen kings, and in the other were the jarls. And then the king Æthelred fought against the kings' force … and Alfred, his brother, [fought] against the jarls' force …[8]

This same type of battle formation was employed in 918 when Vikings departing from Dublin for York attacked the Scots.

> The foreigners of Loch dá Chaech [Waterford], that is, Ragnall, king of the dark foreigners [Danes], and the two jarls, Oitir and Gragabai, forsook Ireland and proceeded afterwards against the men of Scotland. The men of Scotland, moreover,

moved against them and they met on the bank of the Tyne in Northern Saxland. The heathens formed themselves into four battalions: a battalion with Gothfrith grandson of Ímar, a battalion with the two jarls, and a battalion with the young lords. There was also a battalion in ambush with Ragnall, which the men of Scotland did not see. The Scotsman routed the three battalions which they saw, and made a very great slaughter of the heathens, including Oitir and Gragabai. Ragnall, however, then attacked in the rear of the Scotsman, and made slaughter of them, although none of their earls was cut off. Nightfall caused the battle to be broken off.[9]

Diversionary tactics, ambushes and entrenched positions were also in the repertoire of Viking armies.

While it is as raiders and pillagers that the Vikings are best known, when it came to pursuing the conquest of large territories, they were just as capable of drawing up complex and coordinated war strategies. When, for example, in 893, a second Viking Great Army arrived in England with the intention of conquering and settling the remaining free English territory of Wessex, their leader, Hastein, employed a refined version of the successful war strategy used by the Danish Great Army in the campaign against Wessex in 878. Hastein's aim was to drive the Wessex king, Alfred, back into the south-west corner of his own realm, while he subdued Kent and Essex. To do this, Hastein arranged with the Danes of Northumbria to launch a sea-borne attack on the coast of north Devon, probably with the intention of driving south to take the stronghold at Exeter. With Alfred pinned down, Hastein had time to secure his own lines and then travel west to link up with the Northumbrian Danes, leaving Alfred trapped in a pincer movement. Targeted raiding so as to live off the land was calculated to allow this to happen and, so far as commentators and, of course, those caught up in the campaign were concerned, this was the conspicuous aspect of Viking movements. The wider aims were not readily perceived and, presumably, were not meant to be. That Hastein's campaign against Wessex failed does not invalidate the grand design underlying it. For all the informality of the constitution of Viking armies, there was nothing informal about the organization of the land and sea armies. In order to achieve the maximum gain at the earliest point, planning required detailed analysis by a council of war.

In protracted land campaigns, Vikings were often forced, out of necessity, to lay siege to centres of power. Their preferred way of concluding a siege was to take delivery of a large sum of money and then move on. Starving the besieged was preferable to assault, but the difficulty of maintaining a large army permanently at the gate could eventually oblige a more direct approach. There was also the worry of reinforcements arriving to help break the siege. This precisely describes the situation in 885–6 when a massive Viking army laid siege to the River Seine's Île de la Cité in Paris. Having smashed through the defensive fortifications at Pont de l'Arche upriver near Rouen, which had been built in 865 for the sole purpose of deterring Viking raiders, the Vikings settled in on the banks of the Seine beneath the bridge fortifications that connected the island to the mainland both north and south. For over a year, as few as two hundred Franks held them at bay despite repeated attacks across the bridges and from the longships. According to Abbo of Fleury, whose colourful account lionizes the Franks, by the January of 886 the Vikings had grown impatient.

> The Danes then made, astonishing to see, three huge machines, mounted on sixteen wheels – monsters made of immense oak trees bound together; upon each was placed a battering ram, covered with a high roof – in the interior and on the sides of which could be placed and concealed, they said, sixty men armed with their helmets.[10]

Despite these contraptions, the Vikings ultimately failed in their assault and three months later, Sigfred, the leader of the Vikings, accepted a paltry 60 lbs of silver to withdraw, although the bulk of his men stayed on in the expectation of greater reward, which they duly received from the feeble Charles the Fat. Although this is the only account we have of Vikings applying their engineering skills to offensive machinery, there is no doubt that the Vikings knew a good deal about building fortifications for themselves and about the tactics an enemy might use during a siege.

The Vikings were not a homogeneous brotherhood and fortifications throughout Scandinavia are a fair indication that Scandinavians had much to fear from each other. The Danes also had reason to worry about cross-border incursions from non-Scandinavians, and at Hedeby, in south Jutland, which was particularly exposed to attack, the 30-kilometre-long Danevirke rampart spanning the Dano-Frankish border was regularly refortified after it was built in 737. Semicircular ramparts overlooked by wooden towers and reinforced by rows of stakes in the water also protected the prosperous, and therefore vulnerable trading centres at Hedeby, Århus, Birka and Västergarn. Presumably, in these cases, fortifications were built in anticipation of the designs of neighbouring Viking raiding parties and of the Slavic Wends from the eastern shores of the Baltic or, as time went by, in anticipation of the larger threats posed by rival Scandinavian kings. The most impressive fortifications were all Danish. At Aggersborg in north Jutland, Fyrkat in north-east Jutland, Nonnebaken on Fyn, Skåne in Danish-controlled southern Sweden, and Trelleborg on Sjaelland, royal fortresses were built during the late tenth century by Harald Bluetooth (d. *c.* 998). Located on important land routes, all of them had access to waterways into the Baltic with ship moorings lying just outside their perimeters. Known as the Trelleborg ring forts, these were wooden-built, circular structures circumscribed by a ring road and with gates at the four main compass points. They ranged in size from 120 m (390 ft) in diameter to the largest, at Aggersborg, which measured 240 m in diameter (780 ft). The forts were divided symmetrically into three or four main areas, each subdivided into uniformly constructed bow-sided wooden buildings. At a conservative estimate between two to four thousand men were garrisoned inside the fort. If buildings outside the ramparts are also taken in account, an overall population of nine thousand, including women and children, and twice that figure at Aggersborg, is conceivable. Their function – part administrative and part military – evidently signified an assertion of Danish royal power across the region. The kilometre-long Ravning Enge bridge, built across the River Vejle near Jelling around the same time as the forts, is further evidence of Harald Bluetooth's desire to flaunt his military might and extend his realm.

The Trelleborg ring forts, although they were operational for little more than a generation, are testimony to both the increasingly centralized power and prosperity of Viking operations in the later Viking Age. According to the largely fictional *Saga of the Jomsvikings*, Harald Bluetooth also built a stone fortress on the Wendish coast of the Baltic from where he sponsored an exclusively male Viking war band in possession of over three hundred ships. While this is doubtful, the underlying principle of launching raiding campaigns from fortified hideouts is not. This, after all, was what the Viking Great Army did in the late ninth century when they established themselves in the fortified Five Boroughs in English Mercia, and it was probably one of the functions of the Trelleborg forts. What can also be deduced from the Jomsvikings legend is that Scandinavian kings who sought to expand their influence abroad had first to ensure their position at home, and that the former financed the latter. As had always been the case, the means to expansion lay in shipbuilding.

Nothing expresses more precisely the spirit of the Viking Age and the disposition of the Viking than the longship. For almost three hundred years, domination of trade, success in war and conquest, and the colonization of new lands were all a result of the remarkable shipbuilding feats of the Scandinavians. Seaworthy craft had been fundamental to the survival of Scandinavian tribes for six thousand years and their evolution can be traced through several key stages. The first stage consisted of the primitive dugout of the early Stone Age, which was little more than a single tree hollowed out. The dugout was fit only for the inshore waters of fjords and lakes and was notoriously unstable. It took a further three thousand years before greater manoeuvrability was achieved when the idea of splitting a tree trunk across the diameter and inserting a planked hull took hold. These boats are among the first examples of the use of lapstrakes, or overlapping planks, in northern Europe. During the first half of the last millennium BC, war canoes beaked at prow and stern and carved with animal heads evolved, giving Scandinavian vessels the beginnings of the distinctive shape and style that later characterized the fearsome Viking longship. Significantly, Bronze Age art depicts these canoes being guarded by dragons, a beast that was to symbolize warlike intent through into the Viking Age. By the fourth and fifth centuries BC, a uniquely Scandinavian double-beaked canoe that could be rowed both backward and forward by twenty warriors had developed. One such boat from Hjörtspring, Denmark, reveals that the base of these canoes was pared down to a narrow plank curving from prow to stern, taking the first step toward the keel of a Viking Age ship.

New technologies and more sophisticated carpentry techniques emerged by the fourth century AD, leading to the gradual abandonment of the Hjörtspring design. An oared warship found at Nydam, Denmark, features an evenly curved clinker-built hull fixed with clenched iron nails and with a rudder attached on the starboard, or 'steering side', of the ship. Three centuries later a design feature critical to the success of the longship emerged in the form of an embryonic T-shaped keel. The Kvalsund ship found in western Norway, and the Sutton Hoo burial ship found in Suffolk, England, are both ships of this kind and are the clear forerunners of the Viking longship. One last development remained: the addition of a mast for a single square-rigged sail. Picture stones from Gotland, Sweden, illustrate sailing ships from as early as AD 700, but these are unlikely to have been Scandinavian craft. Exactly why Scandinavian shipbuilders resisted sail power is hard to determine; it has been suggested that the reason was cultural rather than technical, in as much as the traditions of rowing were cherished inordinately. Nevertheless, once the advantages of sail were appreciated in the early eighth century, all the accumulated experience and expertise of the Vikings' forebears was rapidly turned towards developing ocean-going warships, capable of travelling long distances at high speed, and towards ever more efficient merchant ships.

Our knowledge of the details of Viking maritime craft is not precise. Much has been learned from voyages in replicas, and some of the literary evidence, such as descriptions from the Icelandic sagas, can now be tested empirically. It is clear that the design of ships, though adapted for purposes ranging from the transportation of cargo, to warfare, to ships built for largely ceremonial purposes, had certain fundamental characteristics. The Viking Age ship was clinker-built with overlapping strakes, joined with precisely spaced iron rivets and caulked with animal hair. It had a T-shaped keel tapering from prow to stern in elegant symmetry. Oak was favoured for the hull, though pine and larch were also used, the latter having the advantage of not cracking when overwintered and housed in a dry berth. Timber was split and trimmed, sometimes to a width of 2 centimetres, but never sawn, thus gaining the maximum from the natural strength of the wood by following the grain of the timber. Where possible, joints were made from a single piece of timber, using the intersections of branches with tree trunks; but, where this was not feasible, ties and trenails were employed.

The distinctive curvature of Viking Age ships was a feature of the lines from keel to gunwale, from keel to prow and stern, and from prow to stern. The hull, rarely with a draught of more than 1.5 metres, was reinforced with framed structures and cross-beams throughout its full width. A steering paddle was mounted on the right-hand side of the stern. Masts, often made from pine, could be unstepped with ease on warships, so allowing passage under bridges and, by deception, gaining the element of surprise for raiding parties. Cargo or merchant ships usually had fixed masts. Sails, which could be reefed or reduced, could be as large as 100 square metres. In the case of warships, oars flanking both sides of the ship were projected through oar ports, which could be closed when not in use. Cargo ships, which were less dependent on speed, had less conveniently and effectively angled oars on the raised gunwales on either side of a central hold. The self-evident purpose of oars was to enhance both speed and manoeuvrability, as well as to act as substitutes for sail. This twin propulsion was critical to the warlike intentions of the longship. Yet, for both warship and cargo ship, the overarching aim of shipbuilders was to maximize speed and efficiency by constructing ships that rode the waves, rather than ploughed them. Lightness, strength and flexibility were the immediate objectives.

Despite the exquisite craftsmanship and the sophistication of their archi-
tecture, Viking ships were not impervious to water. Leakage was a perennial
problem for boats that were both low in the water and pared to the last possible
ounce for the sake of hydrodynamics. One Icelandic saga says that while seven
men rowed, six baled; and the sagas are full of accounts of ships that foundered.
Exposure to low temperatures, with virtually no shelter available on board,
also meant that mortality rates were high. Keeping in sight of the coast was
obviously one way of ensuring a degree of safety and the shallow draught
of the longship increased the opportunities of making landfall after a day's
sailing and proceeding the following day. Ohthere's month-long voyage from
Hálogaland to Sciringesheal in Southern Norway, as told to Alfred the Great in
the late ninth century, was undertaken in this way. But such precautions were
simply not possible for crossings of the North Atlantic, on voyages of discovery
to Iceland, Greenland or Newfoundland, or even on a voyage from England to
the Baltic, which, according to another of Alfred's informants, Wulfstan, could
take seven days and nights.

Many ingenious suggestions have been made by experts in maritime technology concerning how the Vikings managed to navigate the oceans so accurately,
and much has been assumed about devices that they might have had at their
disposal. A sun-stone, or *sólarsteinn*, using the polarizing properties of feldspar
crystal, may have assisted orientation along with some type of sun-compass. A
fragment of circular wood with evenly spaced notches on the circumference,
found in a monastery in Greenland, may have served as a sun-compass by
adding a short gnomon, or pointer, raised at the centre in order to take readings
from its shadow. The obvious shortcomings of sun-stones and sun-compasses
are that they required the observer's zenith to be unclouded and, moreover,
an independent source of time was needed to establish direction from the
sun alone.

Some assistance may have been gained from a device such as the Anglo-
Saxon portable sundial discovered in the cloister garth of Canterbury Cathedral
in 1938 and dated to AD 1000. This remarkable instrument has settings for
each month and indicates the time of day according to four divisions. It would
have been useful for taking bearings at latitudes of 50° to 60°, but it would be
ineffective at times when the sun was reclusive. It should also be borne in mind
that both the Greenland and Canterbury dials were designed for religious
purposes, notably to determine the hour of prayer. The advances in ecclesiastical
astronomy should not necessarily be equated with those in nautical astronomy,

and certainly not before the conversion of the Vikings. Taking bearings from the sun and fixed stars was, however, an important aspect of Viking navigation and it makes sense to believe that Vikings attempted to sail according to latitude by correlating celestial deviations with those of the home port. It is not impossible that charts or calibrations tabulating the sun's position during the course of the year were being refined throughout the Viking Age. It was certainly the case that by the early twelfth century the Icelander known as Star-Oddi had developed sophisticated astronomical tables.

Even if it is accepted that they were able to calculate latitude using a combination of devices, the Vikings had no way of calculating longitude. The answer to questions about Viking navigational techniques is probably much simpler and, in some ways, more impressive. Setting aside hypotheses about navigational calculators, and given the fact that sea-charts were not in use until the fifteenth century, experience and common sense were the likeliest aids to navigation. According to a remark in the early twelfth-century Icelandic *Book of Settlements*, it is apparent that coastal navigation was aided by oral reports, for instance:

> Learned men state that from Stad in Norway it is seven days' sail west to Horn in the east of Iceland; and from Snæfellsness, where the distance is shortest, it is four days' sea west to Greenland. And it is said if one sails from Bergen due west to Hvarf in Greenland that one's course will lie some seventy or more miles south of Iceland.[11]

Advice on pilotage, when land could be sighted, was similarly available:

> From Hernar in Norway one must sail a direct course west to Hvarf in Greenland, in which case one sails north of Shetland so that one sights land in clear weather only, then south of the Faroes so that the sea looks half way up the mountainsides, then south of Iceland so that one gets sight of birds and whales from there.[12]

In addition, where caution made it advisable, soundings were taken from fathom lines, as was the case on Wulfstan's crossing of the Baltic. The most valuable navigational aid was therefore age-old wisdom and local knowledge passed from generation to generation, and ship to ship, although expertise may have been a closely guarded secret. One obvious aid to navigation was the repetition of success. Leif Eiriksson did precisely this on his voyage from Greenland to North America when he followed in reverse the land sightings of Bjarni Herjolfsson.

Supplementing the lessons of trial and error was a sense of speed and time, and perhaps an innate sense of magnetic north. Wave formations and fish migrations helped indicate currents, and cloud formations and the presence of birds were indicators of land; indeed birds, notably ravens, were sometimes carried on board and released in the search for land. This technique is described in the early twelfth-century Icelandic history the *Book of the Icelanders* in which Iceland is discovered by Floki Vilgertharson, much in the manner of Noah seeking a berth for his ark. It was in the very nature of Vikings to be risk-taking adventurers and, sometimes, maiden voyages of discovery had as much to do with good fortune as good judgement. The first sightings of Iceland, Greenland and North America were all the result of voyagers being blown off course.

For many years what was known about the design and structural efficiency of Viking ships was predicated on the excavation of two burial ships of the type known as *karves* (O.N. *karfi*). The first of these, indeed the first ever Viking ship to be excavated, was found at Gokstad in the Vestfold district of Norway in 1881 and has been dated by dendrochronology to the last decade of the ninth century. Measuring 23.3 m (76 ft 5 in) by 5.2 m (17 ft) amidships and 2 m (6 ft 6 in) deep and propelled by sail and sixteen pairs of oars, and with a large projecting keel, it has been deduced that the Gokstad ship was designed for deep waters. Three four-oared rowing boats, or *faerings*, were stowed aboard. As replica trials have shown, the ship could achieve considerable speed, perhaps as much as 12.5 knots in favourable conditions. But at such speeds, given the shallowness of the draught and the width of the hull, Gokstad would have been extremely difficult to control in poor weather. In the open sea it would have been liable to ship a perilous amount of water. The conclusion has now been drawn that the ship was primarily a prestige ship used by high-status individuals, much in the manner of a royal barge. The same is true for the Oseberg ship, excavated in 1904 in the same region as Gokstad. Oseberg was built around 820 and has thus the distinction of being the earliest Viking longship to have been recovered. Oseberg's proportions are similar, if slightly smaller, to those of Gokstad but, unlike Gokstad, whose exquisite craftsmanship is spare of ornamentation, Oseberg is richly decorated with high-quality carvings. This was the work of the royal 'school' of Vestfold carvers and among them was the supreme artist identified by archaeologists as the 'academician', a man whose work was among the finest that has survived from the Viking Age.

Ship burials in richly furnished ships that could have fulfilled a practical purpose are suggestive of the relationship between religious sensibilities and the pragmatics of commerce and commercially motivated warfare. For example, the Oseberg burial chamber, which was raised above the ship, contains the remains of a woman, surrounded by horses and dogs sacrificed at the graveside. Almost certainly, she was a member of the Vestfold royal family. Beside her, along with a number of fine wooden artefacts, there was an elaborately carved wagon or chariot that clearly had a ceremonial purpose. On the tapestries found in the grave a wagon similar to this is depicted in which a woman sits amid a reverential throng. Most likely, the deceased woman in the Oseberg find was associated with a female fertility cult as a priestess of the Vanir gods. In the second century AD, Tacitus, the Roman ethnographer of the Germanic tribes, described a ritual in which a goddess was represented visiting the people in a wagon, whereupon sacred objects were cleansed by slaves who were then drowned in a sacred lake. The powerful religious significance of the grave goods from Oseberg are indicative of the continuing influence of ancient cultic practice among Scandinavians in the ninth century and of the subordination of all earthly power to the honour of the deities.

It could, of course, be argued that ship burials were fashions indulged by a privileged few to the glorification of themselves and their line. Yet because they were ostentatious does not discount the likelihood of religious sincerity. Since at least the Bronze Age, Scandinavian vessels had been thought of as ways of extending tribal power. To this end, superstition attended their making and their use. The old myths suggest that all ships were dedicated to the fertility gods, among whom Njord was the god of shipping, and the sea itself was perceived as embodying the life–death cycle. The myth of the death of Baldur, which is recounted in various eddic sources and is clearly central to the cycle, tells how his father Odin laid him in his longship *Ringhorn* which was then cremated as Baldur's spirit journeyed to Hel. While ship cremations cannot be proven archaeologically, there is sufficient evidence from written sources to lend credence to the practice. Inhumations or cremations in ships were ways of ensuring that the deceased made his or her journey from this life to the next. The longship, and not only the *karve*, was not just a type of transportation, it was an icon. Every nail and plank carried sacred significance and it is said that in pagan times the launch was ritualized by human sacrificial blood anointing the prow. Viking longships carried both warriors and an ideology.

A transformation in our understanding of the various types and purposes of Viking Age ships and shipbuilding took place in 1962 at Skuldelev on the

Roskilde Fjord in Sjaelland, Denmark. In 1075, whilst under threat from hostile ships, the residents of Skuldelev sought to obstruct their enemy's progress by lading various craft with boulders and sinking them across the fjord. Two main classes of ship can be identified from the five wrecks recovered: the *drakkar* and the *knörr*. The *drakkar*, or 'dragon ship', although varied in size, is the typical Viking longship of the late Viking Age. Skuldelev 2 is 28 m (92 ft) long and 4.5 m (14 ft 9 in) wide with thirty pairs of oars and was built in Dublin some fifteen years before it was scuttled, although repair work shows that it had spent most of its time in Scandinavia. Skuldelev 5, of Danish origin, is 18 m (59 ft) long and 2.6 m (8 ft 6 in) wide and had probably been in service for thirty to forty years. This size of ship would have been ideal for raiding in the Baltic or up rivers. Replica trials have established that longships such as Skuldelev 2 and 5 could overtake their prey in any conditions short of a head-on gale. Replicas have proved that 10 knots is possible in a good wind and that 6–8 knots is the mean average over long distances. Speeds of up to 2 knots were possible when tacking (see p. 63 for scale drawings of the Skuldelev craft).

Skuldelev 1 and 3 are representative of the other class of ship, the *knörr*, or cargo ship. Typically broader and higher in relation to length than the *drakkar*, with oar ports only located in the forepart and afterpart of the ship, and evidently more reliant on a fixed sail, these were the workhorses of the Viking Age. The larger Skuldelev 1 was a Norwegian craft of pine construction, measuring 16.3 m (53 ft 6 in) by 4.5 m (15 ft). It could carry as much as 24 tonnes in weight, or 40 cubic metres by volume, and could be manned by as few as six men, each taking an equal share in the cargo. Skuldelev 3 is built of oak from the Roskilde region and measures 13.5 m (43 ft 6 in) by 3.2 m (10 ft 6 in) with a loading capacity of 4.6 tonnes or 12 cubic metres by volume. A crew of five would have been required to sail this ship. These cargo ships were clearly not meant for river traffic, where oars would have been essential. It is likely that ships for rowing up rivers and, when necessary, for being drawn overland were adapted as a kind of hybrid combining the most useful features of the *drakkar* and the *knörr*. Ocean-going Skuldelev *knerrir* functioned as supply ships for Viking armies or as transport for the families and livestock of colonizers in the later Viking Age. Twenty-five *knerrir* transported Eirik the Red's company of settlers bound for Greenland in around 983. Judging from one ship found at Hedeby, which was capable of carrying up to 60 tonnes, sizeable families could have been transported in a single *knörr*; lock, stock and barrel.

With the exception of the Oseberg burial ship's unusually elaborate carvings, featuring dragon posts and writhing shapes of gripping beasts, little of the finishing touches of the Viking ship has survived, not even a dragon prow or its fittings. Fortunately, the literature of medieval Iceland and of contemporary sources gives us some idea of the impression that a fleet of Viking ships made. A monk from the monastery of St-Omer in Flanders, recalling in the 1040s Cnut's fleet of 200 ships that invaded England in 1015, gives us a vivid picture replete with classical flourishes:

> So great, also, was the ornamentation of the ships that the eyes of the beholders were dazzled, and to those looking from afar they seemed of flame rather than of wood. For if at any time the sun cast the splendour of its rays among them, the flashing of arms shone in one place, in another the flame of suspended shields. Gold shone on the prows, silver also flashed on the variously shaped ships. So great, in fact, was the magnificence of the fleet, that if its lord had desired to conquer any people, the ships alone would have terrified the enemy, before the warriors whom they carried joined battle at all. For who could look upon the lions of the foe, terrible with the brightness of gold, who upon the men of metal, menacing with golden face, who upon the dragons burning with pure gold, who upon the bulls on the ships threatening death, their horns shining with gold, without feeling any fear for the king of such a force?[13]

The Vikings, themselves, were just as impressed as their victims with the spectacle of their creations and skaldic poets were often called upon to compose in tribute to their patrons' magnificent vessels. This verse from Thjotholf the Skald celebrates one of the many forays of the Norwegian king Harald Hardrada against the Danes:

> Much ill will suffer oaken
> Oarlocks, ere by rowers
> Seventy sweeps from stormy
> Sea be lifted sithen:
> Onward, Northmen urge the
> Iron-mailed great dragon,
> Like as, with outspread wings, an
> Eagle, on hailstruck sea-stream.[14]

Similarly, this verse by Arnor Jarlaskald eulogizes the power of the longship, *Great Bison*, as King Magnus the Good (d. 1047) set out for Denmark:

Hatefully, the spume and spindrift
Spattered 'gainst poop and rudder,
Gusts of wind did shake the galleys'
Gold-decked yardarms, low them bending,
As you steered past Stafang southward
Steadfastly – the waters parted –
Up above there burned like fire
Burnished mastheads – toward Denmark.[15]

The prime function of a Viking fleet was to carry warriors to land. Battle for domination of the seaways was, however, not an entirely meaningless concept, and this was clearly the intention of Vikings in the Irish Sea and the North Sea. Where maritime nations could mount serious opposition on the high seas, the Vikings rarely emerged victorious. Alfred the Great's fleet was an important deterrent in the late ninth century, and Vikings were frequently routed by Byzantine and Muslim fleets as a consequence of their technologically superior weaponry. Although large-scale naval battles were infrequent, skirmishes between rival Viking forces were not uncommon. Battle tactics at sea were simple: sail alongside, grapple and clear the decks. Perhaps the finest description of a large naval battle is Snorri Sturluson's account of the defeat of the Norwegian king Olaf Tryggvason at Svöld in 1000 by a coalition of Viking adversaries from all parts of Scandinavia. Olaf's ship, *Long Serpent*, built in Trondheim in 998, was reputed to have been almost 50 m (160 ft) long with thirty-five pairs of oars and able to carry more than two hundred warriors. Snorri describes how, as the two opposing fleets closed in on each other amidst a rain of arrows and spears, Olaf commanded that *Long Serpent* be lashed between two smaller longships, *Short Serpent* and *Crane*, gaining a firm platform from which to resist the attackers. The tactic proved to be of no avail and Olaf's chief adversary, the Danish Earl Eirik of Hlathir, succeeded in clearing the decks of the smaller ships and cutting the hawsers holding them together. As *Long Serpent* came under direct attack, Earl Eirik was able to exploit his numerical advantage:

The strongest defence on the *Serpent*, and the most deadly, was made by the men in the forward compartment and those in the forecastle. There were both the pick of the men and the highest gunwales. Now when the crew amidships had fallen and only few men were still standing by the mast, Earl Eirik attempted to board the *Serpent*, and managed to get up on it with fourteen others. Then Hyrning, King Olaf's brother-in-law, fell upon him, and there ensued the most furious fight, with the result that the earl had to fall back and get down into his ship *Barthi*; and of the men who had followed him some fell and were wounded ...

Then there was another terrific fight, and many of the *Serpent*'s crew were cut down. And as the ranks of the defenders on the *Serpent* grew thin, Earl Eirik again tried to board the *Serpent*. And again the resistance was fierce. When the men in the forecastle of the *Serpent* saw Earl Eirik's attack they came aft and turned against him, giving him a stiff reception. However, since so many of the *Serpent*'s crew had fallen that there were gaps between the defenders along the gunwales, the earl's men began to climb aboard in many places. But all those still able to stand up on the *Serpent* retreated aft to where the king was.[16]

At the end, Olaf was forced to leap overboard and so, in a sense, into legend, for his body was never recovered and reports of his continued good health circulated for many years to come. What became of Olaf is uncertain, but Snorri asserts that he never returned to Norway.

It is not impossible that such huge ships as *Long Serpent* existed, for Snorri, writing over two hundred years after the event, says 'the stocks on which it was built still exist and can be seen'.[17] In 1997 a longship nearest to the dimensions of Olaf's ship was found in Roskilde, measuring some 35 m (114 ft), but, as Snorri's account indicates, what such leviathans gained in accommodation they lost in manoeuvrability. Numerous other finds have been made throughout Scandinavia revealing something of the range of seaworthy longships. Some were designed for freebooter flotillas, some for sizeable fleets intent on large-scale conquests across the North Sea. Given the current evidence, the warlike longship had a crew of anything from thirty to a hundred men who worked in shifts when oar power was required. A trip from western Denmark to north-eastern England in such finely tuned craft could have been made in little more than two days and a night with a full wind in the sail. Whilst it should be borne in mind that building a *drakkar* or a *knörr* was a costly business, as time went on and the revenue of Viking depredations flowed to a more centralized leadership, fleets of hundreds of ships are not impossible. The two fleets of the second Great Army that invaded England in 892 were estimated by the *Anglo-Saxon Chronicle* to number three hundred and thirty. Given the extent of the campaign and numbers of men confronting Alfred the Great's forces for the next four years, the estimate is not wholly incredible. Yet it would be unwise to assume that contemporary accounts of Viking fleets were always impartial and precise. Abbo of Fleury's account of the siege of Paris in 885, which claims that an army of 30,000 Vikings entered the River Seine in seven hundred ships, is highly doubtful.

The longship did not long outlast the Viking Age. When William the Conqueror, a descendant of the Viking overlords of Normandy, crossed the English Channel in 1066 to assume the throne of England, it was to be the last great military campaign bringing victory from a vessel of the longship design. The Bayeux Tapestry (*c.* 1080) shows William's shipwrights building his fleet of six hundred longships (one source says three thousand!) and the success of his naval onslaught. By the early middle ages, however, the sealed deck had marked the next important stage in shipbuilding, and the bulkier, slower but more capacious cog, preferred by the German traders of the Hanseatic League, had replaced the sleek proportions of the *drakkar* and the *knörr*. Scandinavians, by this time, were either fully integrated into the communities they once terrorized or had long since retreated to their homelands, where their descendants contributed to Christian Europe's holy wars against Islam. Expansionist tendencies and general belligerence did not, however, disappear from their agenda but were disguised as forceful missions to Christianize Baltic and Slavic neighbours, harnessed to the broader mission of the church.

It is perhaps no coincidence that the demise of the longship and of Viking shipbuilding energy fell hard on the heels of the Christian conversion of Scandinavia. In medieval Christian Europe, dynastic unions, treaties, and wars sanctioned by popes were the way of things. Freebooter mercenary adventurers numerous enough to destabilize kingdoms were a thing of the past. Moreover, Europe had learned much from the Viking Age, and a common enemy had led to a better preparedness – political and military – for any future surprises. The blunt features of the cog in certain ways mirrored the blunted ambitions of the Scandinavians.

# 4

# England, Ireland and Wales, 789–900

The *Anglo-Saxon Chronicle* entry for 789 reads:

> Here Beorhtric took King Offa's daughter Eadburg. And in his days came first three ships of Northmen from Hordaland: and then the reeve rode there and wanted to compel them to go to the king's town because he did not know what they were; and they killed him. These were the first ships of the Danish men which sought out the land of the English race.[1]

At the time, the marriage of Eadburg, the daughter of the Mercian king and self-styled *rex Anglorum* (king of the English), Offa, to King Beorhtric of Wessex would have seemed a far more significant event than the murder of a magistrate, Beorhtric's reeve. But looking back from the late ninth century, when Alfred the Great's historians reconstructed the events of 789, it was the reeve's death that carried far greater significance, for this crime was the start of England's Viking Age. Toward the end of the tenth century, as the Viking Age moved toward its political culmination in England, Æthelweard, ealdorman of the western provinces and a key negotiator in efforts to deal with the new wave of Viking marauders, elaborated further. The reeve was Beaduheard and he had just happened to be in Dorchester when news reached him that the men of three strange ships had disembarked near Portland. He took with him a few companions as a small show of authority, assuming that the strangers were merchants and, therefore, bound by law to present themselves to him and declare their business. Beaduheard was determined that, as the delegate of the king, their compliance should be immediate, so he spoke to them 'haughtily'.[2] It was an error of judgement that few would make after him.

In fact, these Vikings were not Danes but Norwegians and it was from that quarter that the trouble began. Exactly what happened during the next four years is not reported but Beaduheard's death cannot have been an isolated event. It is inconceivable that a king as mighty as Offa would have taken the trouble to fortify the coastline of Kent against 'sea-going pagans with roaming ships' if it had not been for a continuing and serious threat.[3] What was becoming a

mounting problem suddenly turned into a major outrage on 8 June 793, when
the small but richly furnished monastery on the island of Lindisfarne off the
north-east coast of England was sacked by Norwegian Vikings. It was more than
a matter of damage to a kingdom, it was sacrilege. The *Anglo-Saxon Chronicle*
records the event in apocalyptic language:

> Here terrible portents came about in the land of Northumbria, and miserably
> afflicted the people: there were immense flashes of lightning, and fiery dragons
> were seen flying in the air, and there immediately followed a great famine, and after
> in the same year the raiding of the heathen miserably devastated God's church in
> Lindisfarne island by looting and slaughter.[4]

Alcuin, the learned Northumbrian cleric and a contemporary, was in no doubt
about the wider significance of the raid on Lindisfarne. In his letter to Bishop
Higbald of Lindisfarne, Alcuin was certain that 'It has not happened by chance,
but is the sign of some great guilt'.[5] Alcuin had long had misgivings about what
he considered to be the inappropriately low standards set by Higbald. The
death of the 'just and pious' Ælfwald, king of the Northumbrians, in 788, and
the resumption of the kingship of the widely disliked Æthelred, had coincided
with what Alcuin regarded as a moral degeneration in the north. While spiritual
laxity was Alcuin's chief target, in his letter to Æthelred he also suggested that
political and military complacency were part of the general malaise:

> We and our fathers have now lived in this fair land for nearly three hundred and
> fifty years, and never before has such an atrocity been seen in Britain as we have now
> suffered at the hands of a pagan people. Such a voyage was not thought possible.[6]

The attack on Lindisfarne, 'a place more sacred than any in Britain' and the cradle
of English Roman Catholicism, says Alcuin, was portended by 'unusual happen-
ings' and was as a result of 'strange conduct'. Like the *Anglo-Saxon Chronicle*,
Alcuin saw 'the punishment by blood' forewarned in strange phenomena,
significantly the 'bloody rain' that had fallen on the north side of the roof of St
Peter's in York during Lent of the same year. Just as the Old Testament Book of
Jeremiah had prophesied that 'From the north an evil breaks forth, and a terrible
glory will come from the Lord', so had this portent.[7] Materialism, immoderation
and aping pagan fashions, in a time when 'the rich man stuffs himself and
starves the poor', had brought about judgement 'without pity'.[8]

Alcuin's analysis was not simply a matter of religious superstition. The des-
ecration of Lindisfarne, Alcuin had calculated, could be used to reaffirm the

power and probity of the church, particularly as it was demanded from Alcuin's place of work at the right hand of the Holy Roman Emperor, Charlemagne, in Aachen. Perhaps his excoriation did something to rein in excess and dispel apathy but, as Alcuin rightly understood, so far as the pagan terror from the north was concerned, this was only the beginning. The following year, Donemuthan, which Simeon of Durham identified as Jarrow, the site of the interment of the greatest scholar of the century, the Venerable Bede (d. 735), came under Norwegian attack, as did nearby Wearmouth.[9] Yet the outcome for the Vikings was different from that at Lindisfarne. Alcuin had warned his holy brethren at these twinned monasteries to 'Consider whom you have to defend you against the pagans who have appeared on your coasts' in the light of the 'terrible fate that has come upon the church of St Cuthbert'.[10] While the monks were told to put their trust in God rather than arms, common sense suggests that plans were made by monks and local inhabitants in the face of the Viking threat. According to the *Anglo-Saxon Chronicle*, this Viking raiding party suffered its first set-back when one of its commanders was killed, and thereafter, on departure, bad weather wrecked many ships. Those who did not drown but managed to get ashore were put to the sword. Many saw it as divine vengeance for Lindisfarne, somewhat prematurely as it turned out.

One failure was not sufficient to deter the Vikings, for they now knew just how richly stocked the monasteries were and, after Charlemagne's attempts to ransom the abducted clerics of Lindisfarne, they also knew that their inhabitants carried particular value. Contemporary records suggest that the focus now turned to the north west, to Scotland and the Scottish isles, and to Ireland, whilst England enjoyed a period of neglect by the Vikings until the 830s, when the Danes entered the English scene. But this is unlikely. Simeon of Durham, albeit looking back from the twelfth century, says that around the time of the attack on Lindisfarne the Vikings 'overran the country in all directions'.[11] Supporting this is the entry in the *Annals of Ulster* for 794, which speaks of the 'devastation of all the islands of Britain by heathens'.[12] Although the *Anglo-Saxon Chronicle* includes no record of these incursions in England, many Northumbrian farms were probably plundered during the period when Norwegians were attacking and settling round Scotland and Ireland. For the Wessex historians, the theft of livestock and the ruination of farming communities in the north were not the stuff of history.

On their way to mainland Britain and to Ireland, the Norwegians made good use of the island archipelagos of Shetland and Orkney as staging posts. Their initial use of the islands as a base from which to gain access to vulnerable sites throughout northern Britain soon turned to permanent settlement. The next major shock came in 795, when the spiritual centre of Scottish Christianity, the monastery of St Columba on the island of Iona off the north-west coast of Scotland, was sacked. The same fate befell it in 802 and 806, when sixty monks were killed, and again in 807. So beset was Iona that in 814 the monks were forced to relocate to Kells, north west of Dublin, leaving behind only a few monks prepared for martyrdom. In 825, the Vikings returned and martyred these monks, including Prior Blathmacc mac Flaind, who was tortured to death for refusing to betray the whereabouts of the sacred shrine of St Columba. Ireland, however, offered the fleeing monks no safe retreat. Instead, it became a prime target for the Vikings. Perhaps the same raiding party that had attacked Iona in 795 that year raided the island of Lambay, north of Dublin, and overran the remote monastic communities on Inishmurray and Inishboffin off Ireland's west coast. By the end of the second decade of the ninth century, there were Vikings attacks round the entire Irish coastline. So frequent were their assaults, and in such fear were the inhabitants of the monasteries, that bad weather was the only guarantee of a peaceful night. In the margins of a ninth-century manuscript, the *Codex Sangallensis*, one monk gave lyrical voice to his fear of raiders from Norway (*Lochlainn*):

> Bitter is the wind tonight,
> It tosses the white-waved sea,
> I do not fear the coursing of the great sea
> By the fierce warriors from Lochlainn.[13]

While the Celts of Wales proved too hostile and the country's coastal access too daunting to attract more than the occasional raid, Scotland and Ireland proved soft targets for the Norwegian Vikings. With no towns from which resistance could be organised, and deep coastal inlets providing shelter and easy access, raiders came and went at will. In Ireland, twenty-six Viking attacks are recorded in the first quarter of the ninth century. Only on very few occasions were the locals able to put up resistance effective enough to repel them. The problem was not helped by the quarrelsome nature of the Irish themselves, who contributed to their own misery even more effectively than the Vikings. During the same period of the Viking onslaught, the Irish launched over eighty attacks against each other, including attacks on monasteries located in areas of disputed rule, of which there were many. Given this internal disarray, the Vikings' policy of surprise attack

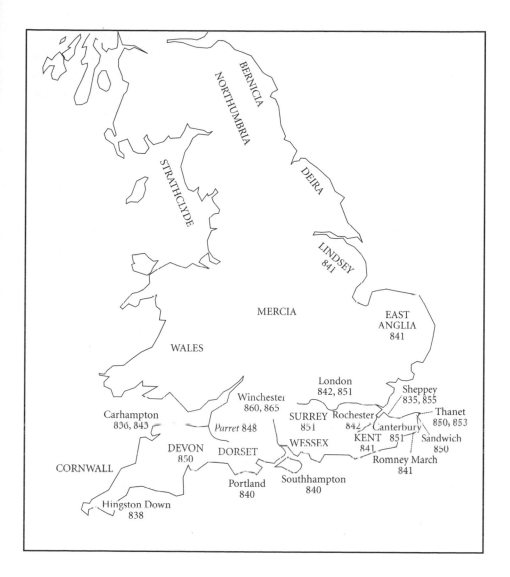

Early viking raids on England (835–65)

was highly effective and it led to them gaining greater and greater territorial influence. So vulnerable were the Irish monasteries to Viking raiders that the major monastery at Armagh was ransacked three times in one month during 832, despite being inland. It was a mixed blessing for a monastery to survive an attack unscathed, as it usually meant that the attackers would return.

By the middle of the ninth century, Vikings were to be found everywhere in Ireland and had founded harbour strongholds, or *longphorts*, around the island, the most important being at Dublin. The Isle of Man in the Irish Sea soon became a Viking stronghold and settlers from Norway streamed to Orkney, Shetland and the Hebrides. Native Picts, Scots and Irish were casually dispossessed, sold into slavery or obliged to collaborate in their own subjugation. As Ireland and Scotland entered a second, more intense, phase of Viking incursions during the 830s, England began to suffer from a startling escalation of Scandinavian aggression. The Danes had, up to this point, largely concentrated on mainland Europe and had contributed to the dismantling of Charlemagne's once great empire, aided by internal dissent among Charlemagne's successors. In 835, the Scandinavians suddenly began to act more concertedly, in greater numbers and with greater ambition. This dramatic increase in Danish activities on the Continent, and in Norwegian violence in the Celtic west, placed England at the centre of Viking attention.

At the outset of the Viking Age, England was comprised of five kingdoms: Northumbria in the north, Mercia in the central and west midlands, East Anglia in the east midlands, Kent in the south east and Wessex in the south west. Whilst Offa had ruthlessly sought to establish Mercian supremacy throughout England, his power disintegrated after his death and by 830 Wessex was in the ascendancy. The Vikings were soon able to exploit the country's fragmentation. The first major Danish attack fell on the Isle of Sheppey in Kent, just to the south of the Thames estuary, in 835. After Sheppey, the Danes were set on testing the strengths and weaknesses of England, identifying the West Country as a vulnerable point. Between twenty-five and thirty-five longships are recorded as having made 'great slaughter' at Carhampton in Somerset in 836. Knowing the disaffection of the Cornish, who were still smarting from the conquest of King Ecgberht of Wessex, the Vikings encouraged them to join forces with them but they did not prevail and were put to flight. Raids and pitch battles, in which the Danes were sometimes victorious and sometimes not, and further great slaughter are recorded across the south of England for the next ten years. Then, in 850, there was an ominous development.

The year was one of mixed fortunes. On the positive side, the men of Devon triumphed over the 'heathen men at Wicga's stronghold'; and at Sandwich in Kent, the Wessex sub-king of Kent, Athelstan, mounted a daring raid on the Danes and seized nine of their ships and dispersed their army. On the negative side, this did nothing to deter the interlopers, and for the first time a Viking army established winter quarters (*wintersetl*) on the Isle of Thanet off the eastern tip of Kent. The following year, the Danes were prepared to make a big impression. According to the *Anglo-Saxon Chronicle*, some 350 ships entered the mouth of the Thames and 'stormed Canterbury and London, and put to flight Beorhtwulf king of Mercia with his army, and then went south over the Thames into Surrey'. Their advance was halted when the Wessex army confronted them and 'made the greatest slaughter of a heathen raiding-army that we have heard tell of up to this present day'.[14]

A precedent had been set, however, and, in 855, Sheppey became the next site for a Danish army to overwinter. Ten years later another precedent was set. In 865 Vikings were once again ensconced on the Isle of Thanet. Rather than enter into the routine of mutual slaughter, the inhabitants of Kent offered money and valuables in return for peace. This was the first time that the English had offered payment to get rid of the Danes. Paying Danegeld would, in years to come, be a common measure of the last resort. Perhaps the English should have learnt something from the extortion in Kent for, as the Wessex historian Asser observed, 'they [the Danes] knew they could get more money from stolen booty than from peace',[15] so having reconciled themselves with the locals the army stole away under cover of night and went about business as usual. Vikings on English soil had become a disturbing year-round presence in the increasingly chaotic situation in the south east. Wales, too, was threatened and it was largely due to the determined resistance of Rhodri Mawr (844–78), the prince of Gwynedd, that Viking interests were prevented from extending much beyond the island of Anglesey. Danish persistence, and a steady escalation of the size and frequency of attacks, were paying good dividends in England and the susceptibility of the English coastline had become widely known among Viking sea kings. Once the Danes had identified England as a place of lucrative reward, it was only a matter of time before they raised the stakes and turned from raiders to conquerors.

The arrival of the Danish Great Army in East Anglia in 865 is one of the most mythologized events in Viking Age history, hardly surprisingly for this invasion would lead to the greatest territorial conquest that the Vikings were to make during their 300 year career. The most likely reason for the invasion of an army numbering thousands was the conjunction of three broader perspectives. First, the Danes, despite losing more often than they won, now fully perceived their potential in England, partly based on a gradual awareness of the lack of coordination among English forces and, after thirty years of Danish trouble-making, partly on a growing readiness among the English to buy peace rather than offer resistance. Records for Viking activity in Northumbria are scant for the years prior to 865 and only the killing of King Rædwulf in 842 is recalled as significant. Nonetheless, it is highly unlikely that Vikings had neglected the north-east coast. The added intelligence that Northumbria was, in 865, engaged in a civil war must have been a persuasive reason to head north instead of south, where Wessex kings could still manage a credible opposition; indeed the Wessex performance was, even at this point, exemplary. Second, the prospects for Vikings in Ireland were less clear-cut than they had been, as Norwegians, Danes and Irish kings were too often locked in mutual conflict for possession of the chief assets. In this three-cornered fight, Ireland was exhausted. Third, in West Frankia, many targets, including monasteries, had been deserted and their valuables moved to regions that offered greater security. Besides this limitation on booty there were also limitations on movement, as systematic defences built in the early 860s had closed down opportunities. These were the underlying strategic causes behind the Great Army's invasion of England, but medieval Scandinavian writers preferred a story with a more personal touch.

According to Saxo Grammaticus and the Icelandic sagamen and poets, the leaders of the Great Army were the sons of the notorious Viking warlord Ragnar Hairy Breeches, said variously to have been a king of Denmark, a king of Dublin, the scourge of the Franks and the Viking world generally, and the son-in-law of the greatest hero of the Old North, Sigurd the Dragon Slayer. Taking into account variants in the telling of the tale, the story is as follows. After having harassed and outmastered King Ælla of York for several years, Ragnar Hairy Breeches was eventually captured and consigned to Ælla's snake pit and an inglorious death. As the poison worked on him, Ragnar recited his death-poem, which he concluded somewhat cryptically with 'how the little pigs will grunt when they hear how the old boar has died'. The 'little pigs', in this case, were no less than his five sons – Ivar the Boneless, Sigurd Snake in the Eye, Bjorn Ironside, Ubba and Halfdan – all cast in their father's mould.[16] Just as Ragnar prophesied, when news of his death reached his sons in Denmark, they vowed immediate vengeance against Ælla and promptly marshalled a fleet of longships and set out for England. At York, the brothers parleyed with Ælla and, by way of compensation, agreed to accept as much land as could be encircled by a horse-hide. But their agreement was merely a ruse and by slicing the hide into strips they encircled enough land to establish a city and from this they laid siege to York. Ælla was in this way vanquished and, as punishment for his murder of Ragnar, was subjected to the Odinic rite of the 'blood-eagle', whereby the backbone was sliced from top to bottom, the rib cage forced apart and the lungs draped over the shoulders, so resembling an eagle, the bird sacred to Odin. Having so disposed of Ælla, says the legend, the brothers waged war against the kingdoms of England and succeeded in establishing a Danish-held territory stretching from the Scottish border to London.

Little of the intimate detail of this tale can be verified and the interweaving legends associated with the Viking protagonists only serve to obscure matters. The actual career of Ragnar Hairy Breeches is difficult to pin down, partly because acts that are credited to him are chronologically unlikely and may well be drawn from the careers of several Viking warlords. Whether the leaders of the Great Army were motivated by a blood debt and whether Ælla perished in the way described is debatable, although the Vikings were capable of such atrocities. What is true, however, is that the 'unnatural' king Ælla, deposer of the 'natural' king Osberht, was one of the first notable victims of the Great Army and that Ivar, in company with his brothers, two of whom were known to be Halfdan and Ubba, was the driving force behind the invasion. The identification of these Viking leaders as the Ragnarssons, the sons of Ragnar Hairy Breeches, is reasonable enough.

The Ragnarssons' first task was to get horses. This was achieved with some ease from the doubtless terrified residents of East Anglia, who 'made peace' with the invaders. The following year, elements of the army rode north to the River Humber, where they were ferried across by longship. Then they proceeded to where the Humber meets the River Ouse and from there they headed for York. The main city of Northumbria provided little resistance and the Ragnarssons easily established themselves inside the old Roman walls. The following year Ælla and Osberht wisely set aside their differences and, with their own great army, broke into the city. It was a miscalculation, for once inside they were promptly ambushed and virtually annihilated. Both kings were killed, either in battle or as captives. The Vikings now had in England what they had not achieved before: a secure, highly fortified and strategically well-placed base from which to launch their campaigns. The immediate focus of their power was the old Anglian kingdom of Deira, better known from this time forward as the kingdom of York.

The Ragnarssons wasted no time. First, the monasteries on the Northumbrian coast as far as the Tyne were ravaged, including Whitby (then known as Strenaeshalc) and, yet again, Jarrow and Wearmouth. Then, in 867, the army headed south to Nottingham to confront the Mercian king Burgred. Burgred rapidly appreciated the enormity of the threat posed to him and promptly summoned the help of his Wessex allies led by King Æthelred. A stalemate resulted with the Danes besieged but not discomfited. Burgred was finally forced to pay the Danes, which, if the going rate on the Continent was anything to go by, may well have amounted to thousands of pounds of gold and silver. Accompanying King Æthelred in this inglorious episode was his brother, a teenager named Alfred, on his first military campaign. In ten years' time, Alfred was to meet these same Danes in the south west of England as the last hope of the Anglo-Saxons and as a result win to himself the epithet 'the Great', but at Nottingham, like all other Englishmen, he could only look on helpless.

The Great Army now returned to York. The following year, it was the turn of the East Anglians. Burgred stood by as Ivar the Boneless and Ubba passed through Mercia with their host. They camped at Thetford and set about subjugating the people and ransacking the land. According to the *Anglo-Saxon Chronicle*, the East Anglian king, Edmund, was killed in battle, but later accounts of his death tell of his being taken prisoner and informed by the brothers that he could continue his rule under their dispensation, providing he renounced Christianity. In these accounts, Edmund's refusal led to his brutal murder on 20 November 869, perhaps, as some sources allege, by the same ritual torture said to have been doled out to Ælla of York, or perhaps, as other sources allege and some medieval depictions show, by a squad of archers. Whatever actually took place, the death of St Edmund, as he rapidly became, played a significant part in the conversion of the Vikings, in both Scandinavia and England. Notably, the conversion of Iceland in 1000 is marked from the birth of Christ and the death of St Edmund, whilst in England King Cnut identified common Christian ground in St Edmund's death in his efforts to reconcile Anglo-Saxon and Scandinavian factions during his rule in the eleventh century. The tradition that established Edmund as a martyr was a reproach to pagan Northmen for all time.

With much of Northumbria under their direct control, Mercia cowed and Ivar's appointee, Guthrum, king in East Anglia, the Danes now turned toward Wessex, which encompassed the whole of the south of England in a line from just below London across to the Bristol Channel. In 871, the Great Army led by Halfdan established itself at Reading in Berkshire, where longships and the infantry could conjoin. While certainly a grave crisis for the West Saxons, the brothers Æthelred and Alfred could now confront the Danes in the way that they might have wished to at Nottingham four years earlier. It is reported that nine great battles were fought. Not everything went the way of Wessex, but in the course of the conflict nine Danish jarls (earls), an unspecified Danish king and Halfdan's co-commander, Bagsegc, perished. A conspicuous Wessex victory at Ashdown, where Æthelred and Alfred separately took on two Danish raiding armies and where 'many thousands were killed',[17] gave the Danes pause for thought. An outright Danish success at Basing, followed by a pyrrhic Danish victory at Meretun,[18] led both sides to recognize that a truce was necessary for the time being. Yet the year was memorable for another reason, as shortly after Easter, Æthelred died and the young Alfred became king.

The Danes withdrew to their winter camp at London in 871–2 and then moved to the Mercian town of Torksey, a few miles north east of Lincoln. Meanwhile, according to the *Annals of Ulster*, Ivar the Boneless and his brother Ubba were busy extending their influence among the Britons in the Strathclyde region of Scotland in company with Ivar's old comrade Olaf the White, a Norwegian Viking who had shared the kingship of Dublin with Ivar prior to the invasion of England. The thirteenth-century cleric of St Alban's monastery, Roger of Wendover, perhaps drawing on the lost northern chronicle, tells of one particularly gruesome episode where the nuns of Coldingham on the Firth of Forth deliberately mutilated their faces in order to deter Ivar's Vikings from violating or enslaving them. The tactic worked, but Ivar and his companions burnt them alive instead.[19] Apart from brutally despoiling monasteries and nunneries, Ivar's aim was to gather slaves for the market in Dublin and once there to resume his kingship. What befell Ivar will need to be considered in due course but in 872 the matter that preoccupied the Danes in England was the kingship of Burgred of Mercia.

The Danes had already ensured Burgred's compliance. No doubt he was chastened by what had happened to Edmund in East Anglia. He is conspicuously absent from accounts of the clashes in Berkshire, despite his supposed loyalty to Wessex. His non-combatant stance was, however, compromised when, perhaps with his consent, the Mercian ealdorman Æthelwulf lent valuable assistance to Æthelred and Alfred in the confrontation at Englefield just outside Reading and died shortly afterwards in a further clash with Halfdan's forces.

But the Danes needed no such reason to turn against Burgred. Curtailed in their first campaign against Wessex, their priority was to consolidate what they already had in Northumbria, East Anglia and Mercia. In this scheme, Burgred was superfluous and his royal pedigree suggested that at some point in the future he might even become dangerous. The royal Mercian seat at Repton in Derbyshire, where Mercian kings had been interred since the seventh century, proved to be an ideal winter camp for the Danes, both physically and symboli-cally. From there, in 873, they 'drove King Burgred across the sea, after he had held the kingdom twenty-two years and they conquered all that land'. In his place, they set Ceolwulf 'a foolish king's thegn',[20] who, in return for a slice of Mercia, would answer to the beck and call of the Danes. Repton was a turning point for the Great Army, a point at which the conquerors could review their achievements, but something very strange happened that took some of the shine off the trophy of victory.

The question as to what happened to Ivar the Boneless will probably never be resolved. *The Anglo-Saxon Chronicle* makes no mention of him participating in events after the murder of Edmund in East Anglia, while the *Annals of Ulster*, which give a fairly full account of a certain Imhar and his activities on either side of Ivar's time in England, does not mention Imhar during this period. Given the reasonable assumption that the Imhar who ruled in Dublin was the same Ivar who returned to Dublin after the escapade in Strathclyde, and that this was the self-same Ivar the Boneless, it is clear that Ivar's death was in 873: thus, 'Imhar, king of the Norsemen of all Ireland and Britain, ended his life'.[21] Yet this does not mean that he died in Ireland. Could Repton be Ivar's last resting place? One possible answer has its root in a chance finding in the late seventeenth century.

In or about 1686 Thomas Walker, a Derbyshire labourer, had a remarkable encounter at Repton that was later reported to the antiquarian Dr Simon Degge:

> About Forty Years since cutting Hillocks, near the Surface he met with an old Stone Wall, when clearing farther he found it to be a square Enclosure of Fifteen Foot: It had been covered, but the Top was decayed and fallen in, being only supported by wooden Joyces. In this he found a Stone Coffin, and with Difficulty removing the Cover, saw a Skeleton of a Humane Body Nine Foot long, and round it lay One Hundred Humane Skeletons, with their Feet pointing to the Stone Coffin. They seem'd to be of the ordinary size.[22]

Walker removed the skull from the stone coffin and gave it to a local teacher. It was subsequently lost but the 'Gigantick Corps ... was attested to us by several old People, who had likewise seen and measured the Skeleton'.[23] Over the years, the site was plundered numerous times and the skeletons, so meticulously arranged, were disarticulated and piled up. The great skeleton in the stone coffin vanished. A thorough archaeological investigation of the site has been conducted since the 1980s. The remains at the Repton site consist of 'about 200 men of military age and exceptional robustness and of about fifty women'.[24] They are dated precisely to 873–4 and, without doubt, many among them were members of the Great Army. Viking artefacts, including coins, weapons and amulets, confirm this dating. The disposition of the central grave was such that it is clear that this was a burial of someone of great prestige, in effect a royal burial. It is known for certain that four eminent Viking leaders – Halfdan, Guthrum, Oscetel and Anwend – were at Repton, but none of them died there. The case for the royal tomb being that of Ivar the Boneless is, if not conclusive, at least compelling.

According to many medieval Scandinavian traditions, Ivar died in England and was placed in a mound 'in the manner of former times'.[25] The *Saga of Ragnar Hairy Breeches* says that Ivar ordered that he be buried 'in a place which was exposed to attack, and prophesied that, if this was done, foes coming to land would meet with ill-success'.[26] Apart from the Repton burial site matching the topographical requirements of Ivar's last wishes, legend has it that in 1066 two invaders, Harald Hardrada and William the Conqueror, were aware of Ivar's curse and that Harald died as a consequence and that William sought to deflect any ill-success by demolishing the barrow. While this proves nothing in itself and is dubious, not least for geographical reasons, the wide circulation of this story suggests that there could be a grain of historical truth underlying folktale rumours regarding Ivar's dying wishes. As for the immense size of the missing skeleton, this accords to some degree with descriptions of Ivar in later sources and might, by one interpretation, be signified in the epithet 'the Boneless', as meaning someone exceptionally tall. Ivar is reported to have been physically unusual in a number of ways. One source says that he was not as other men and 'that neither love nor lust was part of his nature'. Another reports that he was unable to walk due an unspecified infirmity, leaving open the possibility that his death was the result of a degenerative illness. Yet another source reports that he succumbed to 'a sudden hideous disease'. This last hypothesis is particularly interesting, for, although some of the Repton skeletons reveal signs of physical injury, most do not. It is possible, therefore, that at the very moment that the Danes were celebrating their domination of over half of England, plague entered their camp and killed, amongst others, their most powerful and inspirationally vicious leader.

After Repton, Halfdan went north into the old Anglian kingdom of Bernicia, which encompassed a swathe of Northumbria from the Tees to the Tweed, with the intention of securing his border as far as the Tyne. Then, following Ivar's example of two years earlier, he plundered as far west as Strathclyde. Around this time the monks of Lindisfarne abandoned all hope of the meditative life. With the incorrupt body of St Cuthbert and the Lindisfarne Gospels stowed among their belongings, they set off on what would turn out to be over two centuries of dislocation before Cuthbert was finally laid to rest in Durham. But Repton may have wearied many of the Northumbrian branch of the Great Army in this ninth year of their campaign. On his return, Halfdan set about dividing the land into three main areas, or Þrithings, which still define the Ridings of Yorkshire. The intention that the land they had gained would be settled was clear: 'and they were ploughing and providing for themselves', as it says in the Anglo-Saxon Chronicle.[27] This was no longer a place of plunder for a marauding army; it was a new home. Halfdan, however, was unable to settle. In all likelihood, he died in Ireland in 877 at the battle of Strangford Lough, probably at the hands of Oistin son of Olaf the White, Ivar's one-time partner in crime. Their disagreement almost certainly concerned the entitlement to rule out of Dublin.

While some Northumbrian Danes were turning swords to ploughshares and busily establishing the bustling urban centre of Jorvik (York), Guthrum and his lið were set on revisiting the outstanding problem of Wessex. Along with Oscetel and Anwend, commanders of the other division of the Viking army, Guthrum headed for Cambridge where, on the East Anglian flatlands, he recruited new arrivals from Denmark. Alfred responded with a naval assault and saw off seven longships, capturing one of them. But Alfred's hopes of making a stand at Cambridge were frustrated and, in 876, Guthrum avoided Alfred's army and went to Wareham on the south coast. Alfred followed but could not dislodge him and for the first time was obliged to buy him off. In return, the Danes granted Alfred hostages and swore him 'oaths on a great ring ... that they would quickly go from his kingdom'.[28] It was a lie, for they left stealthily at night, mounted their horses and headed straight for Alfred's stronghold in Exeter. Realizing the treachery, Alfred set off in rapid pursuit but was unable to overtake them. Part of Guthrum's plan may have been to send his longships west and attack Wessex from Alfred's rear, but a great storm wrecked his fleet at Swanage. Meanwhile, at Exeter, another stand-off ensued and a truce became the only option for both the besieged and the besieger. What followed was a repeat of what had happened at Wareham. Although Alfred must have known the whole thing was a charade, as indeed it proved to be, he had little choice but to play along. Alfred was evidently one step behind both the thinking and the movements of the invaders. His biggest miscalculation was, however, yet to come.

After Exeter, Guthrum returned to Mercia, pillaging as he went, and set up winter quarters in Gloucester. From here he shared out the land among his men and gave the obliging Mercian puppet-king, Ceolwulf, his promised dues. Then, in early January 878, with a complete disregard for the truce he had agreed with Alfred, Guthrum marched his men south straight to Alfred's fortress at Chippenham, interrupted Alfred's seasonal respite, forced him into hiding and took over occupation. From here, Guthrum drove deep into Wessex, where many of Alfred's subjects submitted to the invaders and many others took to the sea. Guthrum's audacity was only matched by Alfred's lack of vigilance. All now stood in the balance. Should Wessex fall, the whole of England would become a Danish territory with little chance of recovery.

Without his army and seemingly without any immediate hope of raising one large enough to oppose Guthrum, Alfred and a small band of followers took refuge on the island of Athelney in the marshes of Somerset. The legend, well known to every schoolchild, that during this time Alfred was set the task of minding the baking by a peasant woman but failed and let the cakes burn, is probably a fair indication of his preoccupied frame of mind. Matters, however, were potentially even worse than Alfred appreciated. In Devon, Halfdan's brother, Ubba, was set on attacking Wessex from another direction. Luckily, the Devonshire ealdorman was still able to rally an army and Ubba was routed and killed along with, says the *Anglo-Saxon Chronicle*, eight hundred of his men and forty of his elite bodyguard. It must have been some consolation to the fugitive king.

Alfred had not been idle during his years as king. He had guaranteed many local loyalties in Wessex and, as the ealdorman of Devon had shown, a levy system was still in operation. By Easter 878, Alfred knew he could muster support from across his realm, from Hampshire, Somerset and Wiltshire. A rendezvous was arranged at Ecgberht's Stone east of Selwood, a place that commemorated Alfred's grandfather, the founder of the power of Wessex fifty years earlier. The massed army of Wessex led by Alfred then went north east to Edington, thirty miles east of Chippenham, where they confronted Guthrum's army. Alfred's victory was decisive. The Danes capitulated before Alfred's shield-wall and fled. Alfred's men pursued them to Chippenham, which they regained after a fourteen-day siege. It was a wintry Easter and many surrendered 'thoroughly terrified by hunger, cold and fear, and in the end by despair'.[29] Again Guthrum granted Alfred hostages and made the usual promises about leaving the kingdom, but this time Alfred wanted something extra. As part of the treaty concluded at Wedmore, Guthrum was obliged to receive baptism, with Alfred as his godfather, and to take the baptismal name of Athelstan, an honour that Guthrum was to advertise when he issued coins using his baptismal name in late 880s. As far as is known, this was the first willing Christian conversion of a Dane on English soil and it was without doubt a stroke of political genius on Alfred's part.

Edington was a turning-point, not only for the fortunes of Wessex but also for the whole of England; nevertheless, the situation was still precarious. Guthrum returned to East Anglia after taking winter quarters at Cirencester. Many of his men set about cultivating the land and establishing a permanent settlement, whilst others decamped for Frankia to continue the raiding habit. In 885, Guthrum broke his peace once more but, after Alfred had yet again shown his mettle and seized London, a further treaty was signed, which survives to this day. In this, the borders were clearly defined and terms were set out intending to achieve peaceful relations between the West Saxons and the Danes of East Anglia. Alfred's English domain now ran from London north west to Chester. Guthrum died in 890, the last of the leaders of the Danish Great Army. But this did not mean that England could feel sure of some peace and quiet. Indeed, the whole concept of England as a unified country had little meaning at this time and it was only during the reign of Alfred that a notion of an English people (*Angelcynn*) as an ethnicity began to develop. Alfred and his successors would not be content until the land the Danes had taken was recovered but, no matter how many treaties were signed with Viking settlers, new generations of raiders and prospectors had no regard for them. And Danes already on English soil felt no compunction about supporting newcomers.

Alfred's first task was to fortify his realm and regroup his army. He set about establishing *burhs*, or fortified townships, of which more than thirty are listed in the document known as the *Burghal Hildage*. He also divided his levies so he could rotate duties and have an army permanently in the field, as well as a newly equipped naval force on standby. It has been estimated that Wessex could raise over 27,000 men for garrison duty alone. Alfred's greatest achievement of this period was to persuade the West Mercian English to recognize his overlordship. When he took possession of London in 886, he left the town in the keeping of the Mercian ealdorman Æthelred to whom he had given his daughter, Æthelflæd, in marriage. This union proved vital, as Æthelred's loyalty and courage were critical in the 890s, when a fresh wave of Vikings descended.

Meanwhile, the Danes were also entrenching their positions. They established and fortified the Five Boroughs of Derby, Leicester, Lincoln, Nottingham, and Stamford as a bulwark across the midlands. At the centre of their power in the north was the thriving emporium at York, which maintained close relations with Dublin and functioned as the Viking capital for the colonizers. Colonization was, indeed, developing at an alarming speed. In the East and North Ridings of Yorkshire, Viking settlement can be traced in as many as 40 per cent of the place-names with the Norse endings –by and –thorpe, signifying the quality of the land, and Scandinavian personal names in the first element signifying ownership. One promising development at York was the acceptance of a Christian baptism by Halfdan's successor, Guthfrith, in 880. The redoubtable Archbishop Wulfhere, who had weathered the Viking storm almost from the outset, was responsible for Guthfrith's conversion. This reflects the gradual assimilation of the Scandinavian settlers into Christian culture, and carved stones found in north and east Yorkshire show Christian and pagan sentiments merging at this time. There was, nonetheless, a long way to go before Scandinavians in England saw themselves as part of a unified Christian realm.

Apart from piratical raids around the Wessex coastline and the inconstancy of Guthrum, the 880s was a period of relative, if edgy, peace. Things changed in 891–92 when a second Great Army, comprising two hundred and fifty longships, made the short crossing of the English Channel from Boulogne. Having disembarked in southern Kent, it quickly overran one of Alfred's unfinished burhs near Appledore. Then, worryingly, a further eighty ships arrived in northern Kent. At the helm was one of the most feared Vikings in Europe, Hastein, whom Dudo of St-Quentin later described as a 'fomenter of evil', among other equally unattractive qualities.[30] This army had found life uncongenial in the Loire valley and Brittany and was unambiguously set on settlement and conquest in England, for these Vikings brought with them their womenfolk and their children. They soon dominated the coast on either side of the Thames.

For the next three years, the Danes probed and raided, but on every occasion Alfred, ably supported by his ealdormen and his son Edward, was there to confound them. When the Danes set their sights on Chester, Alfred's army adopted a scorched earth policy and set fire to all the surrounding crops, forcing the Danes into Wales and a circuitous return journey to the south east via the safety of Northumbria and East Anglia. When they drove deep along the Severn valley, Alfred's army was there to harass and disrupt them and oblige their withdrawal. When they congregated on the River Lea, north of London, Alfred's men blocked the river and improvised two forts on the riverbanks hemming in their ships. When Viking armies joined forces at a massive encampment at Benfleet on the north bank of the Thames, Alfred's men stormed the place while the leaders were off raiding, reclaimed stolen goods, scuttled or confiscated their ships, and took captive their women and children, who were duly returned unharmed.[31] Throughout, Alfred was distracted by spoiling tactics from Vikings inside Danish-held territories, who on one occasion, in 893, sent a fleet of a hundred ships to north Devon, forcing Alfred's army into a protracted but ultimately successful siege. By 895, Hastein's whole conquest project was stalled and his army wearied and depleted. Alfred calculated correctly that a joint payment from Wessex and Mercia would be enough to dismiss them for good.

The Danish strategy had been sophisticated. They had planned to overrun Kent then, in a series of pincer movements from Devon in the west and from their East Mercian strongholds, to compress Alfred's armies in Wessex. But they had reckoned without two things. First, the *burh* system allowed Alfred's men a secure footing and fresh reinforcements across the south and west of his realm. Second, Alfred, as commander in chief, determined exactly what kind of war he wanted to fight. His defensive strategy anticipated each move. He challenged the enemy when it was vulnerable, only attacking when the odds favoured him, and he did everything he could to prevent large numbers of Vikings gathering in one place. He received pledges of peace without giving them credence, and paid over geld when it helped to dislodge a concentration of warriors. In the main, Alfred beat the Vikings at what was traditionally their own game. In 896, the frustrated Danes either retreated into established territories to buy land or put to sea and headed for the River Seine in Frankia. It had been a worrying time made all the more unhappy by unmanageable miseries. The *Anglo-Saxon Chronicle*, now a contemporary of events, assessed the period from the perspectives of the natural disasters and the depletion among the ruling class that had coincided with Hastein's attempted conquest.

The raiding-army, by the grace of God, had not entirely crushed the English race; but they were a great deal more crushed in those three years with pestilence among cattle and men, most of all by the fact that many of the best of the king's thegns there were in the land passed away in those three years ...[32]

After the departure of the second Great Army, Alfred was clearly keen to emphasize Wessex sovereignty. In 896 he built a fleet of large ships and, when Vikings in six longships from East Anglia set about ravaging the Isle of White and the Devon coast, he put nine of them to good use. Three Viking ships were destroyed. The crew of two other ships were unable to continue rowing and were washed ashore and taken as prisoners to Winchester. Alfred, who had finally run out of patience, hanged them there. The injured crew of the remaining ship made it back to East Anglia, doubtless to report that Alfred was no longer to be fooled with.

Alfred died three years later on 26 October 899, after a period of respite during which he had only to contend with the now familiar treachery of his neighbours. His military achievement laid the foundation for his successors to pursue his ideal of an England unified by law and faith. But his overall achievement was far more than this. Alfred's formidable efforts in the areas of literature and scholarship, as a translator of classical and religious texts, and his determination to revive religious learning, established a cultural strength in England that would outlive both its conquest by Viking kings in the early eleventh century and by the Normans in 1066. Alfred deserves his reputation as the greatest Englishman of the Anglo-Saxon period.

While England was rapidly being divided into Danish territory and Wessex, Ireland was also suffering. In the first four decades of the ninth century, Norwegian Vikings took advantage of Irish political chaos. The history of the Vikings in Ireland, however, is less one of their territorial domination than one of increasing embroilment in native Irish conflicts and rivalries. Ireland, unlike England, brought Norwegian and Danish Vikings together in the same place with the same greed and obduracy and, as a result, an intense distrust of each other.

Ireland's internal politics were largely in the hands of five high kings, but in the layer of authority below them there were numerous petty kings who took little notice of their regal superiors. Constant strife was the way of things and, for a while, this suited the Vikings. Raiders penetrated deeper and deeper inland

and by the mid 830s large fleets were arriving from the Scottish settlements, devastating the land and rounding up slaves: 'After this there came great sea-cast floods of foreigners into Erinn, so that there was not a point thereof without a fleet', says the *The War of the Irish with the Foreigners*.[33] Vikings were clearly taking winter quarters by 836 when Clonmore in County Carlow was burned to the ground on Christmas Eve. The coastal islands not only provided security for the raiders but also served as prison camps for hostages and slaves. The *Annals of Ulster* reports numerous incidents of 'countless slaughter' and of Viking marauders teeming up the broad rivers and plundering almost at will. There was, however, no unified Viking leadership in the country and no plan for complete territorial domination. Then, a particularly ambitious Norwegian Viking took the situation in hand.

The Viking known variously as Turgeis, Turgesius, Thorgestr, Thorgils and Thorkils in Irish and Scandinavian sources has attracted as much legend and lore around him as Ragnar Hairy Breeches; indeed some have argued that Turgeis was Ragnar. Unlikely though this identification is, Turgeis certainly made a great impression. He seems to have been responsible for the construction of the safe-harbour *longphorts* at Anagassin, Dublin, Wexford, Waterford, Cork and Limerick. He first arrived at the head of his fleet on the River Shannon, which he followed as far as Lough Ree in the centre of the country. From there he sacked the monasteries at Clonmacnois and Clonfert and persecuted the monks. Next, exploiting local factional conflicts, he occupied the country's monastic centre at Armagh, which he is reputed to have rededicated to Thor, and proclaimed himself high priest with bloody rituals. His wife, Ota, is similarly said to have taken over the altar at Clonmacnois and to have invoked the pagan gods.

Turgeis attracted to him the Gall-Gaedhil, or Foreign Irish, a disreputable gang of hoodlums of mixed Celtic-Norse parentage who had renounced Christianity in favour of Thor worship. *The Three Fragments* report that 'However much the Northmen proper had behaved evilly to churches, they [the Gall-Gaedhil] were worse by far, in whatever part of Ireland they used to be'.[34] With the aid of these followers, Turgeis brought a sort of power structure to Viking affairs in Ireland. It was not welcomed by the indigenous population and Turgeis was murdered in an Irish conspiracy in 845. The story runs that Turgeis was smitten by the daughter of the Irish king Mael Sechnaill. The king agreed to send the girl to Turgeis in company with fifteen maidens for the delight of Turgeis's nobles. Too late, Turgeis and friends discovered that these were not the girls he expected but armed warriors in women's clothing. He and his companions were surprised and stabbed to death. The more sober *Annals of Ulster* tell a less glamorous tale: 'Turgeis was taken prisoner by Mael Sechnaill and afterwards drowned in Loch Uair.'[35]

Turgeis had done nothing to enhance the reputation of the Norwegians and, after his death, the Irish, sensing their enemy's disarray, inflicted many defeats on the Vikings. In 850 a new power arrived in Ireland in the form of the Danes, who took harbour in Carlingford Lough on the southern edge of County Down. Their first act was to challenge the Norwegians, who they overran at their centre in Dublin, confiscating their valuables and abducting their women. A year later, in 852, the Norwegians mounted a response and came upon the Danes at their harbour. After a three-day battle, the Danes emerged victorious and, by way of thanks, offered tribute to the patron of Irish Christianity, St Patrick. The Irish were temporarily deluded into thinking that the Danes were a new type of pious Viking.

The following year a powerful Dano-Norwegian alliance emerged with the arrival of Olaf the White, a Norwegian, and Ivar the Boneless. While sources claim that these two were brothers, they cannot have been related in the biological sense, though their lifelong alliance may have been based on the Viking bond of blood brotherhood. Olaf's actual pedigree is hard to determine, but it is likely that the Irish records of the exploits of the Viking king in Dublin known as Amlaíbh, and that Scandinavian and Anglo-Saxon references to Olaf, are one and the same person. Olaf's royal demeanour commanded respect from Norwegian and most Danish Vikings, and from many Irish factions. He established himself as king at Dublin in 853 and, for the next twenty years, the kingship passed between Olaf and Ivar without quarrel, depending on duties or opportunities elsewhere. Olaf's policy of hiring his muscle and his fleet to the highest bidder soon dragged him deep into local feuds. His support of Cerball mac Dúnlainge, king of Ossory, in the invasion of Meath in 859, and his embroilment in the civil war between northern and southern Uí Néill, the rival dynasties of high kings, in 862, made him many enemies. When, at Ivar's instigation, Olaf insensitively excavated the prehistoric burial mounds on the banks of the River Boyne in a hunt for treasure in 863, the Irish were outraged and, by 866, Olaf deemed it wise to spend time out of Ireland massacring and enslaving the Picts in Scotland. On his return, he faced an insurgency, in retaliation for which he laid waste to Armagh and either enslaved or killed one thousand people.

In 871 Olaf was for a second time in the Strathclyde region of Scotland,

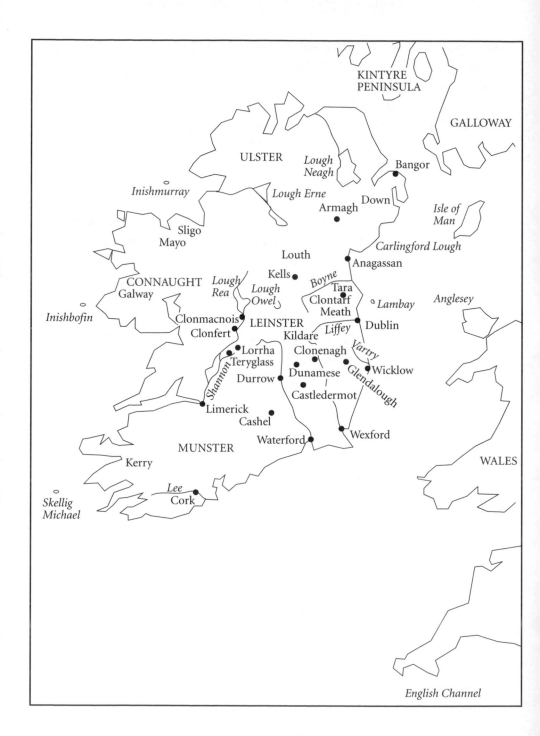

Ireland in the Viking age

this time with Ivar the Boneless. Having destroyed the power base of the Strathclyde Britons and asserted their authority over them, Olaf and Ivar may have returned to Dublin together. With them were two hundred ships bearing in chains Angles, Britons and Picts. After this Olaf simply disappears from Irish records. Perhaps he was killed in battle, perhaps he returned to Norway and the dynastic wars that were raging there. Ivar's rule did not last long and, after his death in 873, a power vacuum opened. What followed is commonly referred to as the Forty Years Rest, signifying that very few Viking longships arrived. It was just as well, for those Vikings already in Ireland created enough confusion on their own. Dynastic rivalry, underhand murders and blood feuds dominated Irish political life until 902. The Irish, however, proved unusually united and, under the leadership of Cerball of Leinster, took decisive action and attacked the 'Foreigners' in Dublin. Their overwhelming victory was indicative of the incoherence of the Viking presence. The departure of the Vikings was in deep contrast to their arrival: 'The heathens were driven from Ireland ... and they abandoned a good number of their ships, and escaped half-dead after they had been wounded and broken.'[36] That may be so, but some of the expelled Vikings managed to rouse themselves sufficiently to attack the Welsh coast before moving on beyond Chester to settle in the north west. Though the Irish could find little peace among themselves, for the next twelve years their shores remained free of Vikings.

At the beginning of the tenth century, both England and Ireland were at a watershed. With Alfred the Great dead in England and the Danes, at least for the present, returned to the lands that they dominated to the north and east, it was to the descendants of Alfred that the burden fell of defending Anglo-Saxon rule in England. Consolidation was not an option. The Danes were not to be trusted, for it was not in the character of the Vikings to be content with what they had got. Wessex was secure for the moment, but the future meant that the Danes had to be engaged and, if possible, expelled.

Ireland, on the other hand, had emerged from the first period of Viking domination relatively intact. The country had not been in danger of being completely dominated by Vikings, as the Irish were too warlike and too fractious to be brought to heel. Indeed, setting aside the decimation of the monasteries, and other acts of Viking savagery, the Irish had, at least in one way, benefited through Viking commercial activities at the *longphorts*. But therein lay the problem. The Irish lacked an Alfred in the early tenth century and this remained the case until the emergence of Brian Boru almost a hundred years later. Ireland was vulnerable to a renewal of Scandinavian raids at any time. Moreover, it was the long-held Viking ambition to make Dublin and York twin seats of power in the British Isles. The expulsion of the Vikings in 902 had strengthened the number of Vikings in north-western England and the Scottish lowlands, and the potential for a Viking trade route between Dublin and York could only be disturbed by their own disputatious nature. The prospect of a northern alliance spanning the Irish Sea pitted the descendants of Alfred the Great against the descendants of Ivar the Boneless for the next fifty years.

# 5

# England, Ireland and Wales, 900–1070

After the death of Alfred in 899, his son Edward the Elder succeeded to the throne of Wessex. Edward had assisted in the repulsion of Hastein during the 890s and seems to have spent more time in action than his father, often having to make critical decisions about troop deployments. He was more than ready to be king and his plan was, perforce, to take on the Danes and win their territory. Two things were in his favour. First, Alfred had married off his daughter, Æthelflæd, to the Mercian ealdorman Æthelred, determined to strengthen an alliance founded as much on a common enemy as on mutual regard. Æthelflæd was made of stern stuff and was every inch her father's daughter. Her commitment to the Wessex cause was absolute. Secondly, the Vikings of Northumbria and East Anglia had given up something of their most valuable asset: mobility. The Vikings now had their families with them and had land and property to protect. It was thirty years since Viking leaders had shared out the lands and a generation of Vikings had grown up in Danish-dominated England, and this new generation needed security. Northumbrian identity was nonetheless jealously guarded by both Anglo-Saxon and Scandinavian contingents. Apart from the obvious difficulty of the task ahead of him, however, Edward had one thing that was most definitely not in his favour. It came in the form of his cousin Æthelwold, son of Æthelred, the king of Wessex before Alfred.

Edward's reign began with open defiance from Æthelwold, whose petulant first act was to seize the royal manor of Wimborne and the *burh* at Twinham. Then, knowing that Edward was on his way to remonstrate with him, Æthelwold barricaded himself and his army inside Wimborne. Æthelwold dramatically declared that he would 'live or die there' but evidently thought better of the situation and 'stole away by night to seek out the raiding-army in Northumbria'.[1] In his flight, he added a fine of 120 shillings to his treason by abducting a nun. If, as may have been the case, the nun was a daughter of Alfred the Great, then Æthelwold's intention was to strengthen his claim by marrying into a competing line. Once in Northumbria, the Vikings were delighted to accept him as their king and, as 'king of the Danes and pagans',[2] he now managed to draw the

Vikings of East Anglia into his insurrection. A rash of raids against Edward's
kingdom accompanied the whole affair. Edward responded by pursuing
Æthelwold into the Fenlands, where, after confusion between the West Saxons
and their comrades from Kent over his orders, he tarried too long and found
himself surrounded by the Danish army led by Æthelwold. The battle that
followed was won by the Danes but at great cost, including the deaths of the
East Anglian king and of the mutinous Æthelwold.

In 905 Edward renegotiated a treaty at Tiddingford with both the East
Anglians and the Northumbrians, ensuring, he hoped, the sovereignty of Wessex
and his alliance with the West Mercians. The Æthelwold rebellion had been
worrying, but it had turned out to be little more than an attempt by the Danes to
see if their unexpected ally could create an opening for them in their long-held
ambitions to extend their dominions in the south. Æthelwold's failure was not
the last attempt by the Danes to conquer England but, for the time being, the
odds favoured Edward. What followed was less a reconquest of Danish-held
land and more an assertion of the might of Wessex over an England that had
never before been politically united. Not all northerners welcomed it. Like
Æthelwold, many preferred submission to the Danes to the rule of Edward.

Danish belligerence resurfaced in 910 with a miscalculated attack on West
Mercia. The *Anglo-Saxon Chronicle* describes what happened:

> Here the raiding-army in Northumbria broke the peace, and scorned every privilege
> which King Edward and his councillors offered them, and raided across the land of
> Mercia. And the king had some hundred ships, and was then in Kent; and the ships
> went east along the south coast towards him. Then the raiding-army imagined that
> most part of his reinforcement was on these ships, and that they might go unfought
> wherever they wanted. Then, when the king learned that they had gone on a raid,
> he sent his army both from Wessex and from Mercia, and they got in front of the
> raiding-army from behind when it was on its way home, and then fought with them
> and put the raiding-army to flight and killed many of it.[3]

Edward's victory at Tettenhall in West Mercia put East Mercia in his grasp. Not
even the death the following year of Edward's chief ally, the Mercian ealdorman
Æthelred, helped the Danes, for now Edward's sister, Æthelflæd, took up the
joint cause of Wessex and Mercia even more vigorously than had her husband.
She oversaw the construction of a system of *burh* fortifications across her
land on the model that had served her father so well against Hastein fifteen
years earlier. Meanwhile, Edward consolidated his victory by seizing control of

London and Oxford and all the lands as far to the north as Cambridge, which he then fortified. Border skirmishes continued while brother and sister mapped out their fortifications in a line across the south and west midlands. Apart from a serious incident in 914, when a vast fleet of Vikings from Brittany entered the River Severn and set about harrying the Welsh borders before sailing for Ireland when threatened by Æthelflæd and Edward, this was a period of forward planning. Edward knew that he was defending his territories not only against the Danes but also against the vastly increased might of the Norwegians, who were now in control of the north west of the country from the Wirral to Galloway.

In 917 Edward and Æthelflæd were able to implement their plan. When, as was inevitable, the Danes from East Mercia and East Anglia yet again broke the peace, Æthelflæd moved on the sparsely defended Danish fortification at Derby, one of the prized Five Boroughs, and took it. The following year she added a second borough and 'peaceably got in control the stronghold at Leicester'.[4] Danish raids were easily repelled by the *burh* defences and eventually Danish armies from East Anglia and East Mercia either capitulated or disintegrated. Soon after, these Danes acknowledged Edward as overlord, saying that 'they wanted all that he wanted, and would keep the peace with all whom the king wanted to keep peace, both on sea and on land'.[5] Edward pressed on and overran a third of the Five Boroughs at Stamford. Nottingham and Lincoln would surely follow, after which the submission of Northumbria would be a genuine prospect. But then Edward got news that Æthelflæd had suddenly died. It was not only personal grief that sent him hurrying to Tamworth, for the succession of Mercia was in the balance and he felt he had no choice but to seize Æthelflæd's daughter and assert his kingship over the territory. He then returned to his campaign and overran Nottingham. The consequence was that 'all the people who had settled in Mercia, both Danish and English, turned to him'.[6] The power of the Danes in England had now been reduced to their kingdom north of the Humber, but Edward's ambition to create an England united under the Wessex royal house was thwarted. The kingdom of York remained beyond his reach.

Viking rule at York had always been connected with their activities in Ireland and, in particular, their rule at Dublin. Ivar the Boneless had set the precedent in 871, when he left York and re-established himself as king of Dublin, giving the Ragnarssons a dynastic seat at both centres. His brother Halfdan tried to do the same a few years later with fatal consequences. The importance of Dublin as a slave market and as the centre of a sea kingdom encompassing the Irish Sea, the Isle of Man, the Hebrides, Scotland and northern England, particularly the

Norwegian dominated west, was crucial to the economic and political interests of the Vikings. Should a common Viking rule be established at York and Dublin, the sea kingdom could become a land-based territory for the conquest of both Ireland and England. The difficulties of holding both kingdoms under the same rule were, however, great. Much depended on whether the Irish could be contained and their land controlled by the invaders, and there was also always the problem of whether the Scandinavian factions could cohere on foreign soil. For much of the first half of the tenth century, the effort to unite the interests of Dublin and York came entirely from the descendants of Ivar the Boneless.

In 914 the Vikings had returned to Ireland and 'a great new fleet of the heathens' entered Waterford harbour.[7] Shortly afterwards, a second force arrived in Waterford and another on the Leinster borders. Commanding these fleets were the grandsons of Ivar the Boneless: Ragnald I to the south and Sihtric Cáech to the north. Ragnald had already established himself as pre-eminent by his victory over the Northumbrians and Scots at Corbridge and by his domination of Cumbria. He bore the title 'king of the Danes'. Coins issued in his name at York earlier in the decade indicate that he had already ruled there. Despite the violent resistance of Niall Glúndub, king of Tara, and the Leinstermen, Sihtric managed to retake Dublin in 917. This was the cue for Ragnald to return to York the following year and establish a Dublin–York axis.

Ragnald was politically astute. He recognized from the outset of his rule at York that King Edward's hold on territories south of the Humber was, as things stood, beyond contention. New fortifications bridging the River Trent near Nottingham, a stronghold at Bakewell in the Peak District, and reinforced townships at Manchester and Thelwall were compelling signs of Edward's intentions toward the north. In 920 Edward's power was acknowledged not only by Ragnald, who could evidently speak for great swathes of Britain to the north, but also by independent territories in western Scotland.

> And then the king of the Scots and all the nations of the Scots chose him as father and lord; and [so also did] Rægnald and Eadwulf's sons[8] and all those who live in Northumbria, both English and Danish and Norwegians and others; and also the king of the Strathclyde Britons and all the Strathclyde Britons.[9]

This did not mean, however, that the Vikings and colonists of Northumbria submitted to Edward in all things, and the title of king of York remained Ragnald's. It is reasonable to assume that Ragnald's choice of Edward as 'father and lord' was little more than a way of buying time while he consolidated his power, and that of his brother Sihtric, across the north of Britain and in Ireland.

When Ragnald died in 920, Sihtric immediately left Dublin for York. En route from the Wirral, he stopped off at Davonport in Cheshire and laid waste to it. Sihtric's raid may have been no more than a gesture, reflecting custom among the high kings of Ireland, but the location was well chosen. Cheshire lay at the intersection of Welsh, English and Hiberno-Norse interests and was itself the home to restive Mercians at the farthest reach of Edward's borders. The power of the Dublin–York axis, and encouragement from the Welsh, may well have been the inspiration for disenchanted Mercians to rebel against Edward at Chester in 924. Mercian dissidence had been fired by Edward's assertion of the power of Wessex over Mercia at the expense of Æthelflæd's daughter Ælfwyn. Perhaps the Mercian insurgents had also interpreted one of Æthelflæd's last acts of diplomacy as signifying that she had been about to make an accord with the Danish Northumbrians, whom they preferred to Edward. If this was the case, they were mistaken, for in fact Æthelflæd had been on the brink of concluding an agreement which would have placed the kingdom of York under English rule. The rebellion remained localized but was of sufficient importance to warrant Edward's personal attention. The suppression of the Mercian rebels was to be Edward's last intervention, as a few weeks later he died.

Edward's death in 924 brought his son Athelstan to the throne of Wessex. It was a timely succession, for Athelstan was more acceptable to the people of Northumbria. As Athelstan had been raised by Æthelflæd, the Mercians regarded him as almost one of their own and had no problem in accepting him as their ruler. At Tamworth in 926, Sihtric Cáech, king of York, and Athelstan, king of Wessex, East Anglia and Mercia, met and hammered out the details of a treaty. To seal the deal, Athelstan gave Sihtric his daughter in marriage and Sihtric accepted baptism. The marriage, however, was a disaster almost from the outset and Sihtric rapidly resumed his pagan ways. Luckily for Athelstan, Sihtric died within a year of the Tamworth concord. His widow, yet chaste it was said, took the veil.

During Sihtric's absence from Dublin, Guthfrith, a third grandson of Ivar the Boneless, was left in charge. After Niall Glúndub, the most powerful Irish opponent to Viking rule in Dublin, had been killed in battle against Sihtric in 919, the way was open to extend the authority of Dublin across the east of Ireland, imitating the Viking kingdom in northern Britain. Guthfrith went about the task with enthusiasm but only modest success. The royal heir of Ulaid was murdered and Viking fleets based in Strangford and Carlingford Loughs plundered along the coast, attacking fortresses and raiding the monasteries for slaves and valuables. The loss of a great fleet and nine hundred men on the bar of Dundrum Bay did not end the campaign. Five years into Guthfrith's campaign, in 926, the threat he posed to Irish interests provoked Muirchertach mac Néill, the powerful king of the northern Uí Néill, to intervene. He overwhelmed the Carlingford Vikings, killing two hundred of them, then sought out the Vikings of Strangford Lough under the command of Guthfrith's son Olaf. Muirchertach cornered Olaf Guthfrithsson at Newry and laid siege to it, taking two hundred and forty captives, whom he beheaded, exhibiting their heads as trophies. Guthfrith himself was obliged to break the siege and relieve Olaf. With the Irish rampant, Guthfrith returned to Dublin in 926. There he received news of the death of Sihtric Cáech. Within a year, Guthfrith had joined Sihtric's infant son, also named Olaf, in York.

The vacancy in York had not escaped the attention of Athelstan, who was not about to let yet another Dublin warlord settle into the kingdom. Guthfrith's tenancy was therefore short lived and both he and the young Olaf Sihtricsson were ousted by Athelstan in 927. For at least the time being, a king of Wessex could be spoken of as the first king of all the English. After their expulsion from York, Guthfrith and Olaf returned to Ireland, where Guthfrith discovered that rival Vikings from Limerick had usurped his position in Dublin. Although he quickly managed to reclaim the town, for the next seven years, until his death in 934, Guthfrith was preoccupied with preventing the Limerick Vikings from displacing him. The problem was inherited by his son Olaf Guthfrithsson, as were the plan to conquer the east of Ireland and the family claim on York. In 937, he resolved the problem of the Limerick Vikings once and for all by destroying their fleet and taking their leader captive. Buoyed by his success, he now conceived of a plan to recover York. It involved nothing less than a grand alliance with all the powers north of Athelstan's territories.

Athelstan had proved politically the most skilled of the Wessex kings. He had secured marriage alliances with Frankish and German royal families and was regarded by King Harald Finehair, the unifier of Norway, as his equal in rank and authority, and therefore fit to foster his son Hakon. Although his reputation in Europe was assured, at home opinions were divided. Athelstan had good relations with the Welsh, whose borders abutted his Mercian domains. Hywell Dda (926–50), in some ways a Welsh Alfred, was a friend to Wessex and had safeguarded the south of his country, where it was vulnerable to Viking incursions. In so doing, he had also helped prevent Viking attacks on Wessex from the direction of the Bristol Channel. The Scots, however, were less tractable and the prospect of a Norse–Celtic confederacy, drawing on sympathy from the independently minded Northumbrian English, was Athelstan's greatest worry.

The crisis came in 937 when Olaf Guthfrithsson mobilized the Scots under Constantine II and the Strathclyde Britons. Having assembled in York, Olaf set Athelstan a clear challenge. The armies met at Brunanburh, a site that has defied certain identification but one that may well have been in Mercia. According to *Egils Saga*, fighting alongside Athelstan were many Vikings mercenaries, amongst whom was the eponymous hero of the saga, the Icelandic poet-warrior Egil Skallagrimsson. Befitting the greatest battle in Anglo-Saxon history, the *Anglo-Saxon Chronicle* describes the event in a poem of more than seventy lines, celebrating Athelstan's overwhelming victory in company with his sixteen-year-old brother Edmund, where they 'won themselves eternal glory in battle with the edges of their swords'.[10] The battle lasted throughout the day and the casualties on both sides numbered thousands. By dusk, Athelstan's forces had all but destroyed the coalition. The notable dead included five lesser Viking kings, seven *jarls* and the son of Constantine. Among the Vikings driven to ignominious flight was Olaf Guthfrithsson.

> There the Norsemen's chief
> Was put to flight, and driven by dire need
> With small retinue to seek his ship.
> The ship pressed out to sea, the king departed
> Onto the yellow flood and saved his life.[11]

Although the battle of Brunanburh was highly significant in that it subdued Athelstan's enemies, its impact on the struggle for control of York was only temporary. When Athelstan died in 939, Olaf Guthfrithsson seized the moment and returned unchallenged, and perhaps welcomed, to York. Olaf's most significant and in many ways startling coup was to launch a lightning campaign in East Mercia and reclaim the Five Boroughs. He then persuaded the archbishops of York and Canterbury to accept him as a legitimate ruler over this territory. For a time, the efforts of a generation of Wessex kings looked as if they had all been for nothing. The new king of the English, Edmund, half-brother of Athelstan, got off to a poor start when he was unable to challenge Olaf Guthfrithsson's army at Leicester. Having regained much of the territory conquered by his great-grandfather in the 870s, Olaf promptly set about reviving an old family tradition and took to ravaging north of the Tees. Only his death in 941 put a stop to this.

Now came the turn of Olaf Sihtricsson (also known as Olaf 'Cuaran', meaning 'sandal'). This Olaf, it will be remembered, was still a boy when, in 927, he had been forced to flee from York in company with his uncle Guthfrith. He had been raised at his uncle's court in Dublin but, in 941, at the time of his royal cousin's death, he was in Northumbria, probably helping to terrorize the populace in old Bernicia. He was the logical choice for the succession at York, but after two years as king, he was once again forced to leave. There were at least two things that alienated Olaf from his subjects in York: first, he promptly lost the Five Boroughs to a newly invigorated Edmund; and second, in 943, he accepted baptism under Edmund's sponsorship. His 'conversion' proved to be insincere, much as his father's had been, but a conversion at the hands of his triumphant enemy was in all likelihood considered unbecoming of a king of York.

Olaf Sihtricsson returned to Dublin in 945 and assumed his kingship there amid the chaos of Irish rivalries. Meanwhile, another Irish Viking opportunist, Ragnald II, the brother of the late Olaf Guthfrithsson, had taken over at York, but his position was very soon threatened when Olaf Sihtricsson returned, seemingly careless of his previous rejection. Edmund, seeing his chance to cut through the Gordian knot of rival claims, intervened and, to the relief of the Northumbrians, removed both Olaf and Ragnald. This, however, was not the end of the drama. In 946 Edmund was stabbed to death trying to defend his steward from a notorious robber. Eadred succeeded him but was powerless to prevent another Viking claiming the throne at York. This time it was the ousted king of Norway, the aptly named Eirik Bloodaxe.

Eirik had been responsible for the death of a number of his brothers back in Norway and his rule there, alongside his queen, Gunnhild, herself renowned as a witch and a seductress, had been notably unpopular. His reputation as a savage pagan was notorious. The suggestion in the *Anglo-Saxon Chronicle* that the Northumbrians preferred him to Olaf Sihtricsson speaks volumes about their poverty of choice and, of course, about their determination to remain a separate entity from England under the kings of Wessex. An alternative version is provided by the Icelandic *Egils Saga*, which tells us that Athelstan himself granted York to Eirik to make him a bulwark against the Scots.[12] In either case, Eirik quickly let down his supporters. King Eadred had been understandably disappointed by the accession of Eirik and had vented his anger by invading Northumbria, during which he burnt down the Minster at Ripon, probably as an act of vengeance against what he perceived to be clerical treachery. As Eadred journeyed home, Eirik emerged from behind the walls at York and hurried to Castleford where he attacked Eadred from the rear. Eadred, says the *Anglo-Saxon Chronicle*, was so enraged by this 'that he wanted to invade again and completely do for the country'. The Northumbrians, fearful of what was about to happen, 'abandoned Eric and compensated King Eadred for the act'.[13]

There was still no stability at York and a year after Eirik's deposition Olaf Sihtricsson returned from Dublin for a third time. Olaf managed to hang on to York for three years before the Northumbrians again tired of him and decided to give Eirik Bloodaxe another chance. Olaf Sihtricsson made his final return to Dublin, where he ruled for another twenty-five years, proving his great talent as a survivor. In 980 he suffered a decisive defeat and, shortly afterwards, the baptism he had received from Edmund almost forty years earlier finally took on some meaning. One of the most obstinate pagans of the Viking world retired to the monastery at Iona, where for the final year of his life he looked back as a penitent on a career spent persecuting Christians.

Back in York in 952, Eirik Bloodaxe managed to secure the backing of Archbishop Wulfstan I, at one time his most vocal critic, but this availed nothing when Eadred imprisoned Wulfstan. The support of the episcopate at York had been crucial to Eirik's survival and without it his many enemies grew daring. By 954, the Northumbrians had had enough of Scandinavian tyrants. Although they knew that the likely alternative was union under Wessex, Eirik was yet again expelled. This time, the Northumbrians made sure that he would not come back. Eirik's path northward took him along the old Roman road between York and Carlisle. He and his retinue headed for Galloway where they intended to sail for Orkney, where Eirik's wife and sons were already safely ensconced. Earl Oswulf of Bamborough, a man with a grudge against Eirik, tipped off a certain Maccus about Eirik's route. Maccus and his gang ambushed and murdered Eirik 'in a lonely spot called Stainmore', south of Carlisle.[14] It is possible that Maccus was the son of Eirik's archrival, Olaf Sihtricsson.

The death of Eirik Bloodaxe in 954 ended the Viking domination of York. For the eighty years leading up to Eirik's intervention, the descendants of Ivar the Boneless had played out their dynastic squabbles at York. During this time, Dublin had been the base from which the York claimants plotted their campaigns, but that association, so important to Viking traders and raiders, was over. The kingdom of York was quickly subsumed by Wessex and Eadred became the true king of all the English, without rival. Yet Scandinavian traditions in Northumbria remained strong and jealously guarded. When Edgar succeeded Eadred, first as ruler of Mercia and Northumbria in 955, then, in 959, after the death of his brother Eadwig, as king of all the English, he sensibly acknowledged that certain privileges and traditions in this part of his realm needed to be tolerated.

> Further, it is my will that there should be in force among the Danes such good laws as they best decide on, and I have ever allowed them this and will allow it as long as my life lasts, because of your loyalty, which you have always shown to me. And I desire that this one decree concerning such an investigation shall be common to us all, for the protection and security of all the nation.[15]

Under this concession the eastern swathe of England from the Thames to the Tees became known as the Danelaw. Much of what this meant in practice concerned procedural matters. For example, criminal suspects were committed for trial by sworn aristocratic juries, a principle unknown under English law, and the most serious offences were tried by combat rather than by the English practice of trial by ordeal. Landholding privileges were also upheld according to Danish custom and, as a consequence, freeholder peasant farmers, known as sokemen, were more numerous in the Danelaw than in the rest of England. Nonetheless, there was a qualification in that Edgar's laws, however they were enacted, should be 'common to all the nation, whether Englishmen, Danes, or Britons, in every province'. Danish custom and practice may have been a special case, but its context was within a unified England. Archbishop Wulfstan II's early eleventh-century criticism of Edgar, stating that he had brought 'heathen customs too fast into this land and attracted the alien here, and introduced damaging people to this country', was proffered with the knowledge of hindsight and disregarded the political complexities Edgar inherited.[16]

Once the link with Dublin had been severed, English and Irish history took differing paths. Edgar's rule, partly as a result, was one of peace and relative national harmony, as 'without battle he controlled all that he himself wanted'.[17] Ireland, by contrast, was not to experience any such peace for many years. Olaf Sihtricsson's survival had long depended on the support of the kings of Leinster. When this broke down in 976, Olaf nonetheless felt strong enough to act independently. He set about plotting the murder of his eminent neighbours and successfully challenged the power of Leinster. His reward was a violent backlash led by Mael Sechnaill II, king of Meath. In 980, Olaf's army suffered 'a red slaughter' at Tara and was then besieged at Dublin. The defeat of Olaf amounted to the destruction of the military and political autonomy of Viking Dublin. The year 980 may be regarded as the date from which the Viking Age in Ireland ceased to be the dominant factor in the country's fortunes.

Around the same time that Olaf lost control in the east of Ireland, the Irish kings of Munster in the south were set on ridding themselves of the Vikings of Limerick. King Mathgamain of Dál Cais attacked and destroyed the Limerick fleet in 975 but was then himself murdered in a dynastic intrigue in 976. Mathgamain's successor was Brian Boru. Brian's ambition was to be high king of all Ireland, and the politics of Ireland for the next forty years were to be dominated by Brian's ruthless campaign to achieve this. Brian's first act was to murder Ivar, the leader of the Limerick Vikings, and then pursue Ivar's two sons, who had taken sanctuary in the church at Scattery, to their deaths. Brian then turned on the Vikings and emasculated their power in the *longphorts*, using their fleets as suited him. By the end of the tenth century, Ireland was divided between two great Irish warlords: Mael Sechnaill II in the north and Brian Boru in the south. Dublin fell under Brian's control.

One other Viking ruler of Dublin had a hand to play in Ireland's affairs. This was Sihtric Silkenbeard, son of Olaf Sihtricsson. Sihtric was unnerved by Brian Boru's authority and feared a further diminution in his power. His reaction was to ally himself with the king of Leinster and launch a rebellion. It was a catastrophe, for Brian easily overwhelmed the rebels and imposed direct rule over Dublin. Brian, however, had married Sihtric's mother and he reinstalled Sihtric as a tributary king, granting him his daughter in marriage. Although Sihtric continued to plot Brian's undoing, Brian went from strength to strength and, after a showdown with Mael Sechnaill in 1004, became the overlord of all Ireland.

Sihtric's plots eventually bore fruit in a second rebellion in company with his Leinster allies in 1013, during which the rebels kept Brian at bay and inflicted as much damage as they received. Encouraged by this, Sihtric engineered an alliance of the Leinstermen with Viking leaders from Orkney and Man. Their force met Brian at Clontarf north west of Dublin on 23 April 1014. Bolstering Brian's ranks were the Vikings from Limerick, while Sihtric absented himself and delegated his brother to lead the Dubliners into battle. Sihtric is said to have watched the events unfold from the ramparts of Dublin, wisely as it turned out, for Brian's forces routed the rebels. But Brian's victory was bought at great cost. The aged Brian was killed in his tent by the fleeing Viking leader

Brodir, the commander of the Viking fleet from Man. More importantly in the long term, so many of his descendants were killed that the Munster dynasty was damaged almost beyond recovery. At Clontarf the winner turned out to be loser.

A hundred years later, Irish historians did not see things this way. According to the chroniclers of the twelfth-century *The War of the Irish with the Foreigners*, Brian, the *imperator Scottorum* (emperor of the Irish), had salvaged Ireland from Viking domination at Clontarf. That, of course, was nonsense. By the early eleventh century, the Vikings were little more than pawns in the Irish dynastic struggle. Nevertheless, the propaganda produced one of the most enduring and powerful myths in Irish history. A passion for Irish independence, led, of course, by the kings of Munster, is revealed in the wild prose describing the characteristics of the opposing sides. Against Brian were the

> shouting, hateful, powerful, wrestling, valiant, active, fierce-moving, dangerous, nimble, violent, furious, unscrupulous, untameable, inexorable, unsteady, cruel, barbarous, frightful, sharp, ready, huge, prepared, cunning, warlike, poisonous, murderous, hostile Danars; bold, hard-hearted Danmarkians, surly, piratical foreigners, blue-green, pagan, without reverence, without veneration, without honour, without mercy, for God or for man.

Supporting Brian were the

> brave, valiant champions; soldierly, active, nimble, bold, full of courage, quick, doing great deeds, pompous, beautiful, aggressive, hot, strong, swelling, bright, fresh, never-weary, terrible, valiant, victorious, heroes and chieftains, and champions, and brave soldiers, the men of high deeds, and honour and renown of Erinn ...[18]

This polemic had a greater effect on Irish politics and the cause of nationalism than Clontarf itself. As for Sihtric Silkenbeard's cause, Clontarf did nothing to help it, for, despite the much-weakened power of Munster, he soon found himself as tributary king to Brian's rival, Mael Sechnaill.

Sihtric, supported by Cnut the Great, the king of the English and much of Scandinavia, continued to meddle in Irish power struggles from behind the stockades of Dublin until his abdication in 1036, but he could not revive Dublin's political fortunes. His most enduring legacy to Dublin was the foundation of Christ Church cathedral in 1030. He was murdered on his second pilgrimage to Rome in 1042. The power of Dublin continued to decline after

Sihtric's death, as successive Irish kings tried to conquer it. It was not until 1170, when a Norman army, led by Dairmait Mac Murchada, king of Leinster, invaded Ireland and seized land for the English crown, that Viking Dublin lost its independence. By that time, Viking influence in Ireland was solely that of entrepreneurs with connections in Norway and Iceland. Pure Norse blood soon disappeared from Irish society, and the Hiberno-Norse community in Dublin was known not as one of Vikings, nor even identified as Scandinavian, but simply referred to as 'Ostmen', men who lived in the east of the country. Old Norse, however, continued to be the language of commerce in Dublin through into the thirteenth century.

After the Viking rule of York was ended by the English in 954, a period of peace followed; indeed, the south of the country had been largely unaffected by northern controversies since Athelstan's victory at Brunanburh in 937. Scandinavians in East Anglia, Yorkshire and Cumbria were content to assimilate with the native population as Christian farmers and traders. Then, in 980, five years after King Edgar's death, the Vikings returned. To begin with, the raids were similar to those at the start of the Viking Age almost two hundred years previously. But behind them lay a motive more menacing than those early attacks, for these Vikings were not solely looking to profit where they could, they were looking to replace a source of income that had underpinned Viking interests almost from the outset. Trade with the Arab caliphate had brought vast amounts of silver coin to Viking traders and warlords since the early ninth century, but during the 970s the Arab silver mines ceased to be productive and trading arrangements between the Vikings and the caliphate broke down. Added to this, Norwegian and Danish Vikings had suffered an irrecoverable blow to their power in Ireland, whilst on the Continent the Vikings who had invaded and settled during the ninth and early tenth centuries had achieved respectability, either in autonomous regions, such as in Normandy, or as Christian communities fully integrated into mainstream European affairs. Territorial and pecuniary gains there were exhausted. Moreover, in Scandinavia, the move toward nation states was reaching completion and newly powerful kings were once again looking for a means to expand. In Denmark, this meant that Harald Bluetooth's huge Danish army looked eagerly toward new horizons, while the contenders for the throne of Norway looked to refresh their claims with new income. With all these pressures at work, the Vikings turned once again to England.

What the Vikings could not have known in 980 was that the spirit, and, perhaps, the luck of Alfred the Great, so vital among his descendants in unifying England, had dwindled. Edgar's son, Æthelred, came to the throne in 978 after the murder of Edward, his half-brother, in circumstances that implicated Æthelred's mother. When what at first appeared to be a resumption of sporadic raiding turned into a major crisis, Æthelred soon proved that he had neither the political skill nor the military strength to deal with it. Many of Æthelred's problems in his thirty-eight-year reign were rooted in his choice of advisers. Æthelred's posthumous epithet 'the Unready' tellingly puns on his name, meaning 'noble counsel', indicating to the contrary *un-raed* or 'ill-advised counsel'. Æthelred could not command the loyalty of the English aristocracy and was, therefore, also dogged by treachery.

In fairness to Æthelred, the problems of the first few years of his reign cannot fully be ascribed to his mismanagement, as he was only twelve years old when he succeeded. Nevertheless, Æthelred's strategy of paying to get rid of the Dane in order to secure the country, the so-called *gafol* payments, had the opposite effect to the one intended. Recent attempts to explain Æthelred's policy as an ingenious device aimed at securing winter truces or mercenary allegiance are unconvincing, not least because it was at best a short-term strategy and at worst an invitation to the invaders to return.[19] In the end, Æthelred's attempt to buy his way out of trouble effectively guaranteed that England's security could only be achieved under Scandinavian rule.

The first raids occurred in the south and west of the country. The *Anglo-Saxon Chronicle* records seven ships raiding Southampton, followed by raids throughout Devon, Cornwall and Dorset in the years immediately following. Part of London was burned in 982 and, in 987, Watchet, the site of a royal mint on the Somerset coast, was attacked. In Wales, coastal monasteries were sacked, St David's being attacked three times between 980 and 1000, and Viking armies set up bases on Anglesey and in Pembrokeshire. Only in retrospect is it possible to see that these attacks were probing English defences and the country's resolve. By 991 the Vikings seem to have drawn their conclusions:

> Here in this year Olaf came with ninety-three ships to Folkestone, and raided about it, and then went from there to Sandwich and so from there to Ipswich, and overran all that, and so to Maldon. And Ealdorman Byrhtnoth came against them there with his army and fought them, and they killed the ealdorman and had possession of the place of slaughter.[20]

1. The late ninth-century Gokstad burial ship. Now in The Viking Ship Museum, Oslo.
© Museum of Cultural History – University of Oslo, Norway.

2. Representation of the battle of Hafrsfjord *c.* 872, showing Viking weaponry. Berserk warriors are depicted in the foreground. Osprey Publishing Ltd from Mark Harrison, *Warrior 3, Viking Hersir, 793–1066AD.* © Osprey Publishing Ltd, www.ospreypublishing.com

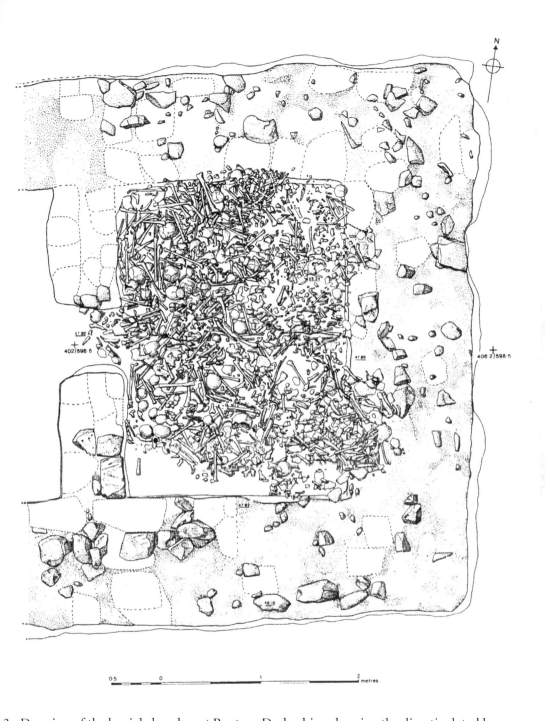

3. Drawing of the burial chamber at Repton, Derbyshire, showing the disarticulated bones of more than 250 ninth-century bodies. The probable site of the death and interment of Ivar the Boneless. *Drawing by* Judith Dobie in Martin and Birthe Kjølbye Biddle, 'Repton and the "great heathen army", 873–4' in James Graham-Campbell et al., eds, *Vikings and the Danelaw* (Oxbow Books, 2001). © Repton Excavation.

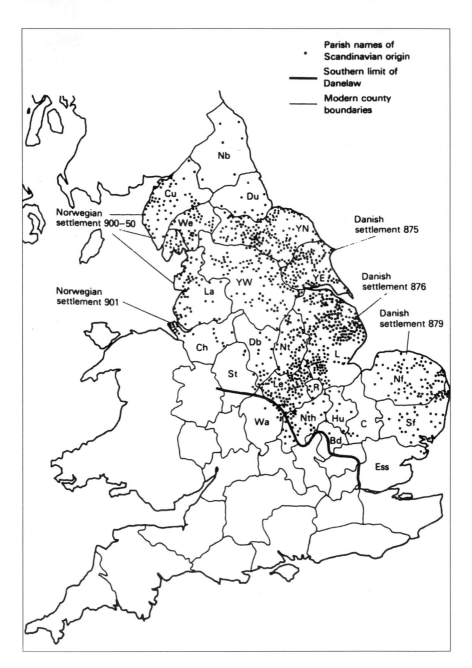

4. Scandinavian settlement in England. A.H. Smith, *English Place-name Elements*, vol. 25 (1956). © English Place-name Society.

5. The Hon hoard found in Norway, which includes coins from across the Viking world and items of Carolingian gold plundered in Frankia. *Photo by* Ove Holst. © Museum of Cultural History – University of Oslo, Norway.

6. Reconstruction of Eirik the Red's turf longhouse at Brattahlid, showing Thjodhild's church in the foreground. © National Museum of Denmark, Copenhagen.

7. The remains of Eirik the Red's Brattahlid estate at Narssaq, Greenland.
© National Museum of Denmark, Copenhagen.

8. Statue of Leif Eiriksson in Reykjavik, Iceland. *Photo by* Peter van der Krogt
http://leiferiksson.vanderkrogt.net

The battle of Maldon was a clear indication of the true nature of the resumption of Viking belligerence. The Viking army was not looking for settlement but conquest. The pedigree of the Viking leader at Maldon suggests the scale and seriousness of the undertaking, for the Olaf named by the chronicler was none other than Olaf Tryggvason, the future king of Norway and grandson of Harald Finehair. In all probability, his chief accomplice, although unnamed on this occasion, was Svein Forkbeard, the king of Denmark and son of Harald Bluetooth. English resistance at Maldon was immortalized in a fine poem written shortly after the event. It tells of a heroic last stand of Englishmen represented by all parts of the country and all classes, and it contrasts the slippery-tongued heathen 'wolves of war' with the plain-speaking Christian English, who see noble sacrifice and fair play as moral absolutes. Prophetically, given the way events were to unfold, the poem blames the defeat of the English on the treachery and cowardice of a handful of deserters.

The defeat at Maldon had to be resolved diplomatically, for the English seemed to have no other response. It is said that the idea of paying Danegeld was first proposed by Archbishop Sigeric and 10,000 lbs of silver was duly handed over. Three years later, in 994, Olaf and Svein returned with ninety-four ships, this time to London, intending to raze it to the ground. Despite the fact that 'they fared worse than they ever imagined',[21] Æthelred and his councillors decided to expend a further 16,000 lbs of silver to make them desist. As part of the settlement, Olaf accepted baptism under Æthelred's sponsorship and promised never to return. Olaf kept to his promise and returned to Norway to seize the kingdom and ultimately to die in 1000 in a sea-borne ambush orchestrated by his probable co-commander at Maldon, Svein Forkbeard.

Other Vikings did not feel bound by Olaf's oath. Between 997 and 999, a Viking army was raiding and devastating across a wide area of the south. Attacks involving 'indescribable war booty' took place in Cornwall, Devon, Dorset and Wales. The Isle of Wight provided a good base while the Vikings 'ate out of Hampshire and Sussex'. When the army of Kent 'submitted too quickly and fled' from the invaders coming up the Medway to Rochester, and Æthelred delayed confronting them on land and sea as he had promised, the chronicler at Peterborough expressed the general dismay:

And always whenever matters should have been advanced, the slower it was from one hour to the next, and they always let their enemies' strength increase; and always the sea was retreated from, and they [the enemy] always moved up after. And then in the end the ship-army achieved nothing, except the people's labour, and wasting money, and emboldening of their enemies.[22]

The drain on resources was a serious problem for Æthelred. During a brief lull in 1000, when the Viking army decamped to Normandy, he set about replenishing his coffers by raiding the Scandinavian populace of Cumbria and then, more daringly, the Viking stronghold on the Isle of Man. The following year the Viking army was back revisiting the same places as before and was free to travel about 'just as they themselves wanted, and nothing withstood them'.[23] Æthelred acted as before, this time with a payment of 24,000 lbs of silver. Then, after taking advice as to how to contain the problem, Æthelred enacted a decree stating that on St Brice's day, 13 November 1002, 'all the Danes who had sprung up in this island, sprouting like weeds amongst the wheat, were to be destroyed by a most just extermination'.[24] Such genocide was bound to have serious consequences, despite the fact that Æthelred did not organize the massacre effectively. Among those slaughtered, including those who sought sanctuary and were burned in St Frideswides' minster in Oxford, were a sister and brother-in-law of Svein Forkbeard.

Æthelred may have felt emboldened to take such a drastic step after his marriage earlier in the year to Emma of Normandy, sister of Richard the Fearless, the ruler of Normandy, but if this was the case no help came when, as was now all the more certain, Svein returned. Svein harried Æthelred's realm for the next two years only briefly withdrawing in 1005 when a famine swept across the country. With cowardice and incompetence rife among his generals, Æthelred again resorted to bribery and in 1007 doled out a further 30,000 lbs of silver to his enemies, but again it changed nothing. Æthelred's attempt to defend the country by building a fleet of eighty ships foundered when twenty of them defected and the rest were burned during a confrontation not with Vikings but with the English defectors. The king's efforts at restructuring his armies were equally marred by the appointment of Eadric Streona to the position of ealdorman of Mercia. Eadric turned out to be a thief, a liar, a double-dealer and a traitor. Meanwhile, Vikings continued to arrive as news of English disarray and their king's generosity spread. Among them was Thorkell the Tall with a great fleet of Vikings from across Scandinavia. By 1011, Viking armies had overrun Bedfordshire, Berkshire, Buckinghamshire, Cambridgeshire, East Anglia, Essex, Hampshire, Hertfordshire, half of Huntingdonshire, Kent, Middlesex, Oxfordshire, Surrey and much of Wiltshire 'and all these misfortunes befell us through lack of decision, in that they were not offered tax in time; but when they had done great evil, *then* truce was made with them'.[25] Danegeld continued to flow.

In the same year, Archbishop Ælfheah of Canterbury was seized and held hostage along with a number of other notables. By Easter of the following year, no ransom had been agreed. Complicating the protracted negotiation for 48,000 lbs of silver in Danegeld was the refusal of the archbishop to accept or assist in any transaction that might be made on his behalf. One night shortly after Easter, the Vikings holding him got drunk and took to pelting him with 'bones and the heads of cattle', then 'one struck him on the head with the butt of an axe, so that with the blow he sank down and his holy blood fell on the earth, and sent forth his holy soul to God's kingdom'.[26] The archbishop's body was delivered to London and interred with all due ceremony at St Paul's minster. The murder was so shameful an event that Thorkell the Tall, who had tried to intervene on the archbishop's behalf, promptly offered his forty-five ships to the service of Æthelred on the condition that he maintain them. Æthelred eagerly accepted but paid Danegeld to the murderers, nevertheless.

By 1013, Svein Forkbeard was ready to deliver a decisive blow. He sailed with a large fleet to Sandwich in Kent, headed up the coast to the Humber estuary and then moved down the River Trent to Gainsborough, where he placed his ships under the command of his eighteen-year-old son, Cnut. The people of the Five Boroughs and Northumbria submitted to him without hesitation, partly out of traditional sympathies and partly out of sheer weariness. Then Cnut took his land army south to receive the submission of Oxford and Winchester. At London, the fleet of Thorkell the Tall and the valiant defence of the townsfolk forced him to turn toward the west country to complete the subjugation of all but London. Within five months Cnut was back in Gainsborough and all of England was his. London had duly yielded, recognizing the hopelessness of the situation, and offered hostages, tribute and whatever Svein required. Queen Emma and the sons of Æthelred fled to her brother Richard in Normandy. By the end of the year Æthelred had followed.

After over two hundred years of resistance led by the kings of Wessex, England had finally become a Danish province. Despite the years of chaos, it had survived in surprisingly good order. The economy still functioned, Edgar's laws remained effective and, thanks to the efforts of Archbishop Wulfstan, the Benedictine monasteries flourished and vernacular scholarship had never before achieved such excellence. The spoils of victory were, therefore, not inconsiderable. But there was to be one last twist in the tale before Danish overlordship was complete. Within five weeks of successfully concluding his twenty-year campaign in England, on 3 February 1014, Svein was dead. His army immediately elected his son Cnut as their king and commander in the field. In the confusion, English councillors recalled Æthelred from Normandy in the hope that 'he would govern them more justly than he did before'.[27] Cnut and his army had withdrawn to north Lincolnshire but, when Æthelred's vengeance fell upon the country, Cnut put to sea and sailed to Sandwich before heading for Denmark. As a parting gesture, Cnut disembarked the hostages taken from London, minus their hands, ears and noses. One further Viking force remained at Greenwich, that of Thorkell the Tall. Either Thorkell had realized what was going to happen next or Æthelred naively felt that Thorkell's defence was no longer necessary; in either case, 21,000 lbs of English silver concluded the alliance.

Back in Denmark, Cnut's elder brother Harald had succeeded Svein. Having a younger brother in command of a great army in the same realm cannot have been comfortable, so Harald decided to help his brother reclaim England. In 1015 Cnut set sail with a magnificently equipped fleet. With him was the battle-hardened Earl Eirik of Hladir, his brother-in-law and ruler of northern Norway, and Thorkell the Tall, re-enlisted to the Danish cause. The pattern of Cnut's conquest was complicated by the dissent that had broken out between Æthelred and his son Edmund Ironside. Against his father's wishes, Edmund had installed himself as ruler of the Five Boroughs and secured the backing of the folk of North Lincolnshire, who were resentful of both Cnut's abandonment of them and Æthelred's bloody vengeance. Æthelred had no opportunity to remonstrate with his son, for in the latter part of 1015 he was laid up with a sickness. He would die the following year 'after great toil and difficulties in his life', as the *Anglo-Saxon Chronicle* remarks.[28] By that time Edmund and Cnut were engaged in the last battle between Wessex and Denmark. This time the whole of England was at stake.

The war was hard fought and both King Edmund, as he became in 1016, and Cnut were young men in their early twenties, equally eager to win glory. Despite the fact that English troops were not easily reconciled to Edmund, some preferring to remain loyal to Æthelred while he still lived, Edmund believed that he had the measure of Cnut. Unfortunately, he had not reckoned on the duplicity of Eadric Streona, Æthelred's lieutenant in Mercia. After Cnut had achieved victory in Wessex and Warwickshire, calculating the odds,

Eadric defected to Cnut. Cnut then managed to subdue Edmund's allies in Northumbria, leaving the territory in the hands of Earl Eirik of Hladir. For his conquest to have any meaning, Cnut had to take London, where Edmund was installed with his army, but the assault turned into a siege and the siege dragged on. Then Edmund managed to escape and rapidly reclaim Wessex, after which he returned to London and attacked the besiegers, forcing them to withdraw, but such were his own casualties that he too had to withdraw, whereupon Cnut promptly resumed the siege. The Londoners continued to resist and, eventually, Cnut abandoned the effort, removing his forces to Mercia and taking to raiding and gathering provisions.

The first conclusive encounter between the two armies came at Otford, south east of London, where Edmund emerged victorious, putting Cnut's army to flight. At this point, Eadric Streona decided that he had made a mistake and managed to persuade Edmund to make what the chronicler regarded as a most unwise decision to forgive him in return for his allegiance. Edmund was now in pursuit of Cnut. He caught up with him at Ashingdon on the high ground between the Thames and the Crouch estuary in south-east Essex. Given the way matters were progressing, Edmund must have appeared to be the favourite, but Eadric Streona succeeded in reversing the odds by promptly running away with his Welsh infantry, so giving Cnut the critical advantage. Thanks to Eadric, Cnut 'had the victory and won himself all England'.[29] Cnut's victory was not, in reality, absolute and Edmund was not yet done with. There was sure to be further confrontation between the two, but for now they feigned accord and divided the country between them. Edmund was to take Wessex and Cnut the rest. Further confrontation was, however, rendered unnecessary when Edmund died at the end of November from the wounds he had received at Ashingdon. Almost immediately, Cnut was accepted as the rightful and unchallenged king. Englishmen felt a mixture of bitterness and relief.

The new king's first act was to appoint trusted men to govern the regions: Earl Eirik stayed in Northumbria; Thorkell the Tall took East Anglia; and Cnut himself Wessex. This left Mercia, and for a while Cnut left the perfidious Eadric Streona in charge. The arrangement lasted a few months while Cnut settled into his new role. Then Eadric got what many felt was coming to him, when Cnut had him executed along with others who could not be relied on or who posed any future threat to Cnut's power. The earldom of Mercia was given over to Leofric. Although Leofric was the first among the English nobility to find favour from the new king, he is probably best remembered for his pious wife Godiva who became famed in later years for her uncompromising protest against her husband's tax regimes.

Leofric apart, during the early years of his rule Cnut's policy was to prefer men of Danish background. Those with traditional English loyalties were sidelined. As time passed, however, and Cnut became more secure and better schooled in the business of being a Christian king in the Anglo-Saxon tradition, his appointments policy was almost reversed and Danish courtiers became a rarity. Cnut's English courtiers were men from newly elevated families whose connection with the power structures of the past were remote. Conspicuous among them was Earl Godwin of Wessex, a man who had started life among the peasantry, progressed to piracy and would go on to become a kingmaker. Cnut was nevertheless careful to make sure that he himself was well protected by men of his own kind and maintained his royal guard of forty ships, the *þinga-lið*, throughout his reign. As for the invasion army, that was now redundant and he quickly disbanded it at a cost to the English taxpayer of 72,000 lbs of silver. Viking soldiers remembered their profitable times in England on rune stones in Scandinavia, such as this inscription from Uppland:

> And Ulv took in England three geld.
> That was the first which Toste paid.
> Then Thorkell paid.
> Then Cnut paid.

Cnut's reign (1017–35) was characterized by his efforts to reconcile English and Danish factions in his realm by law and by deed. He married Æthelred's widow Emma and she bore him Harthacnut and Gunnhild, the latter of whom he married off to the German emperor Conrad. He took great pains to demonstrate the Christian nature of his rule with visits to Rome for papal blessings, large investment in the Christian infrastructure of England and by placing his faith in English churchmen. By way of disowning and perhaps apologizing for the enormities of his Viking past, he oversaw the ceremonial translation of the remains of the murdered Archbishop Ælfheah from London to Canterbury. More controversially, he maintained a lifelong attachment to his concubine Ælfgifu of Northampton, who bore him Harold Harefoot and Svein. In 1018 he ascended the throne of Denmark and, aware that dividing his time between the two countries pleased nobody, eventually appointed Thorkell the Tall his regent there, perhaps nervously, for Thorkell was not without ambition. In 1030, he forcibly took over the rule of Norway from Olaf Haraldsson, although after this he offended the Norwegians by sending his Northampton concubine and their son Svein to rule in his stead. Their turbulent rule in Norway ended the year after Cnut died. Above all, Cnut sought to reassure the English in public proclamations that under his rule no Vikings would again threaten their shores. No doubt some spotted an irony but few would dispute the wisdom of his governance. Good political judgement allied to a willingness to adapt lay behind Cnut's success as a ruler. His epithet 'the Great' was well deserved.

Less capable men succeeded to Cnut's empire and it did not long outlast his death. The contenders for his throne sprang from three related liaisons: Alfred and Edward from the marriage of Æthelred and Emma; Harthacnut from the marriage of Cnut and Emma; and Harold Harefoot from Cnut's relationship with his concubine Ælfgifu. Rivalry, pitting Emma's English and Danish sons against each other and, more bloodily, against those of Ælfgifu, prevailed for the next seven years. In accordance with Cnut's wishes, Harthacnut was first to succeed. He was opposed by Alfred and Edward, whose royal patrons in Normandy encouraged their ambitions. Yet it was not they who usurped the English throne, when Harthacnut was called away to fight for the survival of Cnut's Scandinavian empire, but Harold Harefoot, supported by Ælfgifu and Earl Godwin.

Dismayed by Harold's elevation, Alfred and Edward were now prompted to make their move. Careful to take separate routes, they arrived in England to discuss their claim with their mother, Emma. But they had completely misread the political climate. Alfred was betrayed by Earl Godwin to Harold's henchmen, who gouged out his eyes and mutilated his body. Edward fled back to Normandy. Harold Harefoot did not last long and on his death in 1040 Harthacnut returned and, as a public demonstration of his contempt, had Harold's body exhumed from Winchester and unceremoniously thrown into the Thames. Two years later an accord was in the offing between Harthacnut and Edward, motivated more by Harthacnut's need to cultivate the sympathies of the Anglo-Saxon earls than anything else. Nothing came of this proposed détente, for in 1042 Harthacnut was seized by convulsions and dropped dead. With his death, Danish rule of England came to an end and the line of Wessex was restored when Edward the Confessor came to the throne. But Edward's values were not those of his ninth- and tenth-century ancestors, rather they were those he had learnt during his Norman upbringing. Powerful Englishmen were less than impressed. Among them was Earl Godwin, the conniver of the murder of Edward's brother and the most influential force in the land.

Edward's rule was dependent on the support of the English earls. Edward's ancient pedigree was not mirrored among his nobility, for they were the eleventh-century equivalent of *arrivistes*, raised to power under Cnut. For them, the resumption of the line of Wessex was not necessarily seen as a realignment of English traditions in accordance with historical justice. So it was that the cunning machinations of Earl Godwin, now the possessor of what otherwise would have been Edward's inheritance in Wessex, dogged the king's career. Political necessity obliged Edward to marry Godwin's daughter Edith, and although Edward was understandably wary of a man more prosperous than himself, he was compromised and could do little to hinder his father-in-law's progress. Nevertheless, Edward tried. In 1051 he successfully manipulated reports of a bloody brawl in Dover between the residents and visiting Norman knights into making Godwin appear disloyal in his unwillingness to take revenge on the town. Confronted with an armed force and a charge of treason, Godwin fled to Flanders and Edward duly his seized his Wessex estates. More than likely, Edward viewed this more as a recovery of his birthright than a confiscation. Edith, meanwhile, was confined to a monastery.

The political fallout from Edward's dispossession of Earl Godwin surprised him, for he suddenly found himself at the centre of a Francophobic storm. Worse still, rumours circulated that the childless Edward was contriving a successor to his throne from among the Norman aristocracy, namely one William, the illegitimate son of Duke Robert of Normandy. The English earls stood on the brink of open rebellion. Godwin watched the country's mood from across the Channel and, a year after his humiliation, boldly sailed his fleet up the Thames. Edward's army declined to confront the earl, thus forcing the king into an embarrassing climbdown and obliging the reinstatement and full exoneration of the man most likely to threaten his sovereignty. Edward's Francophile tendencies and his expensive flattery of Norman aristocrats were abruptly curtailed.

When Earl Godwin died in 1053, the new power in the land was his son Harold, whose successful campaign against the Welsh King Gruffyd in 1062–3 brought him status as a general and even greater power than his father had achieved. Edward was cast in the shade and, for the latter years of his reign, lived up to his appellation, 'the Confessor', all but retreating from affairs of state. When he died in January 1066, still childless, the council of nobles, the *witan*, determined that a new Wessex dynasty should succeed him in the person of Harold Godwinson, just as Earl Godwin had planned.

Edward's twenty-four-year rule had been one of relative peace, so far as relations with Scandinavia were concerned. With the exception of localized Viking activity around the Irish Sea and the Scottish isles, Viking raiding parties had become little more than a memory during the reign of Cnut, largely thanks to Cnut's power in Scandinavia. Despite the collapse of Cnut's empire after his death, little altered in this respect during Edward's reign, largely because Norway and Denmark were engaged in fighting with each other and had no spare energy for English affairs. But this did not mean they had lost interest. The succession issue of 1035 not only threw England into dynastic chaos, it also fuelled the ambitions of Scandinavians. So far as pretenders were concerned, both Edward the Confessor and Harold Godwinson had no more or less claim than they to Cnut's throne. The strongest legitimate claim by blood was that of a nephew of Cnut, Svein Estrithson of Denmark, while the strongest in military strength came from the formidable Harald Hardrada of Norway, who believed that a bond made between his late nephew Magnus the Good and Harthacnut entitled him to rule England.

The war in Scandinavia between these two claimants ended in a relative stalemate in 1064. Edward's death two years later presented a clear opportunity for the reassertion of Scandinavian authority over England. Svein, however, was too preoccupied to pursue his claim. He had tested English loyalty to him in 1047, when he asked for support in his war against Magnus the Good but had found it unforthcoming. Svein decided to bide his time. Not so Harald Hardrada, a Viking of the old school and renowned 'thunderbolt of the north'. His nephew Magnus had tried out English defences to the south in 1058 but had found them resilient. Harald Hardrada judged that the way to establish himself in England was to take the northern route favoured by Vikings of yore. The events of 1066 chimed well with him and his northern plan. He found an English ally in the person of Harold Godwinson's disaffected brother, Tostig, whom Harold had dispossessed of the earldom of Northumbria a year before his election to the throne. With the Orkney earls also eager to advance themselves at England's cost, Harald Hardrada prepared to aim one last thunderbolt against England. Unbeknown to him, but preoccupying the new English king, were the equally advanced plans of a third claimant.

Whether William the Bastard, now Duke of Normandy, had been promised England by Edward the Confessor, or whether it was Harold Godwinson himself who had rashly promised him allegiance during an unintended visit to William's court in 1065, is a matter that remains unresolved. What is clear is that William was serious about his right to rule England. The minute he heard of Harold Godwinson's coronation he began putting together a vast fleet and a large mercenary force with the intention making good his claim. He had also managed to secure the blessings of the pope for his cause. By the late summer of 1066 he was ready. Up in the north, Harald Hardrada was a few weeks ahead of him. Harold Godwinson, meanwhile, looked only across the Channel and to his south coast awaiting the Norman invasion. When news came of Harald Hardrada's landing in North Yorkshire and the massing of an army of some nine thousand men, many of whom had arrived in Harald Hardrada's three hundred warships, the new English king was taken aback and infuriated. According to Snorri Sturluson's thirteenth-century account of Harald Hardrada's life, all that Harold Godwinson was prepared to concede to the invader was 'seven feet of English soil or so much more as he is taller than other men'.[30]

The northern invasion army's first encounter was with the king's earls, Morcar of Northumbria and Edwin of Mercia. Their stand at Fulford, where two hundred years earlier the sons of Ragnar Hairy Breeches had laid siege to York, weakened both Norwegian and English manpower, but the Norwegians had the victory and Harald Hardrada was now ready to enter York. But there were hostages to take and negotiations that would assure him of Northumbrian popular support. He paused and encamped on open ground at Stamford Bridge a few miles to the east of York, oblivious that King Harold Godwinson had hurriedly marched his army north and was but a few days away. The English fell upon the unsuspecting Norwegians and their allies on 25 September 1066 'and there was that day a very hard fight on both sides'.[31] The outcome was unambiguous and the last great Viking invasion force was all but annihilated. Tostig was killed, the remnants of the Orkney Vikings swore their allegiance to Harold and the Norwegian survivors were allowed to depart in their twenty-four remaining ships. Harald Hardrada's thunderbolt had rebounded in the shape of an arrow through the throat.[32]

Harold Godwinson had no time to savour his victory, for four days later news arrived that William's invasion fleet had landed at Pevensey on the Sussex coast. Harold promptly rallied his battle-weary and depleted army and hurried back south. At Senlac, north of Hastings, on 14 October 1066 the English and Norman armies met in one of the longest battles in medieval English history, for here all the centuries of indigenous tribal bickering between Angles, Saxons, Danes, and Norwegians were finally silenced. William's victory was absolute, Harold was killed, having ruled for 'forty weeks and one day', as the *Anglo-Saxon Chronicle* precisely noted. As a consequence, English identity was transformed

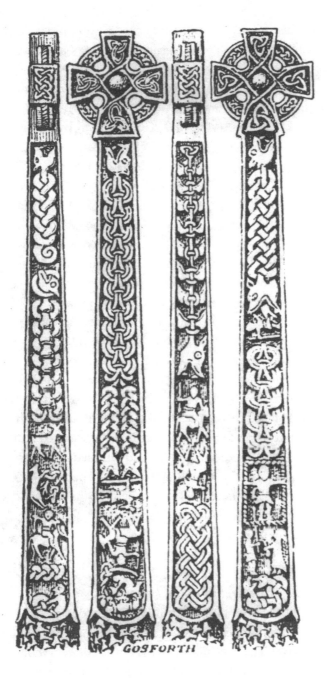

Drawing of the Gosforth Cross in Cumbria. The right face shows Odin
being devoured by the wolf Fenrir. Beneath are images of the crucifixion
of Christ.

forever. From this moment forward for several generations, if you were not French, or at the very least a French speaker, you did not matter. English social and political life became as simple as that.

Svein Estrithson may have had some hand in William's conquest, at least at the level of diplomacy, but he did not yet believe that his own claim was now obsolete. Indeed, he was encouraged to think this way by dispossessed English noblemen who preferred any Dane to any Norman and pointed to insurgencies in the English Danelaw. Given that it was the same noblemen who had rejected Svein's plea for help twenty years earlier, their change of heart was a measure of the changing times. In 1069–70, Svein sent his fleets first to Dover then north to the Humber, where they set about raiding and stirring up trouble. For a time the Norman conquerors had good reason to worry but William had the measure of the situation. With his longships crammed with loot, Svein accepted William's invitation to leave without further battle.

Just one more sea-crossing aimed at conquest was made in 1075, this time by Cnut II, son of Svein Estrithson. Cnut, like his father, hoped to take advantage of the northern rebellion, but when he arrived in York, William had already ruthlessly quelled the uprising and Northumbrians had no stomach for any further insurrection. Ten years later, Cnut once again considered an invasion but he was inhibited by the threat of a German invasion from the south. His fleet soon dispersed. Cnut responded by severely punishing those whom he regarded as deserters and as a direct consequence provoked a rebellion. Cnut was murdered in 1086 in the cathedral he had founded at Odense. This Danish drama was the last gasp of Viking ambition in England. William, king of England, had gathered both right and might behind him and would not tolerate rivals or dissent. Some in the north of England had good cause to look back nostalgically on Viking domination.

The Viking Age, as it unfolded in England, has been assessed positively by some historians as furthering the cause and the necessity of a united English realm. Certainly, the southern and midland English kingdoms of the ninth century rapidly perceived that a united front against a common enemy was their best strategy for survival. The royal line of Wessex from Alfred to Edgar was responsible for showing the way forward in this regard. Yet this process was already underway before the Vikings arrived. After the mid ninth century and the conquest of the Ragnarssons, England, rather than being the sum of a number of kingdoms already entwined by kith, kin and custom, effectively became two countries. It remained so in territorial terms until 937 and Athelstan's victory at Brunanburh, and in many ways it remained so in law until after the Norman Conquest. The Viking contribution, far from promoting a united country, could just as easily be regarded as having impeded it. A north–south divide was encouraged and an east–west divide was established. Left alone, political marriages, the growing power of the church, and the need to have stable trading relations with Europe would all have contributed to English petty kings diminishing in number. But it might not have taken 250 years and almost certainly it would not have entailed the destruction of centuries of scholarship.

Until the reign of Cnut, the Vikings in England achieved little and destroyed much in the process. Of course, it could be said that from the late ninth century the Northumbrian Viking settlers merged comfortably into existing social structures and that their assimilation through intermarriage and conversion produced a homogeneous society. But it is apparent that this assimilation entailed an affirmation of the traditions of 'northernness' fortified by a contempt for the influences of 'southernness', and that the finer points of Christian theology and piety were secondary to the assertion of cultural traditions imported from pagan Scandinavia. In this last respect, a fine example of Viking 'Christianity' is illustrated on the tenth-century Gosforth Cross in Cumbria. Carved into its sandstone faces are scenes from the twilight of the Norse gods at Ragnarok curiously juxtaposed with scenes from the crucifixion. It is quite wrong to assume that the Vikings as Christians suddenly abandoned their cultural heritage or traded it wholesale for ideals of poverty and peace. The Viking outlook – bold, belligerent, and materialistic – remained bred in the bone of many generations of settlers, and the Viking impact, particularly on northern England, reverberated long after William of Normandy had crushed any organized resistance.

Socially, politically and economically, the Viking Age in England can readily be assessed in negative terms. The monuments in stone that punctuated the wayside tracks to the north and east of the country, and that now reside in village churches and city museums, were small compensation for the terror and mayhem the Vikings brought to bear in their longships.

# 6

# Scotland and the Orkneys

In few places outside Scandinavia is there better physical evidence for Viking settlement than the Scottish isles. Equally, in few places is there such a paucity of contemporary written evidence for Viking activity. Twelfth- and thirteenth-century histories and grand accounts of Viking dynasties, such as *The Saga of the Orkney Earls*, are abundant, mainly due to the Icelanders' fascination with their Viking past. Contemporary sources amount to limited mentions in the *Anglo-Saxon Chronicle*, where the English were involved, and the *Annals of Ulster*, most extensively in respect of the outrages at Iona, beginning in 795. The later sources from both Britain and Scandinavia are, nevertheless, valuable and informative, and much of their historical detail regarding genealogy and territorial conflicts is credible; on the subjects of motivations and politics, however, they include a degree of special pleading and poetic licence.

It is apparent from archaeological evidence in Scotland that the essential character of Viking activity was one that shifted rapidly from the use of the Scottish isles as lairs, from which to launch attacks against mainland Britain and Ireland, to one that entailed permanent settlement with a mixed economy, based in part on piracy and in part on farming and fishing. When and how this shift took place raises difficulties. According to Snorri Sturluson's thirteenth-century history, *Heimskringla*, the point at which lairs turned into settlements was bound up with the efforts of Harald Finehair to unite Norway in the latter half of the ninth century:

> During the times of warfare when King Harald brought Norway under his domination, foreign lands such the Faroes and Iceland were settled [by Norwegians]. There was a great exodus to the Shetlands, and many of the nobility fled King Harald as outlaws and went on Viking expeditions to the west, staying in the Orkneys and the Hebrides in winter, but in summer harrying in Norway where they inflicted great damage.[1]

Although the imposition of Harald's authority certainly caused offence to many, the suggestion that it was this alone that triggered the settlement of the

Scottish isles is now thought unlikely. Viking raiders had been active around the north and west of Scotland since the earliest raids in the late eighth century, and contact with the isles had preceded that by several decades. It is highly likely that Vikings were using the island archipelagos as bases from the early ninth century, if not before. The settlement at Jarlshof on Shetland, which comprised a substantial long house and several ancillary buildings for smithying, corn drying, bathing and livestock, was clearly such a base.

Other than Northumbrian Anglo-Saxons, the Vikings encountered three distinct peoples during the course of their expansion in Scotland. Dominating the Western Isles and the territories around Argyll were the Scots, who had migrated from Dalriada (now County Antrim) in Ireland in the late fifth and early sixth centuries. South of the Scots in the Strathclyde region and the south west were the Celtic Britons. Occupying the Caledonian central and northern territories, including some of the Northern Isles, were the Picts (or 'painted ones'), the aboriginal people of Scotland. It was the Picts in the north that first suffered the Viking onslaught. Material evidence suggests that the Picts were an industrious people who had converted to Christianity at the end of the sixth century. Among them were the *papar*, Irish priests and missionaries. Legend repeated in an anonymous Norwegian history reveals something of the contempt in which the Picts were held by incoming Vikings. In this they are described as a pygmy people who built towns in the mornings and evenings but were bereft of strength at midday and so trembled in fear in underground houses.[2] Although this is little more than caricature, it is apparent that the Picts were no match for the Vikings. As is indicated by settlement evidence at Buckquoy in north-west Orkney, their displacement from the Northern Isles was neither immediate nor genocidal, but it is unlikely to have been peaceful. The fate of the Picts thereafter was to be assaulted by Vikings, who in 839 are said to have wiped out the Pictish nobility, or to be overrun by the Scots, expanding their influence from the west in the mid ninth century. As a consequence of either intermarriage with the Scots or slaughter by Vikings and Scots, they soon ceased to exist as a distinct ethnicity. The Picto-Scottish kingdom envisaged by some historians disguises the political subordination and cultural extinction of the Picts.

The dynastic history of the Scottish isles is said to have begun around 866 with Harald Finehair's punitive mission to the Northern Isles. His aim was to stop those disaffected and exiled Norwegian Vikings from causing the 'great damage' to the Norwegian homeland that Snorri mentions. Having subjugated

Orkney and Shetland, or so it is said, Harald proceeded to the Hebrides and on to Man, which he devastated. Snorri tells us that accompanying Harald was his long-time ally Earl Røgnvald of Møre, along with his son Ivar and his brother Sigurd, who held the esteemed position of forecastleman on Harald's ship. Ivar, however, was struck down in battle. Harald's desire to compensate Røgnvald for his loss is given as the explanation for how Røgnvald subsequently took possession of the earldom of Orkney and Shetland.

Neat though this account is of the origins of Røgnvald's Orcadian dynasty, chronology indicates that Harald's Scottish campaign either did not take place or, if it did, it was at a significantly later date. By historical reckoning Harald would have been a mere boy in 866, and his ascendancy as king of Norway does not appear to have become effective until approximately 880. Just how and from whom Earl Røgnvald took possession of the earldoms of Orkney and Shetland therefore remains a mystery. Whatever the case might have been, it is apparent that Røgnvald had enough to deal with in Norway and was not about to abandon his Norwegian interests for a new home in Orkney. As a consequence, his brother Sigurd was the first Norwegian to take the title of earl of Orkney. Given the subsequent history, we can assume that Røgnvald set the condition that the earldom should pass to his own sons on Sigurd's death. From this point, it is chiefly the documentary evidence provided by the Icelandic sagas, particularly *The Saga of the Orkney Earls*, that gives us insight into how this small corner of the Viking world gradually took on an importance in the wider world of Viking Age politics.

The rule of Sigurd the Mighty (d. *c.* 892) saw an expansion of his power onto the Scottish mainland. He allied himself with the Hebridean Viking Thorstein the Red. Together, Sigurd and Thorstein imposed their authority over Caithness, Ross, Moray, Sutherland and Argyll: 'the Northmen wasted Pictland', says a Scottish chronicler.[3] The Scots, however, did not prove to be easy opponents and their treachery, which encompassed the death of Thorstein the Red, was matched only by that of the Vikings. Having prospered at the expense of the Scots, probably to the point that no further territorial gains could be made, Sigurd realized that a truce was necessary. According to *The Saga of the Orkney Earls*, a meeting was arranged with the Scottish earl, Maelbrigte Tooth, so named because of a dental deformity. Sigurd expected deceit and arrived with twice the agreed number of men, whereupon Maelbrigte and his clansmen launched a reckless assault and were promptly annihilated. By way of a trophy, Sigurd beheaded Maelbrigte and rode home with the head on his saddlebow. As Sigurd spurred his horse, Maelbrigte's tooth scratched against his calf. Sigurd died of blood poisoning and was buried in a mound by the banks of the River Oykell.

The death of Sigurd in the last decade of the ninth century soon led to a breakdown of order on Orkney, and within a year Earl Røgnvald had sent his son Hallad to set matters straight. Unfortunately, Hallad lacked the necessary mettle and after a few months returned to the quiet life in Norway, 'a laughing stock'.[4] Røgnvald looked to his four other sons for a replacement. Hrolf the Walker, so large that no horse could carry him, was obviously the most able and violent of them, but he had incurred the wrath of Harald Finehair and was therefore unsuitable.[5] Røgnvald's next choices were either Thorir or Hrollaug; the former, however, was a stop-at-home and the latter was set on seeking his fortune as a settler in Iceland. This left only the tall, ugly, one-eyed, illegitimate Einar, the youngest and least favoured of the sons of Røgnvald.

Einar (r. c. 895–910) turned out to be a far better choice than his father had imagined possible. Not only did he make an astute marriage to a mainland Irish princess, which brought him a measure of control over the Western Isles, he is also said to have introduced the practice of burning peat to the islanders, so gaining himself the nickname Turf Einar. Less promising were the way things were going back in Norway, for Harald Finehair's sons were showing all the arrogance of the spoilt and greedy. Earl Røgnvald was among those they envied and they shamefully burnt him alive in his home. Harald's fury over the murder of Røgnvald was sufficient to cause his sons to flee; one of them, Halfdan Long Leg, to Orkney. Turf Einar now had no choice but to decamp for the mainland. According to the saga, he returned a year later to avenge his father by capturing Halfdan and performing on him the blood-eagle sacrifice in honour of Odin. As was the way of things concerning family honour, Harald's anger now turned against Einar and he set sail for Orkney to exact punishment. Once again Einar was forced to take refuge on the mainland. Harald held the entire Northern Isles community responsible for Einar's crime and imposed a heavy tax of 60 gold marks, which many simply could not pay. Only when Einar offered to remit the whole sum himself, in return for the right to hold the islanders' lands in fee, did Harald come to terms with him. Einar returned to his earldom more powerful than he had left it, dying in his bed after many years of unchallenged rule.

As is apparent from these ninth-century events, the role of the Orkney earls was an important political link between the Norwegian monarchy and the Celtic west. But, so far as Norway was concerned, it was not intended that Orkney earls should think of themselves as wholly independent. If Vikings in the Scottish isles extended their influence across northern Britain toward Ireland, the Norwegian kings wanted to make sure that it was done in their names. From the latter part of the ninth century through to the mid tenth century, the politics of Viking activity in Scotland were inextricably linked to the prospective union of the Viking kingdoms of Dublin and York. The setting up of a permanent power base in Dublin had been, in many ways, dependent on the involvement of Vikings settled in the Western Isles. These Hebridean and south-western Vikings of mixed Irish and Norse blood, the Gall-Gaedhil, had played a significant role as henchmen to the Norwegian Turgeis during the establishment of the Irish *longphorts* in the mid part of the century. Two generations after Turgeis's death, the Vikings of the Northern Isles added their presence to the political scene, not only in respect of Dublin but also of York. This much is apparent from Sigurd the Mighty's choice of ally, Thorstein the Red, for Thorstein was the grandson of Ketil Flatnose, founder of the Gall-Gaedhil, and the son of a king of Dublin, Olaf the White, who had also been the chief ally of Ivar the Boneless, the leader of the Danish Great Army that conquered York and much of northern and eastern England in the years following the invasion of the Great Army in 865.

Yet Viking designs on Scotland had not been especially successful in respect of their campaigns directed north from England. The attacks launched by Olaf the White and Ivar the Boneless on the Strathclyde Britons in the early 870s had been generally consistent with the aim of creating a land and sea thoroughfare between Dublin and York. But the displacement of the Scots by Vikings from the Inner Hebrides early in the century and their subsequent eastward expansion into Pictland under the leadership of the king of Scottish Dalriada, Kenneth MacAlpin (d. 858), had led not only to the oblivion of the Picts but also to the rise of a Scottish kingdom. Olaf and Ivar's raids were deeply disruptive but permanent domination of any territory on mainland Scotland was beyond their scope.

A second and equally unsuccessful campaign occurred in the early decades of the tenth century. The twelve-year expulsion of the Vikings from Dublin, beginning in 902, had enhanced their presence throughout the north west of England and had stoked their ambitions in respect of mainland Scotland. The Scots under Constantine II (900–43) had, however, overrun the Strathclyde Britons in the 920s to give them formidable territorial control. Vikings probing northward were forcefully repelled and, as Sigurd the Mighty came to realize, a truce with the Scots was the better option. Helping to establish common political ground was the fact that both Vikings and Scots could identify a common enemy in the shape of the Wessex kings. The culmination of this shared antipathy toward the English was the coalition of Scots and Vikings that took to the field at the battle of Brunanburh in 937, where they were defeated, after which King Athelstan came close to governing the whole of Britain.

Nevertheless, the affairs of Dublin and York continued to dominate English, Irish and Scottish affairs until 954 and the death of Eirik Bloodaxe, the last Viking king of York. Eirik may have failed in his bid to establish supreme power in the north, but one outcome of his activities in Scotland was to place the Orkney earls at the centre of Scottish politics, inspiring subsequent Orkney earls to emulate and even surpass his achievements. During the period of Eirik's first expulsion from York in the mid tenth century, he journeyed to Orkney, where he obliged the two eldest sons of Turf Einar, Arnkel and Erlend, to accompany him on his campaigns to the south and west. These joint holders of the earldom may well have been present when Eirik asserted his authority over the Hebrides, bringing the Scottish isles under Orcadian authority for the first time. Although Eirik appears to have had the support of the Scots, he was operating in the face of the intense rivalry of Olaf Sihtricsson, king of Dublin, and the fury of the English king Eadred. In addition to this, his subjects in the kingdom of York were increasingly unconvinced of the benefits of having an ambitious Norwegian sub-king as their ruler. Arnkel and Erlend were unlucky enough to be with him when he was expelled from York for the second time, after which he and his lieutenants were ambushed and murdered at Stainmore as they headed north to take ship for Orkney.

The death of Eirik and the absorption of York by King Eadred finally thwarted Viking ambitions for the union of Dublin and York. With the Vikings of Ireland now isolated, Hiberno-Norse influence over the Western Isles was simultaneously weakened. Yet, as Eirik Bloodaxe had shown, a unified Viking rule over all the Scottish isles was possible. More than this, if the Scottish isles could be brought together, Ireland would be an appetizing prospect for the Vikings of Scotland. Towards the end of the tenth century the incumbent earl of Orkney, Sigurd the Stout, was in a position to see the possibilities. But before this the Orcadians had to weather fifty years of relative inactivity, two decades of vicious fraternal rivalry over the earldom, and the growing political and territorial power of their immediate neighbours, the Scots.

Eirik Bloodaxe's wife, Gunnhild, remained in Orkney after her husband's death. Regarding herself as the widow of the true king of Norway, she viewed the Northern Isles as her sons' birthright. So it came about that the Eirikssons 'took power in the islands and used them as their base in winter, spending the summers on Viking expeditions',[6] arrogating the rule of Turf Einar's only surviving son, Thorfinn Skull-Splitter. Finally Gunnhild and the Eirikssons quit Orkney to take part in Dano-Norwegian conflicts, where they expected to win favour from King Harald Bluetooth of Denmark. Their departure allowed Thorfinn to resume his earldom.

Little is known of Thorfinn's career, except that he was 'a strong ruler and warrior'. His death (c. 963) left his earldom in the hands of his five sons. This generation did nothing to enhance Orkney's power and was fraught with dissent and rivalry. *The Saga of the Orkney Earls* blames much on Ragnhild, the daughter of Eirik Bloodaxe, who Gunnhild had given in marriage to Thorfinn's eldest son, Arnfinn. It is said that Ragnhild married three of Thorfinn's sons, having plotted the death of the other two. If this was vexed domestically, it was matched by the political realities, for each of the brothers had a hand in trying to extend their influence in Caithness. Alliances were made with the Scots but there was no clear outcome. Eventually, open conflict broke out between two of the three surviving three brothers, with the Scots unsuccessfully favouring the younger brother's claim to the earldom. Neither of these brothers survived the hostilities and the earldom fell to the last of the brothers, Hlodvir.

The involvement of the Scots in disputes among Viking leaders over the earldom is revealing, for, in all likelihood, the Scots were happy to play off one Orkney aristocrat against another, as fractures in the dynasty could only serve to advance their own cause. Seemingly, and perhaps not surprisingly, it was during the disarray among the Orkney earls that the Scots became the main power in the north east. Any advance of the Orkney earldom now depended on their favour. The Scots, however, disapproved of the pagan practices of their Northern Isles neighbours, as, unlike the Vikings in the Celtic west, the Vikings of the north had clung to the old faith. This Christian–pagan divide was well illustrated by events in the west in 986 when Godfrey mac Harald, leader of the men of Dalriada, killed three hundred Danish Viking marauders as vengeance for the murder of the abbot and fifteen monks at Iona.[7] Alliances might be made between Christian Scots and pagan Vikings but only from expediency.

After the seemingly unremarkable rule of Hlodvir, his son, Sigurd the Stout (c. 985–1014), assumed control and proved the most energetic and ambitious of the earls since his namesake Sigurd the Mighty almost a hundred years earlier. Sigurd the Stout was politically skilled and cunningly exploited Scottish rivalries with the intention of recovering Orcadian influence over Caithness. Eventually he decided to establish a permanent link between Orkney and the mainland by marrying into the Scottish nobility. According to *The Saga of the Orkney Earls*, Sigurd married into the family of the powerful King Malcolm II (1005–34).

One of Sigurd's first acts as earl had been to guarantee the support of the islanders by returning to them the land rights they had forfeited to Turf Einar. Once married, he soon established himself as overlord in Caithness, no doubt with the assistance of his wife's family, and then turned his attention to the Western Isles. There is reason to believe accounts claiming that Sigurd commanded a fleet great enough to subdue and lay under taxation the Hebrides and Man, where he set up tributary earls. Given this power base, Sigurd was able to raise himself up as the ruler of all the western and northern fringes of Scotland, at least in name.

According to several saga sources, it was during this period of unprecedented Orcadian authority that, in 995, Sigurd almost met his end in the person of the scourge of England and aspirant to the Norwegian throne, Olaf Tryggvason. Olaf was returning to Norway from Dublin and had put into port at Osmundwall on Orkney. Aware that Earl Sigurd was nearby preparing his ships for a Viking expedition, Olaf invited him over 'as he wanted a word with him'.

> 'I want you and all your subjects to be baptized', he said when they met. 'If you refuse, I'll have you killed on the spot, and I swear that I'll ravage every island with fire and steel.'[8]

This was characteristic of Olaf's missionary zeal and Sigurd 'could see what kind of situation he was in'. His compliance ensured that his subjects would do likewise. Although other Scandinavian sources relate that Sigurd tried hard to avoid baptism, all are agreed that he eventually succumbed. The Orcadians had had broad experience of Christian neighbours since the settlement, and Sigurd's mother, grandmother and his Scottish wife had all been raised in the Christian faith, but it does not necessarily follow that Sigurd or any of his predecessors had converted before Olaf insisted they do so. The Viking adoption of Christianity, at least in the first place, rarely had anything to do with piety and usually much to do with pecuniary advantage. This can certainly be said of Olaf Tryggvason's own conversion by the English king Æthelred the year before he arrived in Orkney. But before Olaf made Earl Sigurd a demand he could not refuse there had been no obvious advantage in abandoning pagan religious traditions in the Northern Isles. It is, then, quite conceivable that Christianity came to Orkney in precisely the way described in the sagas, although given the reports of Sigurd's death there is, as we shall see, some reason to doubt just how much he personally understood or cared about his conversion.

During the 980s, Sigurd had seen for himself the riches of Ireland, when he raided there on three separate occasions. By the early eleventh century, he was able to look west across the Irish Sea, assured of his position in Scotland. As his Viking mentality would not allow him to sit back and enjoy the trappings of power, the prospect of a permanent stake in Ireland's prosperity beckoned. The opportunity came when Sihtric Silkenbeard of Dublin raised a coalition against the mighty Munster leader Brian Boru. Although modern historians rightly see the encounter at Clontarf in 1014 as an after-event in the decline of Viking power in Ireland, contemporaries are likely to have viewed things differently. When Sihtric called on Sigurd to join forces, perhaps even promising him the kingship of Ireland, he eagerly accepted and brought with him leaders from across the Viking settlements, including the great fleet of Brodir of Man. That, on the day, Sihtric himself failed to turn up may have given Sigurd second thoughts, but by then it was too late.

It is at this point that Sigurd's Christian credentials can be questioned. *The Saga of the Orkney Earls* weaves into Sigurd's life the story of a magic banner, embroidered with the raven insignia of the devotees of Odin. This particular banner brought victory to those who followed it but death to the one who carried it. This is how Sigurd the Stout died at Clontarf, furled in the raven banner of Odin that no one else would carry, his dreams of an Orcadian empire in Ireland in ruins. Brodir, Sigurd's accomplice from Man and the slayer of Brian Boru as he prayed in his tent, was unlucky enough to be taken alive. His fate, say the sagas, was to be tortured to death by Viking supporters of Brian by having his intestines ripped out and nailed to a tree. The Viking catastrophe at Clontarf, for it was nothing less, is described in *Njal's Saga* in supernatural terms. It is said that on the morning of the battle – in Caithness, the Faroes, the Orkneys, Iceland and the Hebrides – showers of blood fell in churches, the ghost of Sigurd went riding and visions were seen of ghastly Valkyries weaving the entrails of those that fell.[9] Such apocalyptic language is understandable, given that a generation of Viking leaders in Scotland had succumbed through greed and miscalculation. Clontarf was remembered in Scandinavia as a terrestrial Ragnarök.

Sigurd's dominions beyond the earldom in Orkney fell to pieces after his death but his career had shown what could be achieved. For the moment, however, it was hard to see how it could be matched, for Sigurd's three sons from his first marriage, Sumarlidi, Brusi and Einar Wrymouth, divided the earldom between them. A fourth son, Thorfinn, the sole male progeny from Sigurd's Scottish marriage, was excluded on the grounds that he was merely five years old and was placed under the protection of his grandfather, almost certainly King Malcolm II of Scotland. Of Sigurd's four sons, it was Thorfinn whom fortune favoured. As soon as Thorfinn came of age his grandfather granted him the earldoms of Caithness and Sutherland, and on the death of his brother Sumarlidi he laid personal claim to a third of the Orkney earldom, which he gained despite the objection of the overbearing Einar. The bad feeling between Thorfinn and Einar erupted into violence (*c.* 1020) when Thorkell Amunderson, Thorfinn's one-time foster-father in Caithness, slew Einar in the certain knowledge that deadly treachery was afoot. Einar's third of the earldom now went begging.

Initially, Thorfinn demanded a full half share of the Orkney earldom, but the resistance of Brusi, who was concerned about the future inheritance of his son Røgnvald, and the subsequent self-interested arbitration of King Olaf Haraldsson of Norway (1016–28), obliged Thorfinn to withdraw his claim. Olaf, himself, assumed control of one third of the earldom, which he then handed to Brusi to oversee as his regent, with the boy Røgnvald being retained by the king in Norway as surety. Some years later, when it became clear that Brusi had insufficient resources to maintain the defence of the isles, he and Thorfinn came to an understanding that lay outside the terms dictated by the king, whereby Thorfinn agreed to take sole responsibility for the island's security in return for the disputed third of the earldom. Thorfinn and Brusi held to the terms of their partnership until Brusi's death (*c.* 1030–35), whereupon, in the absence of Røgnvald Brusason, Thorfinn assumed sole control. The question of the original three parts of the earldom emerged as the source of major tension in later years.

Thorfinn the Mighty's career (*c.* 1020–65) had three clear stages. The first, spanning his partnership with Brusi and the return of Røgnvald Brusason, was largely a matter of maintaining his hold on his Scottish territories and, as a consequence of this struggle, expanding them. The second stage encompassed the years in which Thorfinn took Orcadian authority to unprecedented heights. In the final stage, until his death, Thorfinn concentrated on establishing the Christian and administrative infrastructure of his realm. Throughout, Thorfinn was wise enough to acknowledge the sovereignty of the Norwegian kings over the isles; that is to say, Olaf Haraldsson and, after Olaf's death in 1030, his successor Magnus the Good (r. 1035–47), though neither of these relationships was easy.

Thorfinn's talents as a warrior chieftain were first called upon when he was still in his mid teens, for although his grandfather exercised great power he was not without rival. In the latter years of Malcolm's life, and more so after his death in 1034, disputes arose concerning the legitimacy of his dynasty. Among the chief dissenters were the men of Moray, led by their chieftain MacBeth,[10] who believed he had legitimate claim to Caithness. When MacBeth demanded tribute from Thorfinn, not unnaturally Thorfinn refused to pay. The open confrontation that resulted was to occupy Thorfinn throughout most of the 1030s. At the outset of hostilities, Thorfinn is said to have chased MacBeth's forces out of the region and, in the pursuit that followed, to have conquered Sutherland and Ross. MacBeth retaliated by sending eleven ships north to Caithness and ordering his infantry back into the region from the south, with the intention of catching Thorfinn in a trap. Thorfinn, realizing he was outnumbered, deemed it wise to sail his five longships across the Pentland Firth to Orkney. MacBeth gave pursuit and Thorfinn, typically unwilling to back away from a fight, turned to engage him in the waters off Deerness. The hard-pressed encounter that followed eventually went Thorfinn's way and MacBeth was forced to retreat to Moray and regroup. MacBeth's forces from the south, led by MacBeth's nephew Muddan, had meanwhile penetrated as far north as Thurso, to which Thorfinn dispatched his old protector Thorkell Amunderson to dislodge the invaders. Thorkell moved stealthily through the country and coming upon Muddan's quarters by night set them alight. When Muddan leapt to safety from a high balcony, Thorkell was on hand to decapitate him as he fell.

MacBeth, now all the more determined to subdue the earl, set about raising a great army of Scots and Irish. The opposing forces met at Tarbat Ness on the south side of the Moray Firth. The Scots had the numerical advantage, but Thorfinn took the initiative and 'marched before his ranks, a golden helmet on his head, a sword at his waist, wielding a great spear in both hands'.[11] Such was the courage and leadership shown by Thorfinn that MacBeth's armies crumbled and abandoned the field. Thorfinn now went on the rampage and it is said that he conquered as far south as Fife. When he divided his army and sent Thorkell back north to secure his northern territories, certain of the Scots seized the chance to rebel. Thorfinn quickly crushed the rebellion and as punishment for what he perceived to be Scottish treachery the earl's men went from village to village, burning everywhere so that not a single cottage was left standing. They killed all the adult men they could find, and the women and old people ran off into the brakes and forests.[12]

There is little doubt that Thorfinn's territorial power greatly increased in eastern Scotland during the 1030s, but whether it happened in precisely the manner described above, and whether in the process Thorfinn gained nine Scottish earldoms, as the saga claims, is difficult to substantiate. Evidently, the confrontation with MacBeth ultimately went Thorfinn's way, but the fact that it was MacBeth, who in 1040 murderously usurped Malcolm's successor Duncan I, and who was thereafter forced to spend much of his seventeen-year rule dealing with trouble in the south of his realm, suggests that Thorfinn's expansion was made possible by a power vacuum in the north. If saga chronology can be trusted, Thorfinn was already turning his attention to the west before the end of the decade, an indication that matters nearer home were largely settled. It should also be borne in mind that MacBeth's war against Thorfinn was not wholly representative of Scottish attitudes to the earl, as patronage from opponents of MacBeth was a feature of Thorfinn's success throughout his career. Some territories may simply have been placed in his keeping while the Scots focused on other rivalries.

In 1037–38, Røgnvald Brusason returned to Orkney from exile in Russia to claim his patrimony. He brought with him the support of Magnus the Good, Norway's new king, for Røgnvald had become Magnus's foster-brother and his favourite. As it turned out, Thorfinn unhesitatingly relinquished both Brusi's and King Olaf's thirds of the earldom, the only condition being that Røgnvald should show him loyalty and support him in his campaigns westward. Røgnvald, pleased that Thorfinn had responded so swiftly and positively, readily agreed. The two earls now set about restoring the Hebrides, Man and the western littoral to Orcadian rule. Perhaps for the first time, Shetland was also included as part of the earldom. Less probably, the earls are said to have added territory in Ireland to their lands, although there is some truth behind the account of Thorfinn's raids in England in 1042, seemingly in revenge for the killing of one of his raiding parties by English locals keen to defend their property. Once again it was political good fortune that enabled this remarkable expansion of Orcadian power. Sihtric Silkenbeard of Dublin had presided over the Hebrides but had abdicated in 1036. His supporter, King Cnut, had died the previous year and the succession, in both England and Scandinavia, was plunged into chaos. For both these reasons the Western Isles were prey to whoever could command them.

At some point in the late 1030s, just when the earls' power was at its height, events came about that broke their partnership for good. It was not in the first place the politics of the Northern Isles that intruded but those of Norway. During the time of Olaf Haraldsson, Thorfinn had married Ingibjorg, the daughter of one of Olaf's most powerful supporters, Earl Finn Arnason. Most probably the marriage was encouraged, if not insisted upon, by Olaf. But Finn had a brother, Kalf, whose loyalties were not owed to Olaf. According to Snorri Sturluson's account of the battle of Stiklestad in Norway in 1030, Kalf was among those who had delivered Olaf Haraldsson his death blows. Both Magnus the Good and Røgnvald Brusason had been present on Olaf's side.[13] Despite a brief reconciliation between Magnus and Kalf, Kalf soon managed to cause grievous offence. Magnus wanted Kalf dead, so Kalf did the sensible thing and sought out his powerful nephew-in-law, Thorfinn, in Orkney. He brought with him a sizeable retinue. Røgnvald was displeased but Thorfinn was bound by family loyalties. Time passed but Kalf and company showed no sign of leaving, and Thorfinn began to worry about the drain on his resources. Perhaps tactlessly he raised the subject of the disputed third of the earldom with Røgnvald, in the hope of meeting his household costs from the revenue it would provide. Røgnvald said that the third in question was King Magnus's patrimony and that he, Røgnvald, had neither the authority nor the inclination to surrender it to Thorfinn. Thorfinn then set about raising an army.

Realizing that Thorfinn meant business, Røgnvald sailed to Norway and there received support from King Magnus. With his fleet fully equipped for war, Røgnvald's return journey took him via Shetland, where he further increased his force. The fleets of Røgnvald and Thorfinn met in the Pentland Firth and, after a long and arduous struggle, it was Thorfinn who gained the upper hand. Again Røgnvald went to Norway, but this time he returned with just one ship. Cunning rather than force would be his new tactic. Thorfinn was in Orkney feasting with a small group of retainers when Røgnvald arrived outside his hall. Røgnvald put his plan into action, first by blocking the exits and then by setting the building alight. Few men survived but among them was Thorfinn, who smashed his way through a wall and fled the house unseen, carrying his wife in his arms. Røgnvald assumed he was dead. From Caithness, Thorfinn plotted his revenge and at Christmas time caught up with Røgnvald and his men while they were quaffing their seasonal ale on Papa Stronsay. Again a fire was set and again the chief target of the flames managed to make his escape. But not for long. Røgnvald's men were rounded up one by one and killed, among them was Røgnvald himself, his whereabouts betrayed by the yapping of his lapdog.

The slaying of Røgnvald did not endear Thorfinn to King Magnus, and in due course Thorfinn might well have expected reprisal from Norway, but luck was yet again on his side. In the years immediately following Røgnvald's death, Magnus was preoccupied by turbulent relations with Denmark, and in 1047 he died. His successor, Harald Hardrada, had no grudge against either Thorfinn or Kalf Arnason and little immediate interest in the affairs of Orkney. Kalf returned to Norway and Thorfinn remained unchallenged as sole earl of Orkney for the remainder of his life. The vast expansion Thorfinn had presided over did not survive him and Irish Vikings soon reasserted their influence in the Western Isles and Man, while Malcolm III, having disposed of MacBeth in 1057, resumed control of Thorfinn's mainland Scottish territories and is said to have married Thorfinn's widow, although it may well have been Thorfinn's daughter.

Like all great Viking leaders, Thorfinn's military success was based on the loyalty he attracted from his guarantee of booty and on the ruthlessness he showed to his enemies. Yet his political skills indicate that he had a certain subtlety of mind. His Scottish links and his acknowledgement of Norwegian authority were potentially in conflict, so Thorfinn was obliged to steer a careful course in order to maintain a measure of independence. This awareness of the ways of the world was put to good use in his latter years when he set about ordering the affairs of Orkney along the lines of the most progressive of European kingdoms.

In 1050, Thorfinn turned his back on conquest, piracy and political intrigue and set out on a great European tour, during which he paid a visit to King Harald Hardrada in Norway and journeyed to Rome, where the pope absolved him of his sins. On his return, he established his seat of government on Birsay off the west coast of Mainland in the Orkneys and set about restructuring the law and putting in place an ecclesiastical framework. Thorfinn is credited with setting up the bishopric on Birsay under the jurisdiction of the see of Hamburg-Bremen, and with building Christ Kirk, which, although no trace of it remains, was probably on Birsay. Thorfinn died in 1065, having spent the last fifteen years of his life as an enlightened Christian reformer. He was regarded as being among the greatest of Scandinavian rulers, his enduring legacy coming from his work as a reformer rather than from his achievements as a Viking warlord.

The Christian infrastructure of Orkney and its incorporation into the wider European church led to a line of Christian rulers among Thorfinn's successors. Notable among these was Magnus Erlendsson, to whose memory a church was built on Egilsay marking the spot where his brother had murdered him in 1117. In 1136 the foundations of St Magnus's cathedral were laid at Kirkwall. So splendid and so revered was this cathedral that Thorfinn's original religious centre on Birsay was abandoned in its favour. Orkney never again achieved the standing that it had gained under Thorfinn. In 1066, Thorfinn's sons, Paul and Erlend, were obliged to accompany Harald Hardrada on his ill-fated attempt to conquer England. Though they did not share Harald's fate at Stamford Bridge, the adventure was costly and humiliating. Their inability to cooperate during the remainder of their joint rule did nothing to help recover the earldom's fortunes.

The Scottish isles now fell under more localized leadership from the north and the west but remained subject to Norway until well into the middle ages. Godred Crovan founded his kingdom at Man in 1079, having forcefully displaced Godred Sihtricsson, and his authority was later extended to include the Hebrides and, for a time, Dublin. The *Manx Chronicle* (*Chronicon Manniae et insularum*), which details the island's history from 1066, exalts Godred as one of the great Viking leaders of the latter half of the eleventh century. After Godred's death in 1095, civil war broke out. In 1098, Magnus Barelegs, king of Norway, invaded Man, and the Manx kingdom was duly returned to Norwegian rule. The Hebrides finally succumbed to Scottish rule in 1263 after over a hundred years of strife and three years later the Isle of Man was ceded to Scotland. Orkney, whose authority was limited to its own affairs and the strict bidding of Norway from the mid eleventh century, remained a Norwegian province until 1397 and did not become part of the Scottish realm until the middle of the fifteenth century.

The archaeology of the Scottish isles reveals unique attributes among Viking Age settlements. Orkney and Shetland were entirely absorbed into Scandinavian culture, as is apparent from their almost exclusively Norse place-names and the persistence of an Orcadian Norse dialect known as Norn until the mid eighteenth century. Excavations of the coastal settlements have revealed an abundance of domestic paraphernalia and precious artefacts, including 18 lbs (approx. 8 kilos) of valuables in a mid tenth-century hoard at Skaill to the west of Orkney's Mainland, indicating something of the island's prosperity. From tombs and burial sites it is possible to trace the shifts in religious practices among Viking colonists. The particular nature of the Viking conversion to Christianity is especially conspicuous on the Isle of Man, where there are approximately fifty stone crosses in Celtic and English Christian styles but nonetheless illustrated with Scandinavian pagan motifs, runic memorial inscriptions and old northern myths and legends, such as the devouring of Odin at Ragnarök and the heroics of Sigurd the Dragon Slayer. The remoteness of these Viking colonies and their relative insignificance in European affairs after their Viking Age heyday has meant that they have preserved much in terms of Scandinavian tradition, in both their material remains and their culture. But the truly remarkable story of the Viking settlement of the Scottish isles is the extent to which a relatively localized dynasty of Viking warlords could play a significant role in forming the historical identity of large and keenly contested territories across the Celtic west.

7

# Western Europe

'If a Frank is your friend he is certainly not your neighbour.'[1] So went the eighth-century proverb among those bordering Frankish territories or unwillingly drawn into Charlemagne's empire. By the middle of the ninth century, the same was probably being said of the Vikings. When Charlemagne finally overran Saxony in 804, and so brought his northern border to the southern edge of Denmark, neighbourliness toward anyone in the region was never likely to be the outcome. Yet it was not until thirty years after the death of Charlemagne in 814 that the full force of the heathen 'Northmen' was felt in Frankia. The bitter dynastic rivalry among Charlemagne's grandsons effectively opened the door for the Vikings, meaning that the once great Carolingian Empire would fragment and that, by the mid tenth century, a large swathe of West Frankia would lie under Viking rule in the area that became known as Normandy. The long prelude to this was not, however, uneventful.

From as early as 799, when Vikings plundered the monastery of St-Philibert on the island of Noirmoutier in the Loire estuary, Charlemagne had been aware of the northern threat. Events in Britain during the same period only served to reinforce the sense of danger. Yet it was not isolated Viking warbands that most concerned the emperor but the political threat posed by the Danish king Godfred. Charlemagne's conquest of Saxony and his deportation of the indigenous Saxons, whose land he ceded to his allies, the Slavic Abodrites, prompted Godfred to offer the Franks a show of strength. According to the *Royal Frankish Annals*, Godfred 'came with his fleet and the entire cavalry of his kingdom to Schleswig on the border of his kingdom and Saxony'.[2] Godfred probably hoped that the emperor would in some way acknowledge Danish sovereignty, but, rather than parleying with Charlemagne in person, Godfred sent an envoy to express his concerns. In response, Charlemagne delivered a message on the subject of returning fugitives. This oblique exchange was, nevertheless, enough to prompt both rulers to set about reinforcing their borders: Godfred ordered an overhaul of the Danevirke fortification spanning Jutland while Charlemagne established a garrison on the Elbe and, perhaps, began the construction of the chain of eight ring forts across the Low Countries.

Godfred now cultivated the enemies of the Abodrites and in 808 launched an attack, forcing the Abodrites to pay tribute and devastating their trading centre at Reric, whose merchants he transferred to his own trading centre at Hedeby. Charlemagne responded by laying waste to the lands of any tribe who had shown favour to the Danes. The following year there was widespread disturbance across the region and an attempt by Franks and Danes to settle matters diplomatically failed. Matters came to a head in 810 when Godfred launched an attack involving some two hundred ships against Charlemagne's undefended Frisian coastline on the north-western tip of the empire. Godfred exacted 100 lbs of silver from the residents, then boasted that he would march on Charlemagne at Aachen. Charlemagne only aborted plans for a massive retaliation when news arrived of Godfred's murder and, not long afterwards, an urgent appeal for peace from Godfred's successor, Hemming.

Hemming died within two years of assuming power and thereafter Denmark fell into political chaos. Frankish policy was simply to encourage the turmoil. When Charlemagne died in 814, at the age of seventy-one, his only surviving son, Louis the Pious, championed the exiled Danish pretender Harald Klak against Godfred's sons. By the end of the decade, Harald had succeeded in becoming joint ruler of Denmark. But Danish noblemen, dispossessed or alienated during the years of strife, were now looking to retrieve their fortunes. Piracy directed at Frankia was one evident recourse. Although Frankish land and coastal defences proved adequate in the north, several hundred miles of coastline to the south beckoned any ambitious Dane who could muster a fleet. Illustrating the relative security of the north compared to the vulnerability of the south, the first recorded major attack in 820 of thirteen ships entered the mouth of the Seine and was beaten off by defenders with the loss of only a few cattle and the destruction of some huts. Undeterred, the Viking fleet headed south to the coast of Aquitaine where they attacked the village of Bouin 'and then returned home with immense booty'.[3]

The attempts of Louis the Pious to control Denmark from the outside ultimately failed and the emperor's, now apparently Christianized, champion Harald Klak was relieved of his share of the Danish throne in 827, thereafter turning freebooter and becoming one of the many Viking scourges of north-western Frankia during the 830s. The Danish throne now fell to Horik, a staunch pagan far less well disposed toward Frankish authority. In many respects, Louis the Pious should have been able to deal with both the Danish king and the nuisance of Viking raiders. He had inherited strong defences, the country was prospering and the empire was intact. But Louis had domestic problems that went from bad to worse.

Louis had three sons, Lothar, Pippin and Louis the German. In 817, Louis raised up Lothar as his co-emperor and allocated sub-kingdoms to his two other sons. Then, in 819, Louis' wife died and four months later he married Judith of Bavaria. The match with Judith clearly helped consolidate Louis' hold over the German territories but Lothar, Pippin and Louis the German were seriously worried that Judith's influence might affect their inheritance. Their worries were not misplaced, for in 823 Judith bore Louis a son, Charles, later to become known as Charles the Bald. When the boy reached the age of six Louis granted him Alemannia, the German territories, no doubt encouraged by Judith. Lothar had no trouble in persuading his two brothers to join him in open rebellion. Louis was forced from power in 829 and spent the following year in violent confrontation with his sons before he could reclaim his position.

The restored Louis had still not fully grasped the depth of feeling among his three elder sons. When, in 832, Louis reallocated Aquitaine away from Pippin in favour of Charles, civil war again ensued. This time it took two years before Louis could reassert himself. Family unity was, by now, damaged beyond repair and for the remainder of Louis' rule, until his death in 840, his sons were in almost permanent revolt. Thereafter, hardened by resentment and uncompromising ambition, they turned on each other. Nor had the death of Pippin in 838 simplified matters, for his son, Pippin II, inherited his father's claim to Aquitaine. By 843, a stalemate had been reached and Lothar, Louis the German and Charles the Bald met at Verdun and divided the empire between them: Louis became king of the East Franks from Saxony to Bavaria; Charles, king of the West Franks, a territory much resembling modern-day France but excluding Brittany; and Lothar, king of the Middle Kingdom, which stretched from Frisia to northern Italy. Rather than settle the dispute, the partitioning of the empire only served to formalize fraternal rivalry, and the three-cornered war that followed was confused even further by the intervention of Pippin II, who had been effectively disinherited at Verdun.

Meanwhile, Viking warbands poured into Frankia in ever-greater numbers. Not only were they inadequately opposed but also no side in the civil wars was above employing them in their own cause, either as militia against aristocratic rivals or as bulwarks against other Viking invaders. The monk Ermentarius, a refugee from the despoiled monastery at Noirmoutier, pinpointed the folly of it all:

> Their [the brothers'] strife gave encouragement to the foreigners. Justice was abandoned, and evil advanced. No guards were mounted on the beaches. Wars against foreign enemies ceased, and internal wars raged on. The number of ships grew larger, and the Northmen were beyond counting.[4]

For the Vikings, it was an ideal opportunity.

The 830s had seen a steady escalation of Viking activity in direct response to Frankish disarray. One particular difficulty that surfaced had been unwittingly introduced in the previous decade. In 826, Harald Klak, Louis the Pious' deposed Danish puppet king, had been granted Rustringen on the border between Frisia and Saxony as a refuge. With Louis' sponsorship worthless by 834, Harald was open to offers and so it came about that Lothar encouraged Harald to add to Louis' problems by attacking Frisia. Harald was only too willing to do so but exceeded his brief by sacking the emporium and royal mint at Dorestad where he 'destroyed everything … slaughtered some people, took others away captive, and burned the surrounding region'.[5] Such overstepping of the mark led to Harald being killed by Frankish agents in 852 for fear of possible treachery. In the meantime, Dorestad's riches were plundered annually until 838, and by 840 chroniclers were describing it as a Viking fief. Frisia, forever vulnerable to Viking designs, soon fell entirely into their hands, whilst in the Low Countries the trading centres of Walcheren and Antwerp bore the brunt of Viking greed, while further south on the Loire, the monks of Noirmoutier were forced to abandon their monastery, a desperate measure that they had been contemplating since 819.

In Denmark, King Horik surveyed the growing crisis in Frankia and saw the opportunity to improve his own standing. He began by currying Louis' favour by asserting that he had nothing to do with the attacks on Frisia and claiming that he had personally seen to the execution of the perpetrators. Whoever it was that Horik deemed a perpetrator it was not Harald Klak. More than likely, this was because of Harald Klak's growing power in the region, which would later be enhanced by Lothar's gift of the island of Walcheren and, as such, the control of the trade flowing down the rivers Rhine, Maas and Schelde. Horik's claimed interventions therefore stopped nothing. With the position deteriorating, he now offered to relieve Louis of the burden of Frisia by taking control himself, an offer so transparent in its insincerity that all it did was infuriate the emperor. Horik bided his time.

Louis' death in 840 further emboldened the Vikings. While, by this time, it was not only Danes but also Norwegians and Swedes who were keen to exploit the situation, Horik can be reckoned among the most active rulers in this next stage of Viking activity. Vikings sailed unimpeded up the Seine in 841, exacting tribute as they went and laying waste to Rouen and the surrounding district and leaving the populace 'thoroughly terrified'.[6] In the following year, the trading centre at Quentovic, which housed the bulk of goods heading to and from England, was treated in the same way. Monasteries and local residents soon learned the habit of paying in advance in order to be spared the similar vandalism, but, as ever, this was only a very short-term solution.

In the vain hope of achieving some form of regional supremacy, Viking armies were commonly enlisted by rival Frankish factions, but, once having taken that step, the Franks were unable to control how the Vikings went about their mercenary business. One outcome of this strategy was at Nantes in 843 when Count Lambert, who had repudiated the overlordship of Charles the Bald, guided Norwegian Vikings up river to the town he felt was his by right. It was 24 June, St John's Day, and Nantes was full of celebrations. Whether or not the attack was timed to do maximum damage and inflict maximum casualties is debatable, but there was little left for the rebellious count to recover once the Vikings had finished. In a day of bloodlust they slew everyone they met: the bishop, the clergy, men, women and children. Anything of value they carried off to their new base at Noirmoutier. There they 'brought their households over from the mainland and decided to winter there in something like permanent settlement'.[7] Count Lambert must have thought his 'victory' hollow.

The attack on Nantes was, in miniature, representative of what was happening to the whole of Frankia. 'It was a crying shame', said the chronicler at St-Bertin, for while many ordinary folk were reduced to a diet of earth mixed with flour, 'there was plenty of fodder for the horses of those brigands'.[8] Driven from their homelands and starving, peasants banded together in militias and sought to come to terms with the Vikings on their own account, sometimes with a degree of success. The response of the Frankish nobility to the efforts of the peasants to secure their own livelihoods was to turn violently on them. The common folk were thus caught between two evils, for those who did not strike deals with Vikings were taxed to the point of penury by local rulers anxious to buy off Viking raiders or ransom their own property.

The Loire Vikings were evidently sufficiently confident of their position in Frankia to contemplate exploring the opportunities further south. In 844, having brought destruction on the Garonne, a fleet of around one hundred longships rounded Cape Finisterre and put ashore in Christian Galicia on the north-west corner of the Iberian peninsula. They encountered forceful resistance from the locals and were soon persuaded to leave. The fleet pressed on to the Umayyad emirate of Cordoba and to Lisbon, which they easily entered and ransacked. Encouraged, they added Cadiz and Medina Sidonia to their tally and then decided on the audacious plan of seizing Seville. This they did, killing most of the male population and taking captive women and children, whom they imprisoned at their base on the island of Qubtil (now Isla Menor). Initially, the Moors were stunned by the unprovoked and unprecedented violence of these northern brigands, but they soon rallied their forces. The Arab historian Ibn Kutia recorded the response of his countrymen:

> The arrival of these barbarians struck terror into the heart of the inhabitants. All fled and sought a refuge, partly in the mountains of the neighbourhood, partly in Carmona. In all the west there was none who dared to meet them in battle. Therefore the inhabitants of Cordoba and the nearest districts were called to arms. Our leaders with their troops took up a position at Carmona, but dared not attack until the arrival of the soldiers from the border. The border chieftains demanded news of the movements of the enemy, then asked, if there were not, near Seville, a place where they could lie in ambush without being seen. The commander told them of the village of Quintos-Maafir, south east of Seville. They moved there in the middle of the night, and sat in ambush. One of their men, with a bundle of faggots, was set to keep watch from the tower of the village church. At sunrise, the guard made known that a host of 16,000 *Madjus* was marching on Moron. The Moslems let them pass, cut them off from Seville, and cut them down. Then our leaders advanced, entered Seville, and found its commander besieged in the castle.
>
> When the *Madjus* saw the Moslem army coming, and heard of the disaster that the detachment marching to Moron had met with, they suddenly embarked. When they were sailing up the river towards a castle, they met their countrymen and when all these had also embarked, they all together began to sail down the river, while the inhabitants of the country poured on them curses and threw stones at them. When they had arrived a mile below Seville, the *Madjus* shouted to the people, 'Leave us in peace if you wish to buy prisoners of us'. People then ceased to throw stones at them, and they allowed everybody to ransom prisoners.[9]

Ibn Kutia's account was doubtless partial, and somewhat exaggerated in the numbers of Vikings involved, but the general picture of the humiliation of the Vikings is accurate enough, if not understated. Quite clearly the Moorish emir, Abd ar-Rahman II, was no Charles the Bald and the Vikings not only suffered on land but also at sea. Inflammable naphtha shot destroyed their ships, thirty or so being sunk in a single encounter at Talayata. And this was not the only way the Moors defended themselves. In Seville, gallows were soon in use and palm trees groaned under the weight of hanged Vikings. Those the Emir chose not to hang he beheaded, and he was said to have sent two hundred Viking heads to his cousins in Tangier. Passage off the island of Qubtil very soon became impossible and the Vikings were forced to come to terms. On this exceptional occasion, the captives of the Vikings were returned for nothing more than food and clothing. As many as 1400 Vikings lost their lives, either in battle or in captivity, and those who made it back to the Loire reported their ordeal as a caution to others.

One unlikely outcome of this disastrous sortie against the Spanish Moors appears to have been the establishment of trade between the Vikings in the north and the Moors of Spain. In 845, just a year after the siege of Seville, Abd ar-Rahman II sent his ambassador Al Ghazal to the 'king of the *Madjus*', who may either have been King Horik in Denmark or Turgeis in Dublin. Furs and slaves were probably the merchandise that the emperor wished to acquire. Having dealt Viking warlords such a crushing blow, he was able to negotiate from a position of some strength. Although there are records of isolated and unsuccessful attacks on Moorish Spain during the 850s, it would be thirteen years before a large Viking fleet again tried to exploit the Moors through piracy.

While the Loire Vikings were licking their wounds and settling back into the less arduous business of terrorizing the district around Noirmoutier, Viking aggression far to the north was taking a more sinister turn. Two major attacks occurred in 845 with unexpected consequences. King Horik was almost certainly behind many of the raids along the coastline and up the rivers during the early 840s but, with the northern Frankish borders now completely undefended, he clearly felt able to express his belligerence more openly. According to an exaggerated account in the *Annals of St-Bertin*, early in 845 Horik sent six hundred ships up the Elbe to confront Louis the German but was turned back by a great army of Saxons. Horik then descended on the ecclesiastical centre at Hamburg, where he burned down the cathedral founded by the missionary Anskar, who was himself forced to flee with such valuables and relics as could be carried.

The second attack, this time of a hundred and twenty ships on Paris, is unlikely to have involved Horik in person but it certainly carried his approval and was probably done in his service. The leader was a Viking simply known in the sources as Ragnar. The attack on Paris proceeded despite the deployment of Franks on both banks of the Seine. Ragnar's army overran one Frankish contingent, took 111 prisoners, and hanged them in full view of the contingent on the opposite bank. Charles's horrified men deserted in droves and he was obliged to retreat to St-Denis and pay 7000 lbs of gold and silver, but not in time to stop the Vikings looting the abbey of St-Germain. Ragnar later reported to Horik that Frankish land was exceptionally rich and fertile and that the people were exceptionally cowardly. Yet the Vikings carried off more from St-Germain than they supposed, as on their return to Denmark many 'were struck down by divine judgement with blindness or insanity, so severely that only very few escaped to tell the rest about the might of God'.[10] Among the casualties was Ragnar himself, who, having told Horik that in Frankia only the courage of an old man named Germain was to be feared, fell to the floor, swelled up, burst and died, or so it was reported by one of the monks from St-Germain. So disturbed was Horik that he duly sent envoys to King Louis for peace talks and promised to return all captives and booty from Hamburg and Paris. Horik, however, soon recovered his poise, as is clear from an apparently futile attempt by all three Frankish kings in 847 to persuade him to desist from further attacks under the threat of invasion.

During the following decade, the Viking presence in Western Frankia became ubiquitous. The internecine strife between the brothers not only allowed them many opportunities for lightning raids against defenceless and demoralized targets but also rewarded them with permanent settlement territories for services rendered, as, for example, when Charles the Bald sought their help against his brother Lothar. Frisia, the Seine basin and the Loire valley remained the chief theatres of action, but attacks extended as far south as Bordeaux. In 850, an effort between the three warring brothers to reach an accord allowed some concerted movement against the Vikings in the northern regions but, in the west, the Vikings were too numerous and too evasive to be confronted in any conventional way. Only where specific Viking warbands were entrenched was there any hope of relieving the country of immediate threat.

In 858 Paris was yet again a Viking target. At the abbey of St-Denis, Abbot Louis and his brother had to be ransomed for the astonishing sum of 686 lbs of gold and 3250 lbs of silver, and 'in order to pay this, many church treasuries in Charles's realm were drained dry, at the king's command'.[11] Behind these outrages was Bjorn Ironside, a son of the notorious Ragnar Hairy Breeches. With typical Viking cynicism, Bjorn had visited Charles earlier in the year and sworn fealty 'after his own fashion'.[12] Charles now became painfully aware of exactly what Bjorn's 'fashion' was and laid siege to his army at their camp at Oissel. Assisting Charles in the spirit of the accord of 850 were both Lothar, son of Charles's late brother Lothar, and his rival for Aquitaine, Pippin. It would have been a major victory had it been successful, but distrust once again entered the scene when Louis the German arrived in the Orléans district at the head of a great force, gathering allegiance in Charles's realm as he travelled. Charles promptly abandoned the siege, and turned to meet Louis. Lothar shuttled between his uncles and then went home. Within a few months, fraternal conflict had, yet again, taken precedence over the threat from Viking invaders.

Charles, however, did not abandon the effort of purging the Oissel encampment and engaged a Viking leader named Weland to do it for him in return for 5000 lbs of silver. Weland made a good show of the siege and certainly reduced the occupants to a miserable condition but, rather than pursue his advantage, as Charles would surely have wanted, Weland showed his true Viking colours and suggested to Bjorn that those inside the Oissel encampment might be allowed to depart unharmed on payment of 6000 lbs of silver. Bjorn, rich from his Parisian adventure, did not cavil and promptly paid up. The upshot was two wealthy Viking warbands dispersed around the Seine basin. What was more, such protection as Weland might have offered in the future was obviated when he was killed three years later in duel after attempting to dupe two of his own countrymen. In the face of the disunity and failures of their opponents, the Vikings prospered and multiplied. Ermentarius described the worsening situation:

> Everywhere there were massacres of Christians, raids, devastations, and burnings. Whatever the Northmen attacked, they captured without resistance: Bordeaux, Périgueux, Saintes, Limoges, Angoulême and Toulouse; then Angers, Tours and Orléans were destroyed.
>
>      Then, a few years later, an almost immeasurable fleet sailed up the Seine River. The evil done in those regions was no less than that perpetrated elsewhere. The Northmen attacked the city of Rouen and devastated and burned it. They then captured Paris, Beauvais and Meaux, and they also levelled the castle of Melun. Chartres was also taken. They struck into the cities of Evreux and Bayeux and other

neighbouring towns. Almost no place, and no monastery, remained unscathed …
and the kingdom of Christians succumbed.[13]

Added to this was the attack in 860 on the abbey of St-Bertin, where the raiders
set about torturing the monks for sheer entertainment, inflating one with water
and using another for spear practice.

Among the Viking leaders who continued to harass and oppress the peoples
of the Loire valley was the notorious Hastein. Hastein was, in many respects, a
quintessential Viking. His career, which spanned thirty-five years, was mostly
spent as leader of the Vikings operating out of their stronghold on the island of
Noirmoutier, but included adventures across the Viking world. It is instructive
to follow Hastein's exploits for they give an indication of the problems that
Frankish rulers, amongst others, faced. Hastein clearly had no interest in the
power structures of wherever he chose to target his formidable energies, except
where they were sufficient to prevent him from profiting. He proceeded by trial
and error. When things did not go according to plan, he simply changed direction and started again. Hastein, and those like him, which means all Vikings to
some degree, fought what is now known as an asymmetric war. For those who
opposed him, this meant no coherent enemy, no easily identifiable theatre of war,
no convention of conflict and little chance of negotiating any lasting settlement.
To have to deal with the likes of Hastein was like trying to catch the wind.

Hastein must have been familiar with the humiliation of his predecessors
in Spain some thirteen years earlier, but he was clearly not the type to be put
off by previous failures. In 858, Bjorn Ironside, having bought himself out of
the siege at Oissel, joined Hastein and set sail from Aquitaine with sixty-two
ships intent on profiting at the Moors' expense. Although they collected a large
booty of slaves, gold and silver, they also endured setbacks, first, as had been
the case previously, on the coast of Galicia, where they were driven back to sea,
then at the mouth of the Guadalquivir, where several of their ships, replete with
plunder, were seized. This, and the imminent arrival of Emir Mohammed's
army, was enough to deter them from attacking Seville, so they moved on to
the far south and satisfied themselves by burning down the grand mosque
at Algeciras before heading for the North African coast. Once there, they
rounded up captives, including a number of dark-skinned natives who would
fetch a good price as *blámenn*, or 'blue men', at the northern slave markets.
From Africa they headed for the Balearics and then Roussillon and Narbonne,
looting and burning as they went, and then on to the Camargue where they set

up comfortable winter quarters. According to the Arab historian Ibn Adhari, 'They made many prisoners, took much money and made themselves masters of a city where they settled'.[14]

In the spring, they ventured inland up the Rhône to Nîmes and Arles, which they plundered and torched. Their continued journey to Valence, almost a hundred miles inland, was enough to give the Franks time to gather together a sizeable resistance force. Bruised from the ensuing encounter, Hastein and Bjorn retreated and headed east for Italy. Pisa and Fiesole are said to have suffered their visits but it was at Luna that this murderous jaunt across the Mediterranean reached its grim climax.

According to Dudo of St-Quentin, writing some 150 years later, Hastein is said to have mistaken the gleaming white walls of Luna for Rome. He resolved that the city should be his. Realizing that a direct assault would be pointless, Hastein first sent emissaries to the inhabitants saying that his men were exiles whose chieftain was sick and were all in need of shelter and provisions. Then a second message was delivered, this time saying that their chieftain had died and was in need of a Christian burial. The lie was believed and, with Hastein concealed in a coffin, the Vikings entered the town as mourners. When the bishop and the duke stepped forward to preside over the interment, Hastein leapt fully armed from the coffin, slew the both of them and, in the mêlée that followed, the town was duly taken. Once the truth was revealed to him, that this was not Rome but Luna far to the north, Hastein's rage was such that he ordered the massacre of every male inhabitant. The 'Trojan Horse' motif that underpins this colourful tale and the supposed geographical ignorance of Hastein, in the first place, and the gullibility of the townsfolk, in the second, make the details of the story doubtful, but not Hastein's savagery and cunning.

Whether Hastein and Bjorn's fleet constituted the same band of marauders recorded as raiding Alexandria and Byzantium is unclear, but the return journey suggests that their luck was beginning to run out. The passage back through the Straits of Gibraltar was blocked by a Moorish fleet lying in wait and many Viking ships were lost in the naval battle that followed. Even more foundered in severe weather off the Bay of Biscay. They now deemed it wise to avoid further trouble with the Moors and they did not attempt to add to their spoils until they had reached Frankish territory, whereupon they marched inland from the coast of Navarre and seized its capital, Pamplona, which was then ransomed back to the governor for 30,000 dinari. Only a third of the fleet that had set out for Spain returned to the Loire in 862. Bjorn soon left for Scandinavia and was last heard of causing problems in Frisia. Hastein remained in the Loire as a chronic trial to the Franks.

Charles, meanwhile, realizing that paying the Vikings for peace or as mercenaries was wholly unproductive, set about fortifying his realm with some urgency. Town walls were reinforced, rivers defended with parapet bridges, and lieutenants appointed to oversee the manning of the new fortifications: Count Robert the Strong of Angers would defend the Loire and Aquitaine; and Count Adalhard would take care of the Seine basin. In 864, at the national assembly at Pîtres, Charles issued a series of royal edicts regulating any dealings his subjects might be tempted to have with Vikings. Collaboration of any sort was banned under pain of death. Although such measures could do nothing to stem the tide of Vikings or prevent them setting up camp at river mouths or attacking the coastline, the new fortifications were, at the very least, inconvenient, and an uncooperative populace limited the divide-and-conquer tactics that had so benefited raiders in the past. For some Vikings, it was enough to cause them to decamp for England, where the pickings were rich and the inhibitions fewer. For others, like Hastein, it simply meant a more direct approach to Frankish valuables. As a consequence of Charles's determination to bring order to his battered realm and Viking determination to push deeper and harder into it, the middle years of the 860s present a bewildering picture inside West Frankia.

Count Robert the Strong had partial success in 865 when his forces annihilated five hundred Vikings with little or no loss to his own forces, but not before Hastein's Vikings had allied themselves with rebellious Bretons and caused widespread devastation to Angoulême, Le Mans, Orléans and Poitiers. Robert's victory achieved little more than a hiatus in Viking attacks, for within just over a year they were back in the Loire with the same consequences. If Robert's temporary defence of the Loire can be considered a partial success, Adalhard's attempt to defend the Seine was a complete failure. Adalhard's main task was to guard the upper reaches of the Seine, in particular Paris. But the Vikings had other ideas and, in 865, they launched an attack. Detained by the assault of one Viking force, Adalhard could do nothing to prevent a second force from avoiding the river defences and riding straight for Paris and wreaking their customary havoc. Worse still, having sated themselves at Paris, the Vikings indulged themselves for a further twenty depraved days at St-Denis and then proceeded to Melun to repeat their destruction. Charles intervened, discharged Adalhard and then capitulated. Whether it was the 4000 lbs of silver and a veritable ocean of fine Frankish wine that the Vikings received, the completion of the river defences in 869, or the lure of England that caused the Vikings to quit the Seine for the next ten years is uncertain.

In the Loire, Hastein was now in alliance with the Breton leader, Duke Saloman, and it was this combination of Celt and Viking that brought about the death of Robert the Strong at Brissarthe in 866. The alliance quickly foundered and Hastein was almost certainly the instigator behind the attack on Saloman later the same year. Savage assaults on Bourges and Orléans followed, and the Bretons were sufficiently disturbed to come to terms with Hastein, offering five hundred cattle for peace during the wine harvest and seeking to accommodate him and his followers as settlers and neighbours. But Hastein did not sit around in peace for long and in 872 he sailed up the Loire and headed for Angers. The populace, aware of what the Viking menace meant, hurried into the surrounding countryside. Hastein entered the town unopposed but, instead of razing it, settled in as the new owner, so infuriating not only Charles the Bald but also his Breton neighbours. A lengthy siege followed which was finally concluded when Charles diverted the river on which Hastein's longships were berthed, leaving him literally high and dry. Hastein promised to leave the kingdom in return for safe passage and Charles, perhaps having exacted reparation, accepted Hastein's terms. Hastein promptly broke his promise and returned to his island lair. It was another ten years before Hastein was obliged to leave the Loire and almost another ten after that before he headed across the Channel to fight Alfred the Great.

Charles the Bald died in 877. For the last two years of his life he had been able to style himself emperor, without having gained control of the German territories. He had, nevertheless, been able to extend his realm north to the Rhine, forcing him, out of necessity, into an alliance with Viking chieftain Rurik, who controlled Dorestad and Frisia, an arrangement that led to complications for Charles's successors. Viking activity in Frankia abated to a certain extent during the 870s, the reasons for which were as much to do with the success of Vikings in England as they were with the success of Charles's fortifications. The lull was only temporary, for during the 880s many Vikings recrossed the Channel after Alfred the Great's triumph over the East Anglian Vikings at Edington in 879. For over five years, Flanders, Picardy and the Rhineland territories bore the brunt of the renewed infestation and, with Hastein also in the area, the cost was not inconsiderable. Monasteries at Tournai, those along the Schelde and vulnerable coastal centres were obvious targets, but soon inland monasteries such as those at Cologne and Trier also fell prey to the raiders.

After a period of further fragmentation that followed the death of Charles the Bald, the empire was, through twists and turns, almost reassembled under the rule of Charles the Fat, the son of Louis the German. He began his rule by making precisely the same mistake as his earlier namesake. His response to the situation in the north west was to start paring off land and plucking out property from his empire and giving it to Viking warlords in order to pacify them. He was just as willing to pay over vast sums of money, as, for example, the 2000 lbs of gold and silver that went to the Viking chieftains Sigfred and Gorm. Among the least effective of these bribes was the offer of Frisia to the aspiring Danish monarch Godfred, Rurik's kinsman and successor, in return for Godfred's baptism and his promise to police the border against Vikings looking for profit in Frankia. Godfred foolishly believed he saw further opportunities for advancement and set about plotting invasion. He demanded that his control of Frisia should be rewarded by the gift of certain inland wine-growing regions which, coincidentally, had strategic military value. At the same time, he began putting together an invasion force from Denmark. Charles was astute enough to see through Godfred's ruse and to have him killed. No further deals were done with Vikings concerning Frisia. Yet the deals already concluded suggested to the Vikings that Charles the Fat and largesse were synonymous. Like blackmailers they came back asking for more, but when Charles refused they turned ugly and decided that force of numbers would make their case more effectively.

Charles's ineptitude as a military leader became evident when a vast Viking fleet under the leadership of Sigfred entered the Seine in 885 with the intention of sailing past Paris and heading east into Burgundy. On this occasion, Charles the Bald's Pont de l'Arche fortification near Rouen did nothing to deter the fleet, which was estimated, rather improbably by Abbo of Fleury, to have comprised seven hundred longships carrying 30,000 men. On reaching the Île de la Cité, much to the Vikings' astonishment, the two leaders of the two hundred Franks garrisoned on the isle refused them passage. These were Joscelin, the abbot of St-Germain, and Count Odo, son of the late Robert the Strong, who carried with them the expectations of generations and were not about to let themselves down.

The siege that followed lasted almost a year. The Vikings hurled every available force at the garrison: they attempted to destroy the stone and timber bridges that spanned north and south respectively; they used incendiary boats and siege engines; and they sought access by filling the moats with the dead bodies of men and beasts. Nothing availed. Then, in February 886, the swollen waters of the Seine brought down the weakened timber bridge and many Vikings sailed through and went on to harry the region between the Seine and Loire. But the siege still continued. Finally, Odo managed to carry a message to Charles the Fat, who had been away in Italy, and in the early summer Charles arrived and Sigfred was content to be bought off with a modest 60 lbs of silver. Many Vikings considered the sum derisory and refused to budge. Charles certainly had the opportunity to break the siege by force of arms, as was expected of him, but instead he reverted to his preferred method of dealing with Vikings and allowed them free passage to plunder among the rebellious Burgundians, whom he felt in need of some Viking medicine. More than this, Charles offered to have ready a payment of 700 lbs of silver when they returned after the winter. Odo's and Joscelin's defence, which had cost Joscelin his life in the disease-ridden garrison, had been for nothing. Ironically, Charles's treachery against his own subjects in Burgundy served little purpose, for the Vikings largely ignored the east and set about ravaging to the north. Charles nevertheless paid up as agreed.

Charles the Fat's cynicism and cowardice not only brought about his deposition, it also delivered a fatal blow to any chance there might have been for holding the empire together. Separate monarchies reasserted themselves, never again to be conjoined. Among the northern West Franks, in the region known as Neustria, Count Odo, hero of Paris, was raised to the throne as the only aristocrat with both the means and the courage to rid the land of the Vikings. To the south in Aquitaine, Charles the Simple, Charles the Bald's grandson, set himself up as Odo's rival. Odo's success in Neustria was at first impressive. In 888, he confronted the forces of Hastein at Montfaucon and overcame them, but he still could not prevent yet another attack on Paris a year later. In the end, a combination of force and, perhaps inevitably, money made them leave. Yet the tide was turning against the Vikings and for the next few years both Franks and Bretons had the better of their encounters with Viking raiders. More sophisticated fortifications and better organized and more committed leadership were beginning to make a crucial difference but, despite this, no victory was decisive enough to bring about a complete withdrawal. Then nature lent a hand, for, in 892, famine blighted the land. It was this, rather than any specific military campaign, that persuaded most of the Vikings, including Hastein, to abandon Frankia and head for England. There is some suggestion that the Franks, understandably keen to see the back of their tormentors, provided the ships.

During the last few years of the ninth century and the first decade of the tenth, the epidemic of Viking attacks that had characterized most of the ninth century considerably decreased. When they resumed as a significant threat, the Vikings primarily concerned themselves with Brittany and the region immediately to its north that would become known as Normandy, the place of the Northmen. Brittany had escaped the worst of the Vikings during the ninth century, partly because its leaders were better organized and its people more naturally ferocious, and partly because both Vikings and Franks had distracted each other. Nevertheless, Viking dealings with the Bretons entailed the usual bitter recipe of broken alliances, mercenary employment and temporary intrusion but had no lasting consequences. In 907, things changed when the Breton leader, Alan the Great, died and the country was left leaderless. Then, in 911, a new Viking force arrived that would transform the regions to the south and west of the Seine. Leading them was the Viking referred to in Frankish sources as Rollo (see Appendix, below, pp. 215–216).

Rollo's first campaign led him into direct confrontation at Chartres with the army of King Charles the Simple, who, after Odo's death, had reunited Neustria and Aquitaine. Rollo was repulsed but not expelled. Whether it was at this point that Charles decided on the long-standing policy of using one set of Vikings to control others and offered Rollo the trading centre at Rouen in return for keeping matters quiet in the Seine basin, or whether Rollo simply went to Rouen and Charles made the best of what was beyond his control, is unclear. Whichever the case, royal consent was certainly a reality by 918 and included Charles's daughter Giselle as Rollo's bride. Rollo now bore the title of count of Rouen of the duchy of Normandy and could thus be regarded as a *bona fide* member of the Frankish aristocracy with an extensive territory and an incipient dynasty.

The acceptance of Rollo at the Frankish court was not in all respects a comfortable process. One tale illustrates what may be termed the cultural divide between Frank and Viking. According to the late eleventh-century historian William of Jumièges, Rollo underwent an investiture ceremony, part of which demanded that he should kiss the king's foot. The Viking code of honour obliged Rollo to reject any form of obeisance but, by way of a concession, he ordered one of his men to perform the task. At the crucial moment, instead of kneeling, Rollo's deputy simply raised the king's foot to his lips catapulting his highness backwards, much to the amusement of the common people. This story splendidly caricatures Franko–Scandinavian relations – the mannered and courtly Frank and the loutishly irreverent Viking – but disguises what was in fact a very shrewd and effective move by Charles. The accommodation of Rollo was the most conspicuous success in domesticating a Viking in Frankish history, for Rollo accepted baptism, in body at least if not in spirit, and dutifully cultivated the ecclesiastical centre at Rouen. The nearest parallel would be the schooling of Cnut the Great in the traditions of Anglo-Saxon kingship in England during the eleventh century.

The implications for Brittany of Rollo's arrival on the Seine were felt almost immediately. When Rollo headed for Rouen, a number of his party rounded Brittany's Cotentin peninsula and put ashore with little intention of leaving. From this point onward, Brittany became a focus for Viking raiders and settlers. In the course of the upheaval, nearly all the monasteries were reduced to ruin and many of the inhabitants shipped off to slave markets. In 919, a massive Viking fleet under the leadership of the Norwegian warlord Røgnvald landed at Nantes and exerted great pressure across the region. Røgnvald's impact was sufficient to cause the Breton aristocracy and many leading clergy to take flight for England. In the absence of resistance, the Vikings in Brittany simply took possession.

By 924, Røgnvald and some of Rollo's men had entered into an alliance and set about extending their influence eastward, only to be repelled by Raoul, duke of Burgundy. The following year Rollo broke his oath and raided north of Rouen, but, despite being contained by a confederation of Frankish aristocrats, Rollo managed to exact concessions and further territories to his south. Normandy was becoming a reality. Relief for Brittany, however, did not come until 937 when the exiled Alan Barbetorte gained sponsorship from King Athelstan and returned from England and ousted the Viking invaders. Rollo had died c. 928 but expansion went on under his successor William Longsword, who encroached even further on what had once been Breton territory. By the end of the century Brittany was in all things subservient to the counts of Rouen, and Rollo's Normandy was not only itself secure but also a Frankish powerhouse, militarily and culturally. Viking Normandy had been absorbed into Frankia and then, as Scandinavian gave way to Frankish style, Normandy slowly absorbed much of Frankia into itself. Of this metamorphosis, only the place-names remained to betray a Viking origin.

Rollo's impact on Frankia was unparalleled; indeed, no Viking in the history of the Viking Age, not even Cnut the Great of England, had a more powerful influence on medieval European history than he did, for Rollo's Norman descendants would go on to found royal lines in both England and Italy. Rollo's extraordinary career, culminating in his acceptance as a western European count, signalled the end of the Viking Age in Frankia. Viking raiders came and went throughout the tenth century, and the Christian credentials of Normandy were briefly threatened during the time of William Longsword, when Thor worship was revived, but most Vikings understood that Frankia in the tenth century was not the free-for-all it had been in the ninth. Besides, as the century drew to a close, England in the reign of Æthelred the Unready had far more to offer. This, however, did not mean that Frankia enjoyed peace. Normandy was not an easy neighbour and adjacent Frankish duchies were often placed on the defensive. Yet, aggressively ambitious as the counts of Rouen most certainly were, the dynasty had legitimacy and, as such, required its actions to be legitimized. The one-time Vikings of Normandy were drawn into the world of medieval Christian Europe and, in this regard, the power politics of church and state governed its processes.

The problems that Frankia endured from the Vikings in the ninth century arose, at least in part, because the Vikings recognized none of the political rules that governed the development of Normandy in the tenth. On the contrary, the Vikings of the Loire valley and the Seine basin were politically indifferent. Their simple view was that the problems of the Franks spelt profit. They were, in effect, parasites whose host provided a seemingly inexhaustible supply of nourishment. It has been estimated, for example, that payments made to the Vikings during the ninth century totalled 44,250 lbs of gold and silver. Many other payments must have gone unrecorded. Added to this was booty extracted by direct assaults on trading centres and monasteries, as well as slaves and hostages for ransom. Indirect costs to the Franks due to the Viking presence must also take into account the broader damage to the economy through depopulation and material destruction. Nevertheless, it is interesting to note that the contemporary *Royal Frankish Annals* and its continuation, the *Annals of St-Bertin*, devote only small space to Viking enormities compared to the major subject of their histories, the squabbles among Charlemagne's hapless successors. This gives us a perspective. Whatever problems the Vikings inflicted on the Franks, the Franks managed to inflict more on themselves. By the end of the ninth century Frankia, once at the centre of Charlemagne's Holy Roman Empire, had been reduced to a jigsaw of monarchies rarely able to coexist and themselves riven from within by competing semi-independent duchies. The Viking contribution simply helped matters along.

# 8

# Russia and the East

Whilst it was predominantly Norwegians and Danes who surged across Western Europe, it was mainly Swedes who travelled as much as a thousand miles to the south and east down the network of rivers that run from the Baltic regions to the Black Sea and the Caspian. This Swedish adventure eventually brought Vikings into contact with the riches of the Greeks of the Byzantine Empire, whose ancient capital was at Constantinople, and to the palaces and mosques of the Alid emirates and the Abbasid caliphate, whose religious and economic centre was at Baghdad.

In character, the eastward expansion of the Vikings is often said to be somewhat different from that to Ireland, mainland Britain and Frankia. This is true in terms of the greater emphasis on trade but in terms of violence it is not. Certainly, geography posed inhibitions, for the Slavic regions north of the Black Sea offered no defenceless monasteries replete with valuables or open waters on which longships could vanish with their booty. Raging rivers and the vulnerability of river traffic to hostile tribes meant that Swedish Vikings were frequently obliged to be more circumspect in their approach to the locals than their counterparts in the west. It was therefore as traders not raiders that the Swedes most often presented themselves. Yet trade did not necessarily mean peaceful barter and mutual exchange, and Viking merchants would readily resort to threats, violent assaults and extortion when they did not receive what they demanded. In this way, the disparate Slav economies were organized to the benefit of the Vikings.

Once having reached the broad expanses of the Black Sea and the Caspian, the more familiar face of Viking aggression was shown in surprise attacks and unrestrained savagery. On the shores of these inland seas, monasteries and mosques were the inevitable focus of Viking interest and neither the might of the Byzantine Empire nor that of Islam daunted them. From the mid ninth to the mid eleventh centuries, the Christians of Constantinople suffered from Viking attack at least four times, and the Khazars, who controlled the lucrative trade across the lower Volga, were either unable to prevent them or

were complicit in attacks against the Arabs from the Caspian during the same
period. Towards the end of the tenth century, Viking mercenaries, known and
feared as the Varangians,[1] were widely acknowledged as the most ferocious
fighting men in Eastern Europe and were being employed as an elite militia by
the Byzantine emperor himself. By this time, Swedish Vikings had established
their own formidable kingdom, based initially on the suppression of the Slavic
tribes. The designation of the Swedish Vikings as the Rus is evident in their
territorial legacy, Russia.[2]

Swedes had been making their presence felt across the Baltic for some 150
years before the start of the Viking Age in the late eighth century. If Snorri
Sturluson's history of the Swedish kings, *Saga of the Ynglings*, can be credited,
the earliest sorties there were aimed at conquest.[3] The seventh-century Swedish
king Yngvar is said to have met his death while harrying the Estonians south
of the Gulf of Finland, and, several generations later, Ivar the Widefathomer
emerged as a powerful Swedish king amidst a chaos of rival claims and is reputed
to have established an empire that included parts of the eastern Baltic. Snorri's
history may lack corroboration, but there is little reason to doubt that ambitious
Swedes had long been keen to expand their influence across the Baltic. Swedish
aggression toward the tribes east of the Baltic in the first half of the ninth century
is recorded in Rimbert's *Life of Anskar* (*c.* 870), which relates how the Swedes had
subdued the Kurlanders but had soon been ejected.[4] By Rimbert's time, however,
Swedish ascendancy over the region had been restored. Early ninth-century
Scandinavian interest in the eastern Baltic was also shared by Godfred, king
of the Danes, whose policy had been to secure Danish influence there during
his quarrels with the Frankish Emperor Charlemagne. That the Danes did not
pursue eastward expansion is more to do with the opportunities that they were
able to take in Frankia rather than any specific rivalry with the Swedes.

The view that the Swedish expansion was different in character from that in
the west is most justified with regard to the early stages of the movement east,
for it was as merchants and craftsmen, rather than warriors, that the Swedes first
began to have a lasting impact across the Baltic. Peaceful settlement by Swedes
is suggested by numerous grave finds dating from at least the beginning of the
eighth century, and possibly as early as the mid seventh century, in the Slav
and Balt settlements of Grobin and Elbing on the western and southern edges
of the Baltic. Characteristic items of Swedish jewellery and other household
paraphernalia have also been discovered, further suggesting that the Swedes
were comfortably accommodated among the locals.

By the mid eighth century, the town of Staraja Ladoga on the Volkhov, eight miles south of Lake Ladoga, was developing into a key trading centre under the auspices of Swedish entrepreneurs, attracting merchants from all points of the compass carrying or seeking salt, amber, wax, honey, furs and slaves. During the mid ninth century, Staraja Ladoga became the main transit point for the north–south trade. Ships could be refitted there and provisions loaded for long river journeys, and luxury goods were to be had in abundance. But the town was vulnerable and in the 860s fire swept through its busy streets, most likely as the result of an attack. The town soon revived and, known as Aldeigjuborg in the Icelandic sagas, it was still considered a place of major significance during the early eleventh century. Alongside the development of Staraja Ladoga, further Baltic settlements continued to spring up and thrive, such as those at Wolin and Apulia on its southern and eastern rim.

Most of the Swedes who first migrated across the Baltic came from the island of Gotland, less than a hundred miles off the Swedish mainland, and from the powerful Swedish kingdom of Uppland, which afforded easy access to the Gulf of Finland. Gotland, once an independent island, was incorporated into the Swedish mainland rule sometime before 800; indeed, Alfred the Great's late ninth-century seafaring informant, Wulfstan, remarked on Gotland's long-time status as part of the Swedish kingdom. As northern markets developed, descendants of these early traders soon learned first hand of Arab and Byzantine silver coins proffered by traders heading north from the caliphate and Constantinople. The lure of this precious metal obliged technological innovation and, by at least the mid ninth century, Swedish Vikings had adapted their longships so as to be suitable for river navigation and for the necessary labours of portage, sometimes for many miles over arduous terrain to circumvent rapids or to cross from one river to the next.

Less than two hundred miles east of the upper Baltic is the one of Europe's great watersheds, where rivers drain north and west and open up into huge waterways to the south and east. It was this river system that traders and warrior adventurers learned how to negotiate. The Vistula on the southern edge of the Baltic could take them south to where they could link up to the Dniester, and so on to the Bulgar markets west of the Black Sea. From the eastern Baltic, the Dvina could lead them to within reach of the Dnieper and so due south to Kiev and beyond that to Byzantium. The Volkhov could take them south across Lake Ilmen, either to connect up with the Lovat and so south down the Dnieper, or to head east along the bend of the mighty Volga toward the Volga Bulgars and, after that, southwards to the Khazar markets east of the Black Sea. From there they could travel further east to the open waters of the Caspian, so coming, on its southern shores, to the source of the silks, spices and silver traded by Arab merchants.

Some indication of the scale of the commercial transactions that were stimulated by the Swedes is to be found in the coin hoards in the Swedish homeland, particularly in Gotland. Over half the Arab kufic silver in the form of dirhems, and over three quarters of the Byzantine coins that have been found in Scandinavia were deposited for safe keeping in Gotland. Some thirty-two coin hoards have been unearthed dating from before 890 and approximately 85,000 coins, largely of tenth-century Arab provenance, have been found in Sweden – mainly in Gotland – compared with less than a tenth of that throughout the rest of Scandinavia. This distribution of buried treasure, however, should be seen as reflecting the patterns and practices of circulation across Scandinavia, rather than indicating the wealth of any particular region, for it is evident that Arab coinage was in use right across the Viking world. In reality, the commercial activities of the Swedish Rus for over a century and a half would have meant transactions involving millions of silver and gold coins, as well as a vast store of Russian fixed-weight silver neck and arm rings known as *grivna*.

The net effect of Rus commerce can be regarded as central in financing Scandinavian expansion during the ninth and tenth centuries. When Arab silver mines were exhausted, early in the last quarter of the tenth century, the consequences were significant. The chief Swedish trading centre of Birka seems to have become entirely redundant and the economic consequences of this were felt throughout Scandinavia. In Denmark, relations with Germany were destabilized after decades of relative cooperation. New sources of income were sought and the renewal of Viking attacks on England was directly related to the Scandinavian economic crisis caused by the cessation of the flow of Arab silver.

According to the *Russian Primary Chronicle*, the Northmen, distinguished both as the Rus and the Varangians, entered the political arena of the northern Slavs and neighbouring tribes between 859 and 862.

(859) The Varangians from beyond the sea imposed tribute upon the Chuds, the Slavs, the Merians, the Ves', and the Krivichians.

(860–62) The tributaries of the Varangians drove them back beyond the sea, and refusing them further tribute, set out to govern themselves. There was no law among them, but tribe rose against tribe. Discord thus ensued among them, and

Viking Russia

they began to war one against another. They said to themselves, 'Let us seek a prince who may rule over us and judge us according to the Law'. They accordingly went overseas to the Varangian Russes: these particular Varangians were known as Russes, just as some are called Swedes, and others Normans, English and Gotlanders, for they were thus named. The Chuds, the Slavs, Krivichians, and the Ves' then said to the people of Rus', 'Our land is great and rich, but there is no order in it. Come to rule and reign over us.' They thus selected three brothers, with their kinsfolk, who took with them all the Russes and migrated. The oldest Rurik, located himself in Novgorod; the second, Sineus at Beloozero; and the third, Truvor, in Izborsk. On account of these Varangians, the district of Novgorod became known as the land of Rus'. The present inhabitants of Novgorod are descended from the Varangian race, but aforetime they were Slavs.[5]

The *Russian Primary Chronicle*, it must be understood, was not only composed in the early twelfth century but had as its chief aim the validation of the royal line of the Rus that was established at Kiev. It is a valuable and, in many respects, unique text, but it needs to be approached with caution and its claims must, where possible, be set against any other available contemporary accounts, typically from victims of the Rus. These accounts often flatly contradict the *Chronicle*. The 'invitation' of the Slavs to the Rus to help them put their houses in order may, therefore, disguise a less diplomatic truth. Almost certainly it does. Yet exactly who Rurik and his brothers were is a mystery. Assuming that we accept them as something more than legend, they must have been people of stature in order to assume command of such lucrative trading centres. It is nonetheless curious that they receive no mention in any source, early or late, other than the *Chronicle*.

What is clear is that the *Chronicle* is adrift in its calculation of the date of the ascendancy of the Rus, as in 839, according to the much more reliable *Annals of St-Bertin*, the Byzantine emperor in Constantinople had arranged the safe escort of Rus ambassadors (referred to as Rhos in the *Annals*) to the court of Louis the Pious in Frankia, so that they might avoid the hostility of tribes north of the Black Sea on their journey back to the Baltic regions. Louis, who knew only too well about the menace of the Vikings, detained them while he investigated whether or not they were spies. What we learn from this is that the Rus were not only in significant contact with Constantinople more than twenty years before Rurik and his brothers allegedly went to the aid of the Slavs but also that the Rus who held power in the Slavic regions were definitely Swedes.

A different style of contact with Byzantium followed shortly after the establishment of Rus authority. Within two years, Rurik had, by dint of his brothers' death, assumed full control of the region. The centre of Rus power became Novgorod, not surprisingly given its location on the Volkhov, a little over a hundred miles south of Lake Ladoga and three miles north of Lake Ilmen. Yet other Rus Vikings were not content to remain subject to Rurik's rule. Two of them, Askold and Dir, not kinsmen of Rurik the *Chronicle* points out, sailed south down the Dnieper, intending to set themselves up in Constantinople (Tsar'grad in the *Chronicle*; Mikligard to the Rus). On the way, they noticed 'a small city on a hill', the town of Kiev, which they seized.

These southern rivals to Rurik's kingdom now decided to fulfil their original goal and visit Constantinople. Sources other than the *Chronicle* confirm that they arrived on 18 June 860. With them were two hundred ships and perhaps as many as 8000 men. Their timing was opportune, for the Emperor Michael was absent with his fleet warring with the Arabs. It fell to the patriarch Photius to try and rally the people as the Viking forces plundered monasteries and laid waste the districts surrounding the walled city, slaughtering men, women and children at will and without mercy. 'Why', he lamented, 'has this dreadful bolt fallen on us out of the farthest north?' Like Christian commentators in Western Europe, his conclusion was that the attack was a manifestation of divine wrath, a punishment for the shortcomings of the Christian community. The 'fierce and savage tribe, ravaging the suburbs, destroying everything, ruining everything ... thrusting swords through everything, taking pity on nothing, sparing nothing ... has annihilated whole generations of inhabitants', said Photius. Better, he thought, to have died than to witness 'the disaster that has befallen us'.[6] Word eventually reached the emperor but, despite fighting his way back into the city, he seems to have been unable to do anything to combat the Viking fleet as it sailed past the city, its warriors waving their swords aloft, and on through the Bosporus to the Sea of Marmara and the holy sites of the Islands of Princes, which were then looted and desecrated.

Exactly what made Askold and Dir abandon the Black Sea after ten days of pillage is uncertain. In the *Chronicle*'s view, it was a nightlong vigil of prayer and the dipping of the sacred vestment of the Virgin in the sea, which resulted in a violent storm and the destruction of the fleet of the 'godless Russes'.[7] A less pious explanation is that it was the emperor's plans for a counter-attack that sent the Vikings scurrying back to safety, either this or the likelihood that Viking appetites were already sated and their longships full. Whatever the case,

Photius was not about to let his flock forget what had taken place:

> An obscure nation, a nation of no account, a nation ranked among slaves, unknown,
> but which has won a name from the expedition against us – once insignificant
> but now famous, once humble and destitute but now splendid and wealthy – a
> nation dwelling somewhere far from our country, barbarous, nomadic, armed with
> arrogance, unwatched, unchallenged, leaderless, has suddenly, in the twinkling of
> an eye, like a wave of the sea poured over our frontier …[8]

His description of the wildness and pitilessness of the attack – infants dashed
against rocks, rivers reddened with blood, corpses piled everywhere – suggests
that this onslaught was one of the most barbaric in the entire Viking Age.

Askold and Dir, meanwhile, returned to Kiev. Although nothing is said of
them in the *Chronicle* until their deaths some twenty years later, it is likely
that they were active in laying the surrounding areas under tribute. North in
Novgorod, in about 879, Oleg succeeded his kinsman Rurik and was charged
with the protection of Igor, said in the *Chronicle* to be Rurik's son, although
chronologically this is unlikely. Within three years of his succession, Oleg
paid a visit to Kiev, killed Askold and Dir and set himself up as ruler over
a unified Rus territory with its new centre at Kiev. The *Chronicle* evidently
regards this consolidation as a matter of asserting the legitimacy of the royal
household of the Ryurik Rus over the illegitimate rule of the breakaway faction
in Kiev.

An extensive subjugation of the Slavic tribes east and west of the Dnieper
followed Oleg's conquest, and it is clear that his intention was to extend his
realm south of Kiev to the shores of the Black Sea. He may well have succeeded
in laying tribes to the south west of Kiev under tribute, but to his immediate
south were the ferocious Pechenegs, who received support from the Greeks, and
to the east of them the Khazars, whose vast territory between the Black Sea and
the Caspian gave them control of the passage to and from the caliphate. Against
these, Oleg could not prevail. Despite such limitations, the Rus now controlled a
region stretching some seven hundred miles from Staraja Ladoga to the south of
Kiev, encompassing territories over three hundred miles wide at the narrowest
point. West of the Volga, all traffic to northern climes from Byzantium and the
caliphate fell within the dispensation of the Rus. The riches that could now
accrue should have made belligerence directed at powerful southern neighbours
seem both risky and rather unnecessary. But, if the *Chronicle* is to be trusted,
Oleg thought otherwise.

At some point between 904 and 907, Oleg is said to have raised a great army consisting of his own men and a multitude from the numerous Slavic tribes under his sway. They travelled south by horseback and by ship, which the *Chronicle* numbers at 2000. Forewarned of their coming, the Greeks 'fortified the strait and closed up the city'. Oleg and his men duly set about ravaging and burning all they could find and 'inflicted much slaughter ... after the usual manner of soldiers'.[9] When Oleg fitted wheels to his ships so that they could bear down on his victims from open country, the Greeks sued for peace and Oleg demanded tribute at a rate of twelve *grivny* (twelve pounds of silver) for each of his men. The Greeks now tried to be rid of Oleg and his army by offering them poisoned food and wine. The ploy failed and Oleg presented fresh terms which, curiously, seem to have been less onerous than before the Greeks had tried to poison him. The main clause was the right to trade freely in Byzantium. Given this anomaly in the *Chronicle*'s account, doubts are raised about Oleg's supposed victory, doubts further increased by the absence of any mention of the attack in Greek sources.

What actually seems to have occurred in or around 907 is a negotiation between the Rus and the Byzantine emperors Leo and Alexander concerning trading rights. The outcome of this was that Oleg accomplished through diplomacy, and perhaps a show of strength, what he could not accomplish through force of arms in his efforts to extend his realm to the shores of the Black Sea: in effect, a legitimization of his trading operation from the Baltic to Byzantium. But there were conditions. The Rus would not be allowed to take quarters inside the walled city; any violence from the Rus would find them subjected to Byzantine law; and their traffic to and from the city would be strictly monitored:

> They shall not enter the city save through one gate, unarmed and fifty at a time, escorted by an agent of the emperor. They may conduct business according to their requirements without payment of taxes.[10]

In 912 the agreement was ratified in much greater detail, with all the trappings of diplomatic courtesies, and Oleg 'despatched his vassals to make peace and draw up a treaty between the Greeks and the Russes'. Penalties for murder, theft and fraud were agreed and the mutual regard of each other's citizens was enshrined, even to the extent of ransoming each other's prisoners from foreign lands. Most importantly, mutual assistance during misadventures at sea was subjected to careful protocols, so as to ensure the protection of merchant traffic. Oleg's emissaries to Constantinople are listed as 'Karl, Ingjald, Farulf, Vermund, Hrollaf, Gunnar, Harold, Karni, Frithleif, Hroarr, Angantyr, Throand, Leithulf, Fast and Steinvith', all names of Scandinavian extraction.[11] At Emperor Leo's court they were treated royally, honoured with gifts and taken on a tour of the palace and the city's sacred sites and reliquary. Just how moved Oleg's compatriots were by the Emperor Leo's exposition of 'the true belief' is not recorded.

Two years later, Oleg died after a period of being 'at peace with all nations'. The *Chronicle*'s account of his death has much of the atmosphere of folktale about it. It is said that a magician had warned Oleg that he would meet his death from his favourite horse. Unnerved by the prophecy, he sent the beast away, but after a while he hankered to ride it once more. On being told that it had died, and so now believing the prophecy to be false, he commanded that its bones be assembled so he might once again mount it. As he dismounted, he stamped contemptuously on the skull, mocking his apparent fate, whereupon a venomous snake emerged and bit him on the foot.[12] An alternative possibility is that Oleg died at the hands of the Khazars after raiding in the Caspian. His reign had lasted thirty-three years.

Igor, Oleg's ward, now assumed power, and the peace with Byzantium seems to have lasted for four decades. During this time, both the Rus and the Greeks were engaged in their own private disputes with other neighbours. Igor was forced to suppress an uprising from the Derevlians, north west of Kiev, and then, between 915 and 920, he was led into a protracted campaign against the Pechenegs, whose broad territory north of the Black Sea meant that both the Rus and the Greeks were dependent on their quiescence for trade to run smoothly. Meanwhile, Byzantium suffered repeated attacks from the Bulgars in the 920s and then from the Magyars in the early 930s. On both occasions the Emperor Romanus was forced to make peace, which may well suggest that he paid handsomely to achieve it. It is mere speculation as to how much, if at all, the Rus engaged in the politics of the region at the expense of their Greek trading partners during this time, but they almost certainly watched the situation carefully in order to take what advantage they could. Doubtless, the Greeks did likewise.

Whatever the background to events, Igor cannot have been getting the benefits of trade that Oleg had intended and, in 941, he resorted to open warfare. Having mustered a great fleet, probably a thousand strong rather than the ten thousand that both the *Chronicle* and some Greek sources report, Igor entered the Black Sea, headed round its south-eastern shores and set about looting and burning monasteries, palaces and villages with all the attendant butchery. But the Bulgars had warned the Greeks of the Rus incursion and when Igor entered the waters off Constantinople a coalition of Greek fleets was there to meet him. Having shown great courage against vastly superior numbers in the engagement that followed, the Rus eventually deemed it wise to retreat. The Greeks followed raining 'Greek Fire' on them and causing havoc. So runs the typically partial account in the *Chronicle*. A different account that does slightly less honour to the Rus was given by the diplomat Liudprand of Cremona, whose father witnessed the battle. In this, there was no opposing coalition but an anxious and sleepless emperor who conceived of the idea of fitting out certain of his old galleys with flamethrowers.

> As they [the galleys] lay surrounded by the enemy, the Greeks began to project their fire all around; and the Rus, seeing the flames, hurled themselves from their boats, preferring death by water to live incineration. Some sank to the bottom under the weight of their cuirasses and helmets ... others caught fire even as they were swimming among the billows; not a man escaped that day save those who made it to the shore. [13]

Many of the Rus survivors deemed the Greeks invincible, as they had in their possession 'lightning from heaven'. The *Chronicle* indicates that Igor thought differently and looked to the Swedish homeland to recruit Viking manpower and recover his pride. In 944 he is said to have returned, this time with the Pechenegs as his allies, amongst others.[14] Warnings of the Rus advance, again from the Bulgars, gave the emperor enough time to devise a response, if only in the sense of offering Igor tribute equal to that which Oleg had received. At the very least, this meant a resumption of the trade agreement. To the Pechenegs the emperor sent silk and gold, which they readily accepted, thereafter relieving their pent-up energies by turning west against the Bulgars.

The Rus-Byzantine treaty of 945 reiterates all of the treaty of 912, if at greater length and with greater ceremony. This time fifty Rus envoys were sent to conclude the agreement. Among them are listed a number of names of Slavic origin indicating the gradual integration or Slavicization of the Rus. Igor might well have been satisfied with the state of his realm and the lucrative trade that he controlled, but the classic character flaw of Viking leaders had Igor in thrall: greed. The peaceful outcome of Igor's aggression against the Greeks had left him with a huge army with nothing to do. Perhaps one of those Vikings mercenaries

whom Igor had summoned from the north thought that that he could make a
name for himself by leading the army east to the northern tip of the Caspian
and taking whatever fate would allow among the unsuspecting Arabs. Igor,
who more than likely remained in Kiev, would probably have encouraged the
enterprise and expected his share of any success.

Trade with the Arabs had been crucial to the development of the Rus kingdom since its inception. But such trade involved the approval of the Khazars,
whose territory merchants had to cross. The Khazars, who officially professed
Judaism but tolerated many faiths, including Islam, evidently took their role
seriously and regarded themselves as a buffer between Rus aggression and the
wealth of Islam. As one Khazar leader is said to have remarked in the tenth century: 'I ... do not allow the Russians who come in ships to go against the Arabs
... they would destroy the land of the Arabs as far as Baghdad.'[15] The initial
approaches to the Caspian were, however, peaceful in intent and, according to
the contemporary writer Ibn Khurdadbeh, Swedish merchants trading furs,
sword blades and spears had gained first-hand knowledge of the riches of Islam
in the ninth century and had travelled by camel all the way to Baghdad. The
imposition of a tax on their goods both by the Byzantine emperor, when they
entered the Black Sea, and thereafter by the Khazars, when they entered the
Don, coupled with the wealth they encountered in the caliphate and the relative
vulnerability of Caspian ports clearly stimulated more aggressive Rus interest.

In 912, towards the end of Oleg's reign, the Khazars had foolishly allowed
themselves to enter into an agreement with the Rus granting them passage
into the Caspian in exchange for half of whatever the Rus could plunder there.
Looking back from thirty years later, the Arab writer Al Masudi told how the
Vikings ran amuck among the startled Arab communities, looting, burning and
slaughtering in the towns of Abusgan and Ardebil, among others. The Khazars
clearly had not expected the Rus to be so destructive and the Muslims among
them raised an army and intervened, leaving only a few Rus to live to tell the
tale. Oleg was almost certainly behind this attack and a more likely fate to that
given in the *Chronicle* is that he was the unnamed Viking leader who was killed
as a result of the Khazar reprisal.

In 944, Igor's mercenaries moved in similar fashion against the Arabs. The
Arab historian Miskawaih describes them travelling inland from the west coast
of the Caspian on the River Kura in modern-day Azerbaijan, where they easily
took possession of the town of Berda, despite an army of five thousand sent
by the governor of the town to confront them. They then enslaved the women

and had the audacity to offer the townspeople the freedom to continue their religious practices, providing they accepted them as their new rulers. This was greeted with stone throwing. The enslaved women now took their vengeance and poisoned the food supply and the water. The dysentery that ensued brought about many deaths among the occupiers, and forced many more to quit the region, but it was not enough to loosen their grip entirely. After repeated efforts to force them out, the ruler of Azerbaijan, Marzuban ibn Muhammed, succeeded in tricking many of the Rus out of the town and surrounding them. The Rus commander and hundreds of his men were killed. With numbers seriously depleted and the epidemic still raging, the Rus finally rowed away under cover of night, leaving Berda's women behind.

If Igor had hoped that encouraging mayhem in the Caspian would help improve his position he was badly mistaken, for the Khazars now took against the Rus, as of course did all Muslim people. The damage to trade with the Arabs may have been behind Igor's decision to increase the tribute he levied from the tribes under Rus dominion. 'He thought of the Derevlians, and wished to collect from them still larger tribute,' says the *Chronicle*.[16] Igor attacked the Derevlians in 945, seemingly having already taken one lot of tribute from them. Then, on his way home, he decided that he might as well take a third lot, so, with just a handful of retainers he returned to Dereva, where the indignant Derevlians declined to comply and, instead, slaughtered him and his company.

Igor underestimated the Derevlians, but now the Derevlians underestimated the Rus, for they promptly invited Igor's widow, Olga, to marry their prince. Their aim was no less than to take control of Igor's successor Svyatoslav, yet a boy, and thus the Rus dominions. To this end, they sent a delegation of their senior men by boat to Kiev to bear their proposal. Olga, the archetypical ruthless Viking queen, saw her chance for revenge and, appearing to be compliant, offered to honour the delegation by having them carried in their boat to the royal palace. The credulous Derevlians accepted the honour only to find themselves dropped into a trench and burnt alive. Derevlian leaders back home were clearly oblivious of Olga's vengeance when they sent a second delegation at her behest. Olga's reception was to have them incinerated in a bathhouse. News of this also failed to reach the Derevlians, as Olga now journeyed to Igor's tomb in Dereva where she insisted that a great feast should be held. She waited until the Derevlians were drunk and then instructed her bodyguard to set about massacring them.

Apparently inspired by the enthusiasm of the young Svyatoslav, the Rus now brought their army to bear on Dereva with predictable consequences. The Derevlian survivors retreated to Iskorosten where Igor had met his death and were placed under siege for a year. The *Chronicle*'s account of how Olga eventually achieved the devastation of Iskorosten is little more than a legend that was widely incorporated into tales of other Viking attackers in Scandinavian traditions. Thus it is told that Olga finally offered to leave Dereva without further vengeance and only the tribute of three pigeons and three sparrows from each household. The Derevlians readily accepted and with much relief delivered the tribute. Olga then contrived that each bird be fitted with a flaming match and let them fly back to their coops and nests, so razing the town to the ground and allowing Olga to complete her retribution. Despite the *Chronicle*'s propagandizing mixture of history and legend, it is highly probable that Olga exacted future tribute from the Derevlians with even less consideration for their feelings than had her husband.

Olga retained great influence over the Rus territories until her death in 969 and was to all intents and purposes the supreme authority while Svyatoslav was away on his many campaigns. She oversaw the gathering of tribute throughout the kingdom and saw to the foundation of new trading posts, as well as ensuring that established centres, such as that at Novgorod, remained subject to the rule of Kiev. In 957, she visited the Emperor Constantine Porphyrogenitus in Constantinople. According to the *Chronicle* she received baptism from him during this visit, apparently in order to avoid having to marry him, but this cannot be entirely true, as the emperor's own account makes no mention of this important first conversion of a Rus royal and, in any case, the emperor was already married. Trade agreements seem to have been on the agenda during Olga's visit, for she took away with her many costly items in return for her promise of 'slaves, wax and furs'. But when the emperor sent messages reminding her of her side of the bargain, she peevishly complained that she had been insulted when the emperor's guards delayed her in the Bosporus when she sought entry into Constantinople. We can nevertheless conclude that Olga did, indeed, convert to Christianity at some point in the 950s and that a trading relationship with the Greeks was maintained during her lifetime.

Olga's influence over her son's realm did not extend to matters of religious belief. When she implored him to follow her lead and convert, he replied, 'How shall I alone accept another faith? My followers will laugh at that.'[17] Svyatoslav's obstinate paganism was entirely consistent with his warlike mien, and no neighbour was safe from his ambitions. Svyatoslav's main aim for the Rus was to extend their territory west as far as the Danube and east as far as the Volga, so allowing them to monopolize all the trade routes running from the Baltic to the Black Sea and the Caspian. To do this, he had to take on the Khazars, the Bulgars, both western and eastern, and eventually Byzantium. From the outset, the political dynamics of the region favoured him. The Greeks were distracted by their campaigns against the Arabs to their south and later in the eastern Mediterranean, and the Khazars, for so long the bulwark against Rus aggression eastward, were disunited within their realm, so much so that certain factions of them approached Svyatoslav for his assistance.

Perhaps Svyatoslav had not reckoned on the Pechenegs, whose land in the lower Dnieper north of the Black Sea would need to be traversed, and on whom the Rus were traditionally dependent for livestock, including horses. In the middle years of the tenth century, Emperor Constantine Porphyrogenitus had noted the vital role played by the Pechenegs in Greek foreign policy, particularly in so far as they kept the Rus in check.[18] In order to reach the Black Sea and pursue trade with Byzantium, the Rus needed to negotiate a series of rapids on the lower Dnieper (all of which Constantine lists using Scandinavian names), which rendered them vulnerable to Pecheneg attack. In many ways, the Pechenegs held the key to Rus expansion south and west. But they could not be controlled and could not be trusted. Svyatoslav's disregard for the unpredictable Pechenegs, while pursuing his grander schemes, led to his undoing.

In 964, 'stepping light as a leopard',[19] Svyatoslav set out due east from Novgorod to the limit of his dominions and then along the Volga to the capital of the east Bulgars, which he sacked. He then sailed south to where the Volga flows into the Caspian and set about the ruination of the Khazar capital, Itil. The Khazars, already weakened, never recovered from Svyatoslav's assault and from this point they fade from history. With the obliteration of Khazar power, the Rus had all the lands from the Dnieper to the Volga under their control, albeit somewhat precariously. Svyatoslav now turned his attention to the west and to the Bulgars of the Danube. The Greek emperor, Nicephorus Phokas, initially encouraged Svyatoslav in this enterprise against the troublesome Bulgars by paying over a huge bribe. The emperor's strategy was largely a matter of necessity, for the subjection of the Bulgars would allow him to concentrate on his long-running war against the Arabs. What he did not fully appreciate was Svyatoslav's intention to establish a new Rus capital at Pereyaslavets on the Danube. From the Greek point of view, such a development would take matters from bad to worse.

Svyatoslav's first campaign against the Bulgars was a resounding success and he is said to have captured eighty towns along the Danube and to have set himself up in Pereyaslavets, where 'all riches are concentrated'.[20] Then, in 967, the Pechenegs seized their moment and laid siege to Kiev, trapping Olga and her grandsons inside. Word reached Svyatoslav and he was forced to abandon his new seat of power and hurry north to break the siege. All, however, was not well in his kingdom. Novgorod was demanding a prince of its own and many among the Rus, including the aged and infirm Olga, were discontented by Svyatoslav's declared intention to return to Pereyaslavets. Svyatoslav remained convinced that his future lay on the Danube, and in order to pacify his subjects he appointed his sons to oversee the major Rus centres, including Kiev and Novgorod. It was during this period of restructuring that Olga died, freeing Svyatoslav from any further obligation to remain in Kiev. After the elaborate solemnities, such as befitted the most formidable of Rus queens, Svyatoslav set out to recapture the land of the Bulgars.

The *Chronicle* account would have us believe that, having stormed the city of Pereyaslavets for a second time and so reasserted his authority over the Bulgars, Svyatoslav now threatened to overrun Byzantium. Faced with such a prospect, we are told, the Greeks immediately offered tribute. A more balanced account indicates that Svyatoslav's ambitions exceeded his might. During Svyatoslav's absence, the Greeks had engineered an alliance with the southern Bulgars and sealed it with royal weddings. Rather this than have Svyatoslav in the immediate neighbourhood. It may well have been this alliance that prompted Svyatoslav to turn south toward Philippopolis in the Crimea, where he is reported to have impaled 20,000 Bulgar prisoners. Yet not all Bulgars were opposed to Svyatoslav and, perceiving the opportunities for political advantage, he was able to attract many of them away from any alliance with the Greeks by placing the Bulgar royal family under his protection and guaranteeing them in their position. In 970, the immediate benefit to Svyatoslav was that his army was reinforced with Bulgar warriors keen to profit at the expense of their old enemies, the Greeks. Also enticed onto Svyatoslav's side was a throng of sundry nomads, among whom were a considerable number of Pechenegs. Strengthened, Svyatoslav headed across the mountains into Byzantine territory and, seemingly unopposed, took Adrianopolis. On the way, he showed his dissatisfaction with those Bulgars who had allied themselves to the Greeks by torching the town of Philippopolis. He must have assumed that the coalition he now led and the violence it could offer had persuaded the Greeks to resign themselves to a new power in the region and, without further advance, he headed back north. He was so confident in his position that he left the main pass over the mountains unguarded.

Svyatoslav could not have been more wrong in assuming Greek acquiescence. The new emperor, John Tzimisces, promptly set about blocking any escape up the Danube. Thereafter, in 971, he launched an attack from the south over the unguarded mountains and succeeded in taking the Bulgar capital, Preslav, and in capturing the Bulgar royal family. John then turned north east in search of Svyatoslav. The Rus and Greek armies eventually faced each other outside Dristra (modern Silistra), north of the Dniester, where Svyatoslav had established quarters. The battle that followed was eventually won by the Greeks, but not decisively, for the Rus fell back within the city walls of Dristra. Nevertheless, it was enough to discourage the Pechenegs and many others who, perhaps richer from Greek bribes, abandoned the Rus. More indecisive fighting ensued over the following weeks, with the Rus attempting to break out of Dristra but always in the end being forced to retreat. A final furious battle took place on 24 July 971. Svyatoslav launched a frenzied attack into the Greek ranks and for a while his army had the Greeks on the back foot, but luck was against them and a violent storm broke confusing the Rus and allowing the Greeks to regroup and counter-attack. Apparently inspiring the Greeks was a mysterious rider on a white charger, who they later believed was sent to deliver them by the Holy Virgin. Svyatoslav, wounded and weary, retreated to Dristra, from where the Greeks could hear him as 'he raged all night in anger and pain'. The following morning he offered terms, which the emperor, equally aware that a stalemate had been reached, willingly accepted.

Svyatoslav and John met on the banks of the Danube to agree the terms of a treaty. A Byzantine official, Leo Diaconis, was present and later described the arrival of the Rus leader:

> Svyatoslav crossed the river in a kind of Scythian boat; he handled the oar in the same way as his men. His appearance was as follows: he was of medium height – neither too tall, nor too short. He had bushy brows, blue eyes, and was snub-nosed; he shaved his beard but wore a long and bushy moustache. His head was shaven except for a lock of hair on one side as a sign of the nobility of his clan. His neck was thick, his shoulders broad and his whole stature fine. He seemed gloomy and savage. On one of his ears hung a golden earring adorned with two pearls and a ruby set between them. His white garments were not distinguishable from those of his men except for cleanness.[21]

Emperor John, in golden armour, received no gesture of deference from Svyatoslav, nor is he likely to have expected any: the Rus may have been offering terms but they were not acknowledging defeat and certainly not acknowledging their betters. Svyatoslav and the emperor parleyed as equals, the Rus leader sitting on the mainthwart of his boat. In the end, they agreed to maintain 'peace and perfect love'. What this meant in the short term was that Svyatoslav would depart with his booty from Bulgar territory and, in return, the Greeks would encourage the Pechenegs to allow the Rus safe passage across their land.

Laden with valuables, Svyatoslav and his men set out to reach the lower Dnieper. The winter bit deep and they were forced to pay heavily for food: a horse's head could cost them half a pound of silver. Word got round. Exactly how hard the Greeks had tried to ensure Pecheneg compliance with Svyatoslav's request for safe passage is not recorded, but it was to no effect. In the spring of 972 the Pechenegs discovered the Rus trying to negotiate the rapids and fell on them, relieving them of their spoils of war. They made a drinking vessel of Svyatoslav's skull, as was their way when honouring a great fallen enemy.

Svyatoslav's death triggered a vicious battle for the succession among his sons. It also concluded Rus efforts to expand their influence westward. When Vladimir, prince of Novgorod, emerged as the ruler of the Rus six years after the death of Svyatoslav, paganism, too, came to an end in the Rus lands. Vladimir's rule, which he preferred to exercise from Novgorod rather than Kiev, is chiefly conspicuous for his conversion to Christianity. He appears at first as an unlikely convert, as he did much in his early years to champion the old ways, favouring human sacrifice and sponsoring many expensive monuments to the Slav deities. His indiscriminate womanizing and heavy drinking were legendary even by Viking standards and he is said, for example, to have kept three hundred concubines.

What made him tire of the relaxed standards of paganism and search for a new faith is likely to have been prompted by political considerations, but he was not keen to let go of his habits in so doing. He was attracted to Islam by its polygamy but was forced to reject it because it would have meant abandoning his drinking habits. Christianity, on the other hand, did not mean temperance but it did mean a considerable restriction on his sexual habits. In the end, Vladimir's choice of Christianity was more indicative of the advantages that cooperation with the Eastern Orthodox Church in Byzantium could bring to the Rus economy than of the obduracy of a heavy drinker. The hand of the Byzantine emperor's sister, Anna, and, as a result, her lands in the Crimea must also have been factors in his decision, and Anna was adamant that she would not marry a pagan. But Vladimir's conversion to Christianity was not the only prerequisite before the match could be made, as Vladimir first had to reconcile matters with his current wife Ragnheid, a Swedish princess. One account claims that he was forced to pacify her by building the town of Izaslavl for her and their son. Another claims that she converted and entered a convent. As Ragnheid had witnessed the death of her entire family at the hands of Vladimir before being forced to marry him, and had been obliged to endure her husband's dissoluteness throughout their marriage, she perhaps did not find her fate wholly objectionable.

Negotiating his way into the affections of Anna also involved making sure that Vladimir got the best possible settlement for himself. In order to prove himself worthy of imperial status among the Greeks, Vladimir decided to make a show of both his military strength and his fealty in one single action. He did so by attacking the Byzantine city of Cherson in the Crimea which, it appears, was in the throes of a rebellion against Greek authority. He laid siege to the city from the Black Sea in 989 and, with the unexpected benefit of inside information, ended any resistance by cutting off the water supply. He then restored the town to Greek dominion as a personal gift from him to Basil II. The gesture obviously had the desired effect, for it was at Cherson that Vladimir and Anna married with all due ceremony. Sealing the Greco–Rus alliance was Vladimir's gift of six thousand mercenaries to the emperor for his personal protection, a gesture that appears to have established the precedent for the Varangian Guard. What prompted Vladimir's generosity may have been less a case of honouring an ally and relative by marriage and more one of escaping an expensive commitment.

Vladimir enforced Christianity throughout his realm and it significantly enhanced Rus security. Byzantium and the Rus now entered into unprecedented close and meaningful contact. Nevertheless, Vladimir did not adopt Byzantine ways in all things, and in the churches that flourished throughout his kingdom it was a Slavonic, not a Greek, liturgy that was heard. The fact that it was also not a Norse liturgy is a fair measure of the extent to which the Rus had become assimilated into the culture of the lands they had conquered. Vladimir's conversion can be regarded as a turning point in Rus history, indeed as the point at which the Viking Age in Eastern Europe began to decline in political significance, just as it did in Frankia when Rollo of Normandy converted. Yet Vladimir, king of Russia, did not abandon efforts to extend Rus influence, nor did certain Slav tribes abandon their efforts to reduce it. Once allied to the Greeks, there were both voluntary and involuntary limitations on any increase in Rus territorial power to the south and the west. But there was no such limitation to the east and Vladimir's campaigns against the Volga Bulgars occupied much of his early military career. One possible motive for attacking along the Volga was the decline in Arab silver, but it did nothing to restore the flow from exhausted silver mines. Vladimir's campaign against the Bulgars was evidently successful militarily and was concluded in a peace 'till stone floats and straw sinks', but it may not have enhanced Rus prosperity. There were, as ever, the Pechenegs to contend with and Kiev was frequently threatened by them, forcing Vladimir into protracted and often precarious confrontations in order to maintain his key trading assets. Overall, Vladimir's rule was not significant in terms of territorial expansion; rather it was the Christianization of the Rus that strengthened his authority throughout Christian Europe.

Vladimir died in 1015 and the succession was not resolved for another four years when Jaroslav, Vladimir's appointed heir, defeated his usurper brother Svyatopolk to assume the title of grand prince. Jaroslav's reign was characterized by increasingly close links with the royal houses Europe, including many in Scandinavia. He married Ingigerd, the daughter of the Swedish king Olof Skötkonung, and their daughter, Elisleif, went on to marry Harald Sigurtharson, better known later as Harald Hardrada, king of Norway. Harald's half-brother, Olaf Haraldsson, known later as St Olaf, sought refuge with Jaroslav in the year immediately preceding his ill-fated attempt to reclaim the Norwegian throne in 1030, and Magnus, Olaf's son, remained in Jaroslav's safekeeping until he could return north to rule over the lands his father had lost. The complex of relationships and allegiances that were established with Scandinavia were all part of the development of an acceptable political establishment in Russia that had begun during Vladimir's reign, rather than any special favour toward the ancestral homeland. Noticeably, Jaroslav was not wholly prejudiced in favour of Scandinavia and his daughters were married into royal houses in Hungary, France, Germany and Byzantium.

Jaroslav, who was remembered as 'the Wise', saw to it that Christian culture was the bedrock of his administration and to this end he employed Byzantine architects to build the great cathedral of St Sophia and the impregnable Golden Gate fortification in Kiev, where he ruled. But, as with Vladimir, this did not mean that Jaroslav was set on modelling his kingdom along Byzantine lines, for Christian Slavic identity was reinforced in the tenth century, especially in Jaroslav's determination to have the great corpus of Greek religious literature translated into Slavonic. Churches and monasteries now proliferated throughout the Rus lands and the clergy were granted special protection under new legislation. Jaroslav's reign was that of an enlightened European ruler who sought to affirm the cultural uniqueness and sovereignty of Russia within the context of Christian Europe.

Although Jaroslav's reign marked the apogee of the Rus settlement and their complete integration among the Slavs, the area remained volatile. In 1043, the Rus-Byzantine accord temporarily broke down and Jaroslav sent his son, Vladimir, into the Black Sea with disastrous consequences, due partly to a calamitous storm and partly to the superiority of the Greek galleys and their incendiary missiles. Whether the breakdown was brought about by an attack on certain eminent Rus within the walls of Constantinople, whether it was owing to the refusal of Emperor Michael V to make use of the Varangians, or whether, as one Byzantine writer suggests, it was simply because the opportunity presented itself against a weak emperor is not known for certain; but, according to the Greek historian Cedrenus, 15,000 Rus corpses littered the Bosporus. It took three years before amity was restored between Jaroslav and Constantinople. Other neighbours, for example Lithuanians and Poles, also felt the force of Russian belligerence and any Slav tribe that dared disturb Jaroslav's domestic economy was brutally punished. Judicious political manoeuvring, carefully constructed marriage ties and a grim aspect shown to weakness or any potential threat ensured that, by the time of Jaroslav's death in 1054, European Russia was a political and geographical fact that none could deny.

Jaroslav's Russia was a place that lent particular inspiration to Icelandic saga writers in the thirteenth and fourteenth centuries. Much is told of giants, trolls, dragons, beguiling witches and other exotic creatures enlivening the adventures of the Viking freebooters who searched along the river ways in the east. Yet, among the fictional embellishments, certain details of the fortunes of some of these saga heroes have a real historical basis. The *Saga of Yngvar the Widefarer* tells of the disinherited Swedish prince, Yngvar, who journeyed to the court of Jaroslav, said in this instance to be in Novgorod (Holmgard, as it is called in the saga), where he resolved to trace the source of a river leading to the east.[22] His search took him across the Caspian to the court of a king whose country was in the throes of a civil war. Yngvar won great wealth in assisting him, but at much cost to his army. On the homeward journey an epidemic entered Yngvar's camp and he himself succumbed to its ravages.

Yngvar is said to have been buried in Citopolis, a city ruled over by his paramour, a Russian queen named in the saga as Silkisif. Over thirty eleventh-century runic monuments in Sweden commemorate Yngvar's death as being in 1041 after a five-year campaign in Serkland, the land of the Saracens, so confirming some of the history that the saga author claims was transmitted to him in oral traditions. Apart from Jaroslav, none of the characters that Yngvar encountered on his travels can be historically attested. It is nevertheless clear that Yngvar's fatal voyage was the last Viking adventure in the Arab regions. What would appear to have motivated him was an attempt to re-establish the contact with Arab merchants that had declined toward the end of the tenth century as a result of the dearth of Arab silver. The saga of Yngvar's bootless search for the source of a great river can be read as a metaphor for the loss of what was once the greatest single source of revenue for the Vikings in the Viking Age.

Scandinavian warriors seeking fame and fortune in Russia, or Gardariki as it was commonly known in Scandinavia, most often did so as mercenaries. These Varangians were regarded as foreigners in eleventh-century Russia and enlisting their help could prove to be something of a mixed blessing. The *Saga of Eymund* reflects, in a politically realistic fashion, how Eymund and his Norwegian Varangians placed themselves in the service of Jaroslav in Novgorod during the period of the succession wars with his brothers.[23] Eymund proved to be a skilled general and a sound tactician and succeeded in overcoming the main threat to Jaroslav in the person of his brother, Burislaf. He finally engineered a peace with the third brother, Vartilaf, whose service the Varangians had entered after a falling out with Jaroslav. On the subsequent death of Vartilaf, Jaroslav became grand prince over all the Rus territories, except for Polotsk west of the Dnieper, which was granted to Eymund as his personal kingdom.

Although the names of Jaroslav's brothers in the saga do not correspond with those given in the *Chronicle*, the general account of Jaroslav's rise to prominence broadly parallels history. Yet, while the cool calculations and personal daring of Eymund constitutes the chief course of the action in the saga, it is Jaroslav's unwillingness to pay his Varangians according to their agreements that constitutes the underlying tension. In this respect, Jaroslav emerges as both short-sighted and mean. Interestingly, Jaroslav's faults are ascribed to his father Vladimir in the *Chronicle*, who was similarly slow in paying his Varangians, to the point where they too deserted him. The Varangians, then, may have had their uses in the Rus dynastic wars and among the Greeks against the enemies of Byzantium, but, in times of peace, the presence of thousands of warriors in the region all eager for profit must have proved to be either unnerving or a considerable drain on resources – or both. Jaroslav's supposed meanness in the *Saga of Eymund* was doubtless born out of economic and political realities, and no doubt Emperor Michael's decision to dispense with the Varangian Guard was one that had considerable implications for the stability of Jaroslav's realm.

It is perhaps a little ironic that the Varangians proved to be an embarrassment to eleventh-century Rus rulers, not only because it was they who had in the first place encouraged these adventurers from Scandinavia to profit in their causes but also because the old Viking spirit of the founders of the Rus kingdom lived on in this soldierly brotherhood. It is among the Varangians that we find one warrior who can rightly be called 'the Last of the Vikings': Harald Hardrada Sigurtharson. Several Icelandic sources record the adventures of Harald, perhaps the most notable being Snorri Sturluson's saga history.[24] As loyal half-brother to Olaf 'the Saint' Haraldsson, Harald was on the wrong side at the battle of Stiklestad in Norway in 1030, where Olaf was killed and his army routed. Harald, dejected and bereft, fled to Russia and placed his formidable energies at the service of Jaroslav, where he remained for four years. In all probability it was Harald's desire to win the hand of Jaroslav's daughter Elisleif that prompted him to seek his fortune in Constantinople. Harald served nine years in the Varangian Guard under three successive emperors, not including the tyrannical Michael V whom Harald was said to have helped depose, tearing out his eyes as a popular gesture.

Harald served in campaigns against Muslim forces in the Mediterranean and throughout the Middle East, where he is reported to have seized Jerusalem, against the Normans in Italy, and finally against the Bulgars. According to an anonymous Greek source, he was raised to the rank of *spatharocandidate*, that is to say the third level closest to the emperor,[25] and, according to all sources, his men revered him as a fearless and cunning field commander who led them to vast wealth. Much of Harald's personal fortune was said to have resulted from the death of three emperors during his time in the Varangian Guard, as at each death the Varangians were, by custom, allowed to help themselves to whatever they wanted from the emperor's palace, a practice known as *pólútasvarf* or 'palace plundering'. When he returned to Scandinavia, Harald's treasure bought him his kingdom and 'it seemed marvellous to all who saw it that so much gold should have been got together in one place in the North'.[26]

Harald was imprisoned in Constantinople in 1043, perhaps as a consequence of Jaroslav's rash and ill-fated sortie against the Greeks earlier in the same year. He soon managed to escape and, calling in on Jaroslav to claim Elisleif as his bride, he headed for Sweden to assume a share of the Danish-Norwegian kingdom ruled over by his nephew Magnus the Good. Never willing to let matters rest, in 1066 he set out to lay claim to the English throne and met his doom outside York at the hands of King Harold Godwinson. Three weeks later, when Harold Godwinson fell before the invading William of Normandy, Harald Hardrada's hard-won Byzantine fortune came as an unexpected bonus to the Conqueror.

The Varangian Guard continued to serve successive emperors in Constantinople into the next century, but their ranks gradually slipped into anonymity and their prowess was not long to remain pre-eminent, for disciplined cavalry as opposed to ferocious infantry were proving to be a more effective weapon of war. Such was not the Viking way and those who remained in the Varangian Guard did so alongside many other mercenaries enlisted from other parts of Europe. Despite this, the Vikings in the east became the subject of storytellers and the stuff of legend.

Surveying the history of Viking Age Russia, one cannot help but be impressed by the Rus conquest of the Slav territories. While Vikings in the west were no less formidable, they, generally speaking, had the advantage of a congenial climate and an opposition that was identifiable in its strength and its movements. Not so in the Slavic regions. Nomadic tribes, such as the Pechenegs, were unremittingly hostile and could easily exploit the vulnerability of the Rus as they plied their trade back and forth from their strongholds at Novgorod and Kiev. Disease, difficult terrain, risk of ambush and a climate that ranged from harsh winters to sweltering summers were all part of what the Rus had to contend with in order to achieve fame, fortune and a secure footing.

Compelling accounts of ordinary life among Rus settlers and voyagers have been left by Arab writers. Ibn Rusta, writing in the early tenth century, told of the scene at one Rus settlement, probably Novgorod. It is a far cry from the opulence of the Ryurik princes as described in the *Chronicle*:

> Russia is an island around which is a lake, and the island in which they dwell is a three days' journey through forests and swamps covered with trees and it is a damp morass such that when a man puts his foot on the ground it quakes owing to the moisture.

They have a king who is called Khaquan Rus, and they make raids against
Saqalaba [Slavs], sailing in ships in order to go out to them, and they take them
prisoner and carry them off to Khazar and Bulgar and trade with them there.

They have no cultivated lands; they eat only what they carry off from the land
of the Saqalaba.

When a child is born to any man among them, he takes a drawn sword to the
new-born child and places it between his hands and says to him: 'I shall bequeath
to you no wealth and you will have naught except what you can gain for yourself
by this sword of yours.'

They have no landed property nor villages … their only occupation is trading in
sables and grey squirrel and other furs … and they take as the price gold and silver
and secure it in their belts.[27]

Whilst Ibn Rusta is largely uncritical of the Rus, even seeming to appreciate
their dress sense, he also notes their nervousness of each other, apparent in the
fact that no man would go 'to satisfy a natural need' without a bodyguard for
fear of attack. A far less flattering image of the Rus is provided by Ibn Fadlan,
who deplored their unsanitary habits and their gross practice of copulating
with their slaves in public. More shocking still to Arab eyes were the barbaric
religious ceremonies in which slave girls were ritually sacrificed in order to
accompany their owners to the afterlife. To the great civilizations of the east,
the Rus first appeared as little more than wild men whose cultural values were
both bewildering and shocking.

Quarrelsome and crude in their habits and savage in their religious customs
the Rus may have been, but when it came to showing a united front, as Ibn Rusta
also noted, they were without peer. What bound them together was their desire
to expand their influence, to profit and to defend their gains by all available
means. In this no natural peril and no human opposition discouraged them, not
the Slavs, not even the great fleets and armies of the Greeks and the Muslims.
From the early ninth century, and through the tenth century, the Vikings in
the east moved relentlessly against their neighbours until, as if by osmosis, the
cultures that they sought to dominate and exploit absorbed them. In the end, it
was not as Vikings at all that they commanded their territory but as Christian
Slavs wedded to the same civilizing constraints that, in their ignorance and
greed, they had once sought to master.

# 9

# Atlantic Explorations and Settlements

The Scandinavian search for new land to conquer and colonize involved some of the most daring explorations in maritime history. Land that had only ever been heard of in legend was vigorously sought out as a reality and, in the process, land that no European had ever heard of or even imagined was discovered by luck and accident. Dissatisfaction with emerging power structures in Scandinavia, mainly in Norway, and desperation for good farming land on which settlers might prosper, remote from the interference of kings and petty tyrants, were clearly important factors in these expeditions across uncharted waters to unknown locations. But these things alone cannot fully account for the speculative voyages that, in stages, took Viking ships almost 2500 miles west from Norway to make the first landfall by Europeans on the North American continent. Nor does it explain the depth of feeling that motivated these perilous adventures. To understand this, it is necessary to try and apprehend the sheer will of the Vikings, their fearlessness, their determination to improve their and their descendants' lot, their sense that the world was there for them to encompass, and their belief that death in the pursuit of independence was not tragic but glorious. The terror of the Vikings befell those who were forced to resist their expansion, but in their single-mindedness was a kind of grandeur. Nowhere and at no time in the Viking Age was this more apparent than in the intrepid spirit that drove the Vikings to navigate the breadth of the Atlantic Ocean.

Early in the ninth century, in the same movement that brought Norwegian pirates via Shetland and the Orkneys to Ireland, an archipelago of islands 200 miles north west of Shetland drew their attention, not as raiders but as farmers. The twenty or so islands of the Faroe Isles, meaning 'sheep islands', span seventy miles from north to south with the largest island, Streymoy, covering over 200 square miles. What the Vikings saw was that those islands that were habitable offered not only good grazing but also no significant resistance to their occupation, as the only residents were Irish hermits pursuing the meditative life. These solitary souls had been living out the austere ideal of the *peregrinatio pro Christo* since at least the early eighth century (current archaeology indicates human habitation since the mid seventh century), and were hardly disposed toward a violent assertion of their rights of tenancy. Writing in 825, the Irish monk Dicuil described what would seem to be the landscape of the Faroes, their relative accessibility for monks sailing in their coracles from Ireland, and how, in his time, matters had changed for the worse.

> There is another set of islands, nearly all separated by narrow stretches of water; in these for nearly a hundred years hermits sailing from our country, Ireland, have lived. But now just as they were always deserted from the beginning of the world, so now because of the Northmen pirates they are emptied of anchorites, and filled with countless sheep and very many diverse kinds of sea-birds.[1]

Throughout the course of the ninth century, Norwegians continued to stream toward the Faroes. Stimulating immigration in the latter decades of the century was the rise to prominence of the unifier of Norway, Harald Finehair. This, however, cannot have been the only explanation for a surge in their settlement. Many who settled had no particular quarrel with Harald and had lived far from the reach of his authority. This is apparent from the early thirteenth-century *Saga of the Faroe Islanders*, which credits Grim Kamban as being the first settler in the latter half of the ninth century. While the saga's late dating of the settlement must be wrong, the prominence of Grim Kamban among later settlers need not be disputed, but his Norse forename and Gaelic surname indicate that he originated from the Viking colonies in Ireland or the Scottish isles. More than likely, the lush green pastures of the Faroe Isles were, in themselves, sufficient to entice settlers.

The Faroese modelled their social and legal structures on traditional Norwegian practice. Aristocratic leaders apportioned the land among their families and their followers, and an annual assembly, the *Thing*, was established to preside over legal disputes at Tinganes (now the capital Torshaven). The *Saga of the Faroe Islanders* is partly concerned with the operation of Faroese law in respect of the rivalries over land that sprang up between the settlers. Yet, as the saga dramatically records, the independence of the Faroese was compromised by their continuing commercial attachment to Norway and, despite the resistance of certain farmers to the Norwegian king, Olaf Tryggvason, and his forceful Christian missions, the Faroese were obliged to accept Christianity and concede authority to Norway by the end of the tenth century. By the late twelfth century the Faroes were fully subject to Norway as a 'tax-land'.

The settlement of the Faroe Isles was, in certain respects, the natural outcome of early Viking efforts to establish a sea kingdom around northern Britain and Ireland. The settlement of Iceland was a separate matter, as it had nothing to do with piracy and plunder and was purely and entirely a search for land. In the case of the settlement of the Faroe Isles, only a few sketches of the life and times of the settlers remain, but in the case of the settlement of Iceland a detailed and colourful picture survives to reveal how the settlers fashioned their new world. While the historical forces and the general pattern of events were largely the same for both settlements, the numerous Icelandic histories and sagas amplify the drama of the Icelandic settlement in such a way as to confer upon it an entirely unique character. The sagas are the enduring legacy of what was surely a high point of civilization amid the general chaos of Viking Age violence.

Like the Faroes, Iceland was uninhabited apart from a scattering of Irish monks, whose tenancy can still be discerned in certain place-names given by Scandinavian settlers, such as Papey and Papos in the east, signifying places once inhabited by 'the fathers' or *papar*. Icelandic saga tradition has it that the Norwegians of the western fjords undertook the 600-mile voyage to the west as a direct result of their defeat by Harald Finehair at the battle of Hafrsfjord in the latter half of the 880s. The reason given in Snorri Sturluson's saga composition, *Egils Saga*, for the opposition of many Norwegians to Harald's tyranny was his taxation policy and, in particular, his ruthless claims over lands, known as the *oðals*, which had traditionally been passed on through rights of inheritance.[2] As with the Faroes, this may have accounted for the departure of many, but settlement on Iceland was already well underway before Harald's autocracy, and the initial impulse to put to sea in search of a new home had had its origin some decades earlier.

The existence of an island named Thule, somewhere to the north of Britain, had been remarked upon as early as the fourth century BC by the Greek geographer Pytheus. The Roman geographer Polybius also assumed its existence in the first century BC, and in AD 18 the Roman cartographer Strabo had drawn Thule on his world map with relative accuracy in respect of the actual location of Iceland in relation to Britain, even though Strabo had no idea of the existence of the greater Scandinavian landmass. By the early eighth century, the intuitions of classical writers had clearly become part of a common stock of lore regarding the far north, and the Northumbrian monk and historian, the Venerable Bede, rehearsed speculations about Thule without qualification, stating simply that it was some six days' sailing from Britain. Only in the early ninth century did the guesswork begin to take on the character of fact. Dicuil also knew of classical efforts to identify Thule but felt sure that certain eyewitness accounts, gleaned from clerics of his acquaintance in the last decade of the eighth century, were conclusive. Thule, for Dicuil, was the self-same place where around the summer solstice, by day or by night 'a man could do whatever he wished as though the sun were there, even remove lice from his shirt'.[3]

Firm evidence for the existence of Iceland did not arrive in Norway until after the mid ninth century. The early twelfth-century Icelandic *Book of Settlements* tells of three separate voyages before exploration turned into permanent settlement. In the first, a sea captain known as Naddod the Viking was driven off course during a storm while heading for the Faroe Isles and made landfall in the east of 'a big country'. Having surveyed the land from a mountain top, Naddod judged it to be uninhabited and was later able to give good report of a discovery he called 'Snowland'. In the second, a deliberate voyage of discovery was prompted by Naddod's accounts of 'Snowland'. Urged on by it, and by his mother and a seeress, Gardar Svarvarsson set out and eventually made landfall on the island's eastern shores. Gardar circumnavigated the entire island and, like Naddod, was favourably impressed, so much so that he renamed it, in proprietary fashion, 'Gardarsholm'.

The third voyage was undertaken by Floki Vilgertharson, known also as Raven Floki, who, inspired by Gardar's reports, not only made landfall but also established himself in the west, intent on staying for a while. Unfortunately, Floki was a better sailor than settler. All summer he and his men went fishing but, in their enthusiasm for the bounty yielded by the large rivers, neglected to make hay for the livestock. As a result, when winter arrived all the animals died and in the spring a disgruntled Floki returned to Norway. 'When asked about the place,' says the *Book of Settlements*, 'he gave it a bad name.' The bad name he gave it was 'Iceland'. This poor advertisement was, however, countered by one of Floki's companions, a certain Thorolf, who 'swore that butter dripped from every blade of grass in that land they had found', so winning himself the nickname Thorolf Butter.[4]

Iceland lies in the Gulf Stream just south of the Arctic Circle. It is an oval landmass of approximately 300 miles from east to west and over 200 miles from north to south. The interior of the island is barren and uninhabitable, being comprised of mountain ranges and glaciers, and much land is covered by vast lava fields and deposits of ash caused by the numerous active volcanoes. Only round the coastal areas, and areas which are less than 600 feet above sea level,

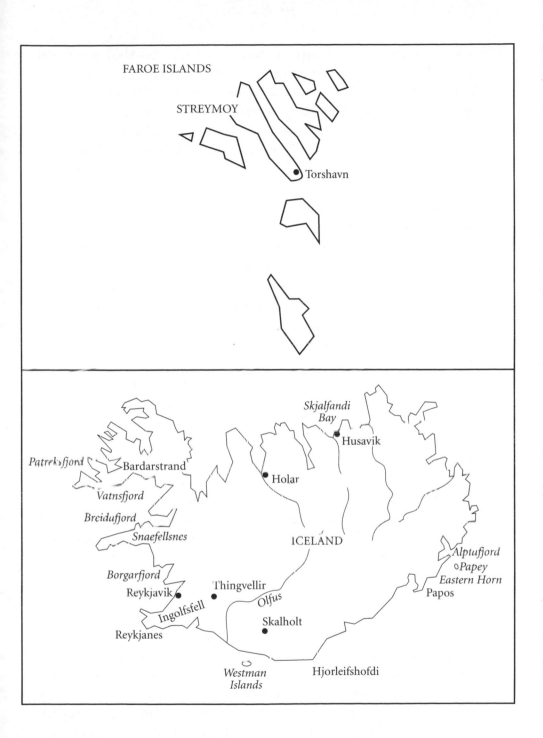

Iceland and the Faroe Islands in the Viking age

can farming economies be supported. Although such land can be found round most of the island, the most extensive fertile areas are to the west, particularly along the peninsula south of Breidafjord and surrounding the wide mouth of Borgafjord. This land yields readily to agriculture and the cultivation of, for example, barley from which beer can be brewed. As Floki discovered, the rivers teem with fish, especially salmon. There is also plentiful bird life and the coastal waters readily support a fishing economy. The reports of the early voyagers, good and bad, would have had sufficient information in them to cause a stir of excitement in Norway, especially among those whose prospects were limited by powerful neighbours or overbearing kings.

The first permanent settler of Iceland is reported to have been Ingolf Arnason. At some point in the late 860s, Ingolf and his foster-brother Hjorleif had made a reconnaissance trip to Iceland and, after one winter on the Eastern Horn, they were satisfied that they could make their way in the country, perhaps further to the south. Consequently, they returned to Norway and set about equipping themselves for a one-way journey of settlement. Both men set sail the following spring with women and livestock aboard their respective ships. Both also had slaves, ten of whom Hjorleif had recently captured on a Viking raid in Ireland. Once they sighted land they split up and, in a ritual intended to secure the blessing of the gods, Ingolf cast his high seat pillars overboard. Wherever they came to land, Ingolf would settle. Thus guided for the time being, he made his first home in the south east.

Hjorleif sailed west along the south coast and made his home approximately 80 miles from Ingolf. Having only one ox, he put his Irish slaves to work ploughing the land. The work was not to their liking and they rebelled, killed their demanding owner and his companions, abducting the women and carrying off the valuables. When Ingolf heard the news, he set out with the intention of bringing the culprits to book. He eventually came across the Irishmen eating a meal on the offshore island of Eid, west of Hjorleif's settlement. They panicked and Ingolf took no time in exacting absolute vengeance just as a foster-brother should. Yet Hjorleif had only himself to blame, thought Ingolf, for he had persistently refused to do sacrifice to the gods. The following summer Ingolf abandoned his settlement in the east and, with his followers and the wives of the men murdered by Hjorleif's slaves, put to sea to explore what other possibilities the island might have to the west. As he rounded the island's south-western peninsula, he once again cast his high seat pillars into the sea. This time they came to rest in a fine natural harbour where, given the name he conferred upon it, he could probably see volcanic activity in the distance. Ingolf called his new home Reykjavik, 'Smokey Bay'. The year was 873.

By 930, less than sixty years after Ingolf's final settlement, all the decent farming land in Iceland had been claimed. The *Book of Settlements* lists some 430 prominent individuals and their families, amounting to 3500 personal names as well the names of almost 1500 farms. Taking into account followers and slaves, we can estimate that the population of Iceland was in the region of twenty to thirty thousand by the middle of the tenth century. Mostly they came from Norway but approximately 7 per cent of the named settlers were of Celtic or Celtic–Norse extraction, and among those not named – slaves, for example – the percentage was almost certainly higher. All of these settlers took land around Iceland's verdant fjords and coastal areas, chiefly in the west, although vigorous settlement also took place in the east, north of the Eastern Horn, up in the far north beside the rivers flowing down from the mountainous interior, and around the fringes of the chilly fjords of the north west. Back in Norway, Harald Finehair was so disturbed by the depopulation of his western fjords that he required every man who wished to go to Iceland to pay him an emigration tax. This did nothing to stem the flow of those who saw great prospects for themselves in a new land.

Given this clamour for a fresh start outside Norway, squabbles over land claims soon forced the need for legal judgements and, where necessary, redress. In the second decade of the tenth century, a leading man in the community, Ulfljot, was sent to Norway to research the law and adapt it according to the needs of the settlers. In 930, the laws of the Icelanders were proclaimed from the Law Rock (*Lögberg*) at the Icelandic parliament, the *Althing*, in the rugged surrounds of the Vale of the Thing, about thirty miles north east of Reykjavik. Presiding over the parliament were thirty-six priest-chieftains (pl. *goðar*; sing. *goði*), who alone had voting rights and who appointed the chief magistrate, the Law Speaker (*Lögsögumaðr*), from among themselves. Thirty-five years later, this number was increased to thirty-nine chieftains, and assemblies were established in the four main regional districts, north, south, east and west, although the *Althing*, where an additional nine chieftains were appointed to the judiciary, remained as the court of referral when matters proved too intractable in the regions. Much of the operation of early Icelandic law can be gleaned from the sagas, and the twelfth-century lawbook, known obscurely as Grey Goose (*Grágás*), is believed to contain elements of the basic legal provision from the tenth century.

The oligarcho-republic that constituted the Icelandic commonwealth was to last for over three hundred years, despite almost constant pressure from Norway to bow its authority and the disapproval of the church, which regarded a country without a king as both wayward and scandalous. Concessions had to be made along the way, for, like the Faroese, good relations with Norway were crucial for both exports and imports, especially the importation of timber which was soon in short supply among the settlers. In the late 990s, when Olaf Tryggvason realized that being a Christian king ruling over a Christian realm was both politically and economically shrewd, Iceland was put under severe pressure to convert. Icelanders in Norway were held hostage and when Olaf's missionary to Iceland, the homicidal Thangbrand, was forced to abandon his murderous evangelizing and return to Olaf declaring that no one could convert such a people, Olaf was barely dissuaded from massacring all Icelanders on Norwegian soil. Such pressures were bound to prevail, besides which Icelanders were moving dangerously close to a civil war between Christian converts and dyed-in-the-wool pagans. In or around the year 1000, Iceland's Law Speaker saw the good sense of religious conformity within the country, consistent with the demands of King Olaf. For a while, pagans were allowed to carry on their practices in private, although a ban on the exposure of weak or unwanted infants was immediately enforced, as was a taboo concerning the eating of horse flesh. A complete ban on paganism came into force within fifty years.

The conversion of Iceland did not have an immediate effect on its social structure, but there were some obvious advantages in adopting Christian culture, not least of which was Latin literacy. The fluidity of the alphabet, far outweighing the possibilities inherent in traditional runic script, rapidly caught on among the Icelanders. By the early twelfth century, Ari 'the Wise' Thorgilsson was able to present his countrymen with a brief history of the settlement in their own tongue which he called the *Book of the Icelanders* (*Íslendingabók*). Not long after this, the comprehensive land registry known as the *Book of Settlements* (*Landnámabók*) supplied both a history of land ownership and a wide store of tales about the early settlers. By the middle of the twelfth century, Icelanders had analysed the grammar of Old Norse and established the principles of its orthography, an undertaking that was unique in the Scandinavian middle ages.

Church learning was central in such endeavours, and the monastic centres established at Skalholt (1056) and Holar (1106) did much to help fashion the literary outpourings for which medieval Iceland has become rightly famous. Hagiographies celebrating the deeds and holiness of Iceland's bishops, the

*Bishops Sagas* (*Biskupasögur*), were at first written in Latin but, when the church in Rome declined to accept Icelandic saints into the canon, the monks abandoned Latin in favour of Old Norse. The combination of history writing and hagiography had an influence on more expansive historiographies known as the *Kings Sagas* (*Konungasögur*), which, like the *Bishops Sagas*, were first written in Latin but later presented in the vernacular. Besides this, a great project of preservation was very soon underway which involved the gathering together of the poetic myths and legends of Norse paganism, the so-named *eddas*. Somewhat ironically, a literary culture that simply could not have developed without the conversion to Christianity devoted much of its energy to ensuring cultural continuity with the pre-Christian era.

While Christian culture brought clear benefits, the longer-term consequences of conversion for domestic politics were not so unambiguously advantageous. The reason for this appears to have been in the abolition of the priestly role of the chieftains and the ascendancy, both religious and economic, of the church. Gradually, fissures were exposed in the post-conversion commonwealth. The chieftains, reconstituted as guardians of the church and collectors of its taxes, who steadily accumulated vast wealth through corruption and intimidation, soon fell into violent competition with each other. As time went on, power accrued to fewer and fewer, and, by the mid thirteenth century, a civil war for domination of the country was in full swing amongst a handful of ambitious families. King Hakon Hakonarson of Norway looked on, anticipating intervention and doing what he could to promote the chaos. In 1262–4, the Icelandic commonwealth was abandoned in favour of rule from Norway and one of the most remarkable political and social structures in European history came to an end.

There was something within the character of the Icelanders that led them to regard their remote commonwealth and their membership of it as a founding of something more than just a fine place to live and farm and, with luck, prosper. Their desire for self-government as a *sjálfstætt fólk*, an 'independent people', was not only a matter of political will but also a philosophy underwritten by a profound examination of the nature and meaning of freedom and responsibility. The mode of this examination took place within the sagas. During the thirteenth and early fourteenth century the literary talents of the Icelanders came to full flower in the writing of what are generally known as the Icelandic Family Sagas (*Íslendingasögur*). This group of approximately forty sagas, some of which are the length of a modern novel, recall events of the tenth and early eleventh centuries when the law was established and Christianity was adopted. Critics often refer to this period of the founding of the commonwealth as the 'Golden Age', and the Family Sagas are sometimes regarded as a body of literature whose purpose was to help the audience and readership escape the troubles of their own day. Although medieval Icelanders may have looked back on their ancestors' days with a degree of nostalgia, it is a trivialization of the profundity of both the themes and subjects of the Family Sagas to label them escapist.

The Family Sagas were presented by their authors as history. They were almost certainly written as such and were based on oral traditions, early written histories and historical references preserved in the elaborate verse art of skaldic poetry. Nevertheless, they are not 'dry' histories and the authors deliberately crafted their tales about feuding farmers, outlaws and family honour into a compelling literary form. Powerful human dramas are delineated with heroes who have convincing psychologies and who are beset by moral dilemmas that have life and death consequences. Sagas such as those concerning the cowardly burning of the pacifist Njal and his family in their homestead, the reformation of the practices, if not character, of the chieftain Hrafnkel the Priest of Frey, the violent jealousies and sexual intrigues that entangled the lives of the homesteaders of Laxardal, the adventures of the great Viking warrior with a poet's soul, Egil Skallagrimsson, and the vengeance and heroic last stand of the principled outlaw Gisli Sursson, are unfolded in realist narratives that are pithy, ironic, sometimes comic, and invariably tinged with both glory and regret. Taken together, the Family Sagas are a national epic and a meditation on what has persuasively been called loss, whether the loss of a limb, a livelihood, a life, or a national identity.[5] Exactly what social or genetic chemistry occurs among a people to give rise to a period in which their uniqueness can be expressed *par excellence* probably defies analysis, but it occurred in medieval Iceland and it placed their saga literature in the top rank of world literature.

Not all of those who quit Norway for Iceland had the good fortune to do so when desirable land was still there for the taking. One such was Thorvald Asvaldsson, father of Eirik the Red, whose life and times were later described in the Icelandic saga named after him. Thorvald's decision to leave Norway for Iceland was not entirely based on a spirit of adventure, for he had been declared an outlaw in Norway for what the saga darkly refers to as 'slayings'.[6] Eirik the Red was still a teenager in the late 970s when his father took him from the fine pastures of the Stavanger district of Norway to the icy windswept fjords surrounding Drangar

in the far north west of Iceland. Thorvald did not long survive the harsh life
they had come to and, soon after his death, Eirik married and moved south to
take land in the Haukadal district, close by where his father-in-law had a farm.
But Eirik had his father's temperament. When a neighbour killed some of his
slaves, after they had brought down a landslide on his property, Eirik retaliated
by killing two men and, as a result, was forced out of Haukadal by the outraged
residents. Eirik now headed for the tiny islands at the mouth of Breidafjord and
in these cramped circumstances soon found himself at loggerheads with his new
neighbours. More killings ensued and this time Eirik was declared an outlaw
and, as a consequence, was forced to leave Iceland for three years. His response
was to set sail for a land in the far west first sighted by a certain Gunnbjorn some
sixty years earlier but never yet explored.[7] So it happened that, in or around the
year 983, Eirik the Red became the first recorded European to set foot on the
vast glacial island of Greenland.

What Eirik and his companions first saw after their four-day voyage cannot
have been encouraging, as forbidding cliffs of ice rising as much as 5000 feet out
of the sea are the monotonous characteristic of Greenland's eastern coastline.
Eirik pressed on and the journey south along the cliff-line led him round
Cape Farewell, Greenland's southern tip, after which he must have felt that all
his hopes were fulfilled, for here there was both a good harbour and ice-free
pasture. Bestowing his name as he went, Eirik sailed into Eiriksfjord and hove to
on the island he named Eiriksey at the mouth of the fjord. During the next three
years, he built lodgings at Eiriksholm and ventured almost 150 miles inland to
the limits of the green strip in the west. He discovered no sign of current human
habitation and sufficient good land to accommodate any who might wish to
follow him. In 986, he returned to Iceland to advertise his discovery, to which,
in order to encourage his audience, he gave it its somewhat hyperbolic name of
Greenland. Those, like him, who had been reduced to eking out a living in the
shadow of their wealthier neighbours, were eager to take their chances. Recent
famine in Iceland provided an additional incentive.

Of the twenty-five heavily laden transport ships of the *knörr* design that
are said to have accompanied Eirik on his return, only fourteen managed to
complete the journey: some foundered, some turned back. Perhaps as many
as five hundred settlers made this crossing successfully and, once there, they
quickly established two settlements on Greenland's western coast: one at the
head of Eiriksfjord, known, rather confusingly, as the Eastern Settlement (in
the area surrounding Qaqortoq); and one, somewhat smaller, 300 miles to

the north known as the Western Settlement (in the area surrounding Nuuk). A third minor settlement developed, later known as the Middle Settlement, approximately half way between the two main settlements. As befitted a founder and self-appointed Law Speaker, Eirik took the best land and built the grandest farm, which he called Brattahlid, in the northern part of the Eastern Settlement. Sources recount that the Eastern Settlement grew to support just over two hundred farms, while the Western Settlement supported just less than a hundred. This would indicate a colony of four to five thousand people at the height of the settlement.

There is no doubting the historicity of Eirik the Red's settlement of Greenland. Not only was it recorded in the *Book of the Icelanders*, the *Book of Settlement*, *The Saga of the Greenlanders* and *Eirik the Red's Saga*, but archaeological finds have provided an almost exact corroboration of the founding of the settlements as described in the literary sources. Eirik's Brattahlid estate has been identified and excavations have revealed the remains of its main hall measuring 15 m (50 ft) by 4.5 m (15 ft). A number of Viking Age artefacts and items of domestic equipment have been found both here and throughout the settlement sites. It is clear that the settlers not only cultivated the land but also harvested the seas and the natural fauna. Their need for metal, timber and grain was met by their exports of sub-arctic animal furs, for example reindeer and bear, and their domestic economy was supported by catches of whale, seal and a variety of fish. In time, the settlers identified an area in the far north between Disco Island and Kingigtorssuaq, which they called the *Norðsetr*, where polar bears could be hunted for their fur or captured alive and sold at great price to the royal courts of Scandinavia. Similarly, ivory from narwhals and walruses brought a handsome return, as did falcons. This hunting economy ensured a plentiful supply of luxury goods, although voyages to the *Norðsetr* were hazardous and often involved great hardship: many simply did not return. The presence of the Greenlandic Norsemen at extreme northern latitudes has been confirmed by the discovery of an early fourteenth-century runic inscription at latitude 73°, hundreds of miles inside the Arctic Circle, and, even further north in Melville Bay, of cairns believed to be of Norse origin dating from the thirteenth century.

Archaeological evidence also testifies to the conversion of the Greenlanders, which, as in Iceland, took place around the year 1000. A small church found on Eirik's Brattahlid estate is probably the one referred to in his saga as having been built at the insistence of his wife, Thjodhild. Eirik, however, was said to have

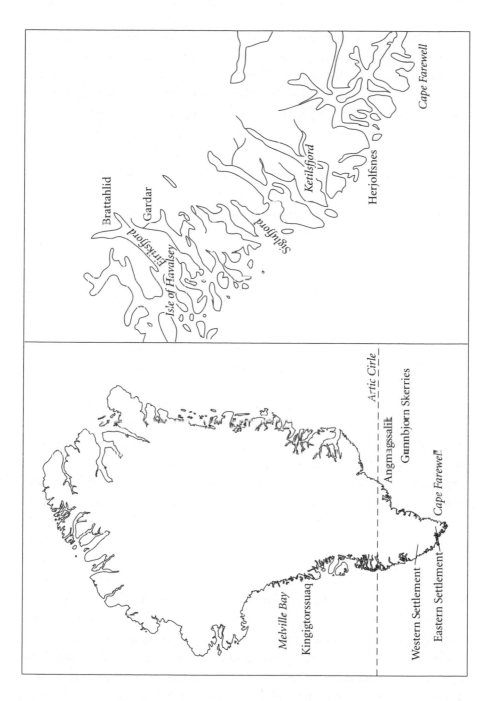

Viking and Greenland and the Eastern Settlement

held no brief for the new faith and to have refused to convert. This obstinacy cost Eirik his place in the marital bed, thus magnifying his resentment of what he regarded as an intrusion into his republic. It is unlikely that Eirik resisted Christianity for long, for, if *Eirik the Red's Saga* is to be believed, pressure to convert came not only from his wife but also from his son, Leif, who had been commissioned by King Olaf Tryggvason to convert all the Greenlanders. It is apparent from the numerous grave finds beside Thjodhild's church that Christianity was rapidly established in the country. During the twelfth century, Gardar in the Eastern Settlement provided the site for the establishment of an episcopal see with a fine cathedral, and in due course the settlement went on to accommodate an Augustinian monastery, a Benedictine convent and as many as twelve parish churches, with a further four in the Western Settlement. Yet, at about the time that Greenland appeared to have been fully incorporated into the habits and structures of Christian Europe, matters began to take a drastic turn for the worse.

The settlement of Greenland took place at the outset of a climatic phenomenon that affected western and central Europe known as the Medieval Warm Period or the Climatic Optimum. During the first two hundred years of the settlement, the mean temperature of the seas around Greenland rose by between 2° C and 4° C. The effect of this was that the ice-floes stayed north of latitude 70°, well above the Western Settlement. After about 1200, a slow cooling began that would last for over two hundred years, by the end of which time sea temperatures were probably as much as 7° C below that which they had been when Eirik the Red first entered Eiriksfjord. The consequences for the settlements in Greenland were disastrous. Numerous accounts by mariners from the thirteenth century onwards record the treacherous ice-floes that eventually drifted down almost the entire length of the country. The winters grew longer and more brutal with the inevitable detrimental effects on livestock, and fewer and fewer ships arrived from Norway, the monopolizing parent country since 1261. By the end of the fourteenth century only the Eastern Settlement was sustainable. Adding to the troubles of the Greenlandic Norse, from the early thirteenth century onward was the increasing presence of another set of colonizers, the Eskimos.[8]

The so-named Thule Eskimos had probably arrived in Greenland about the same time as Eirik the Red. They had migrated east from Alaska, partly as a consequence of the same climate shift that the first Norse settlers had enjoyed. The Eskimos were, however, exceptionally well adapted to arctic climates and until around 1200 they had remained in the northern areas of Greenland, far above the settlements. When the period of cooling began they began to move southward following the creatures of sea and land on which their existence depended. Norse contact with the Eskimos was not peaceful. The settlers referred to them by the derogatory name *skræling*, which simultaneously implies 'ugly, stunted and barbaric', as they did to all the non-European peoples they encountered on their westward voyages. At first, trade opportunities presented themselves with these superlative hunters, but this very soon gave way to violent competition. It was ultimately a battle of wills that the Norsemen could not win. The *Norðsetr*, apart from being increasingly difficult to access from the sea due to drift ice, was soon the domain of the Eskimos and by the mid fifteenth century Eskimos had occupied the Western Settlement. There is even a suggestion in Bishop Gisli Oddason's annal for 1342 that the Norsemen had so completely abandoned the struggle that they had gone native:

> The inhabitants of Greenland of their own will abandoned the true faith and the Christian religion, having already forsaken all good ways and true virtues, and joined themselves with the people of America [the Eskimos].[9]

Much that is reported in Scandinavian sources suggests that the Eskimos were the aggressors against a peaceful Christian community, but Eskimo 'histories' that were set down from oral traditions in the nineteenth century paint a rather different picture. Dealings with the *Kavdlunait*, as the Eskimos called the Norse settlers, are recorded in such tales as *Ungortok, the Chief of the Kakortok* and *Encounter of Kaladit with the Ancient Kavdlunait on the Ice*. In these tales the Norsemen are both vicious and stupid. Eskimo women are abducted and abused, families are slaughtered in their dwellings, and gangs of Norsemen pursue Eskimo hunters to their death; but, in every case, it is the Eskimo who triumphs, not through any moral superiority but through his perfect adaptation to the environment. So it is told that when the Norsemen were leading away captive Eskimo women, the Eskimo patriarch lured them back onto the frozen river at which point they 'lost their footing [and] fell on their backs, others sideways and some went tottering about',[10] so allowing the sure-footed Eskimo to spear them one after another and rescue what remained of his family.

These tales perhaps provide the better information for what took place in the final years of the Greenland settlements. It was not the Eskimos that drove the settlers to abandon their homes or suffer a lingering death but their own failure to adapt to the changing climate. The settlers struggled to maintain a farming economy when all the environmental evidence suggested the futility of this effort. They were slow to change their diets from meat to fish, they persisted in wearing woollen clothing of the European style and, unlike the Eskimos, they did not exploit the full nutritional value of their sea catches; in short, they were wasteful. Rather than persecute the Eskimos, they needed to learn from them. As it was, the remaining inhabitants of the Eastern Settlement became increasingly isolated and fewer in number. Eskimos occupied the land in all directions and the sea groaned with calving icebergs. After 1410, when a handful of Icelanders managed to sail away after being stranded for four years in the Eastern Settlement, contact with the outside world all but ceased. Toward the end of the century, Pope Alexander VI wondered what might be done about this most remote outpost of Christianity:

> Since, as we have been informed, the church at Gardar is situated at the world's end in the country of Greenland, where the inhabitants for lack of bread, wine and oil are accustomed to feed on dried fish and milk, by reason of which there are very infrequent sailings which were wont to be made to the aforesaid country due to the severe freezing of the seas, no ship is believed to have put to land there for eighty years ... [and] no bishop or priest whatsoever has in personal residence been in charge of that church.[11]

The pope need not have worried, for by this time there was scarcely anyone left to attend the church. In 1540 an Icelandic ship sailing out of Hamburg was forced ashore near the Eastern Settlement. The captain later reported the discovery of a solitary body sprawled across the beach, frozen and long dead. His carcass was clothed partly in homespun wool and partly in seal skins, and the knife in his belt was almost worn away through constant sharpening. What befell his companions is unknown: maybe they made a desperate attempt to escape and foundered; maybe they simply died out, as the generations passed. Judged from the evidence of grave finds, life for the majority had been nasty, brutish and short.

Back in the year 1000, in the prime of the Greenland settlement, it must have appeared as though nothing could go wrong. The pasture was rich, the wildlife was abundant, the climate was much like that of Norway, the seaways were free of obstacle and Greenlandic society was self-governing. It was in this heady world of secure and free living that the young men of the settlements began to wonder what might lie beyond the horizons even further west. It is their adventures that occupy the main part of the narratives of the thirteenth-century Icelandic compositions *Eirik the Red's Saga* and *The Saga of the Greenlanders*. These sagas, known collectively as the *Vinland Sagas*, are obviously related but, in places, present conflicting accounts of the actions of those involved and of the order and constituency of the westward journeys of the Greenlanders. For example, in the latter of the two compositions, *Eirik the Red's Saga*, it was the setting forth of the courage of Eirik's descendants and of the most intrepid of the explorers, the Icelander Thorfinn Karlsefni, that appears to be of foremost concern to the author, while the author of *The Saga of the Greenlanders* was less tendentious in respect of the personalities involved and more concerned with mapping the voyages. That said, these sagas have more similarities in their respective accounts than they have differences, and this would seem to indicate a common basis in oral traditions, perhaps dating back to times contemporary with the events recorded. Setting the two sagas together, where we do find significant differences between them, the greater ring of authenticity is to be found in the raw documentary style of *The Saga of the Greenlanders*, rather than among the sophisticated literary techniques of *Eirik the Red's Saga*. Taking into account, where possible, archaeological evidence, it is therefore possible to provide a reasonably credible history of the European discovery of North America, despite our current inability to be wholly precise about certain locations.

The first person to sight land on the western limits of the Atlantic was Bjarni Herjolfsson, an Icelander who was intent on making the crossing to Greenland to which his father had recently emigrated. This must have occurred not long after Eirik the Red had taken his party of settlers from Iceland to Greenland. But wind and fog beset Bjarni's journey and he drifted far off course into the western Atlantic. Bjarni rightly doubted whether the hilly and forested land that eventually came into view was Greenland and he headed north across open seas for two days until he sighted a flat and wooded land. Despite the criticism of his crew, Bjarni obstinately refused their requests to put ashore for provisions and doggedly pressed on farther northward for three days until he sighted a third land of high mountains capped by a glacier. Following the shoreline still further, he guessed that he was tracing the coast of an island, at which point he declared that the country could offer 'nothing of use' and turned eastward into open seas.[12] Four days later he arrived at his intended destination in Greenland's Eastern Settlement, a crossing that must have involved little more than 200 miles of open sea without site of land. In all likelihood, what Bjarni had actually seen were the coasts of Newfoundland, Labrador and Baffin Island. Later, when he reported his strange sightings to Eirik the Red and company at

Brattahlid, 'many people thought him short on curiosity'.[13] Bjarni's tantalizing
story of unexplored land would have become part of the lore of travellers'
tales in Greenland, and as time went by Eirik's first born son, Leif, formed the
opinion that he had the curiosity that Bjarni lacked.

In or around the year 1000, Leif purchased Bjarni's ship and set about badger-
ing the ageing Eirik to join him and undertake one more journey to unknown
lands. Eirik was not keen but nor was he about to admit that age had the better
of him. So, having given in to pressure from Leif, he set out from Brattahlid
to take ship, whereupon he fell heavily from his horse injuring his foot. Eirik
returned home declaring 'I am not intended to find any other land than this
one where we now live'.[14] Leif and his thirty-five companions would have to do
without the luck and pluck of Greenland's founding father.

Leif's crossing followed Bjarni's return journey in reverse and he soon
arrived at the mountainous glacier-capped land that Bjarni had sighted last
on his voyage northward up the coast of North America. Leif, unlike Bjarni,
was not going to be vilified for any lack of curiosity and he immediately put
ashore. He named the place 'Helluland' (Stone-Slab Land) but, having made
his point, did not tarry long. The flat and forested land he encountered next he
named 'Markland' (Forest Land), and here too he briefly set foot. Leif's two-day
journey south from Markland brought him in sight of the northern coast of
Newfoundland. Heading towards it, he came across a small island, possibly Bear
Island, possibly Belle Isle, and went ashore. Here he and his men found the grass
soaked in dew and 'thought that they had never tasted anything as sweet'.[15]

The next leg of Leif's journey took him south down the Straits of Belle Isle
into the Gulf of St Lawrence, beyond Bjarni Herjolfsson's most southern sight-
ing. So much is clear. Yet where exactly Leif arrived after this is uncertain and
the saga's description of the topography he encountered has attracted much
speculation and argument.

> [They] sailed into the sound which lay between the island and headland that
> stretched northwards from the land. They rounded the headland and steered
> westward. Here there were extensive shallows at low tide and their ship was soon
> stranded, and the sea looked far away to those aboard ship.
>
> Their curiosity to see the land was so great that they could not be bothered to
> wait for the tide to come in and float their stranded ship, and they ran aground
> where a river flowed into the sea from a lake.[16]

Leif was so taken with this place that he decided to overwinter and he promptly ordered his men to set about building what the saga describes as 'large houses'. *The Saga of the Greenlanders* is quite specific about what excited the explorers and, again, it has teased speculation about exactly where Leif built his camp.

> There was no lack of salmon both in the lake and in the river, and this salmon was larger than they had ever seen before.
>
> It seemed to them the land was so good that livestock would need no fodder during the winter. The temperature never dropped below freezing, and the grass only withered very slightly. The days and nights were much more equal in length than in Greenland or Iceland. In the depth of winter the sun was aloft by mid-morning and still visible at mid-afternoon.[17]

Once comfortably accommodated, Leif divided his men and began a systematic exploration. This led to their most remarkable discovery yet, and one that presents us with perhaps the greatest puzzle of all in our attempts precisely to identify Leif's final destination.

Among Leif's companions was a man named Tyrkir, a German referred to as 'a southerner', whom Leif addressed by the title 'foster father'. Despite Leif's orders that no one should let themselves be separated from the reconnaissance parties, one evening Tyrkir was found to be missing, much to Leif's annoyance and distress. When Tyrkir at last appeared, he was clearly deeply agitated and for a long time he spoke only in German. Once he had calmed down, he managed to communicate that the source of his excitement was his discovery of grapevines and grapes. Leif's mercantile instincts were aroused.

> 'Are you sure of this foster father?' Leif said.
>
> 'I'm absolutely sure,' he replied, 'because where I was born there was no lack of grapevines and grapes.'[18]

Leif now assigned his men to cutting down and collecting this unexpected treasure and, in the spring, he set sail for Greenland towing a boatload of vines behind his ship. He 'named the land for its natural features and called it "Vinland" (Wineland)'.[19]

So where was Vinland? The most important information in the saga is that it was at a latitude south enough for vines to grow wild and north enough for salmon to be fished. Judged according to our modern climate, this would place Vinland somewhere between latitudes 41° and 42°; that is to say, between New York and Boston. This, of course, is not an accurate calculation of how things might have been a thousand years ago, and Vinland could well have been further north in Maine or even New Brunswick. Some linguists have even suggested that the saga author misunderstood his sources or that manuscript copyists misunderstood the saga author, and that, as a consequence, the problem of the vines might, so to speak, be a red herring. According to this argument, Leif's 'grapes' could just as well have been the berries of an indigenous tree and the vines, in reality, timber. If this was the case, then the saga author or his copyists were not the first to draw the wrong conclusions, for in 1075 the conscientious Adam of Bremen reported information that he had gleaned from King Svein Estrithson of Denmark some fifteen years earlier about the wild grapes of Vinland and the 'fine wine' they produced.[20] As Svein's birth was contemporary with the grape trade that is said to have developed after Leif's first visit, then we have an account that is both near contemporary and, one assumes, discerning enough to know the difference between fermented tree berries and 'fine wine'.

Strenuous efforts to identify Vinland have not been helped by forgeries, allegations of forgery and the romantic enthusiasm of amateurs. The elaborately carved Kensington Rune Stone and the allegedly medieval Vinland Map are among the most famous attempts to validate Norse penetration onto the continent and the location of Vinland. While the former is wholly discredited, the authenticity or otherwise of the latter continues to arouse heated argument, although it is now the case that the burden of proof lies with its defenders, who have yet to explain the presence of twentieth-century chemicals in 'medieval' ink. So far, no authentic archaeological evidence has been found to support the sagas' suggestion of a deep southward penetration by Norse explorers, but, given the hundreds of miles of coastline in question and the intervening time period, this is perhaps not so surprising.

Yet there can be little doubting the presence of Norsemen in the Gulf of St Lawrence. The discovery in the 1960s of what would appear to be a Norse settlement at L'Anse aux Meadows on the northern tip of Newfoundland at least corroborates something of the saga accounts. Although this is unlikely to have been the Vinland settlement, as it is too far north for grapes, it could possibly have been a settlement founded by Leif himself and a staging post for more southerly explorations.[21] A cluster of turf houses, including a boat repair shed, a blacksmith's workshop, a kiln and a furnace, as well as accommodation for approximately ninety people, are a good indication of the seriousness of Greenlanders in establishing a permanent settlement across the Atlantic. The L'Anse aux Meadows colony was only in operation for the first two to three decades of the eleventh century. The reason for its abandonment was probably related to that given in the *Vinland Sagas* for the abandonment of efforts to settle Vinland. Without the freedom to exploit the resources further south, a northern staging post was effectively redundant. It was in this regard that the Vinland paradise that Leif reported back in Greenland soon proved to involve significant trouble, as those who followed his example rapidly found out.

Three more successful journeys to Vinland are recorded in the *Vinland Sagas*. The first of these was made by Leif's brother, Thorvald. Thorvald and his men occupied Leif's settlement and set about exploring to the west. Thorvald quickly concluded that there was no human settlement in the vicinity, despite the discovery of a wood grain cover, and he settled down for the winter. Come the spring, he once again set about exploring, this time to the east, but misfortune befell him when his ship ran aground damaging the keel. Detained while repairs were done, Thorvald named the headland Keel Point (*Kjalarnes*), a location that some have speculated on as being in the far north of Nova Scotia. Once able to put back to sea, Thorvald explored the eastward fjords of the island and, on encountering what he considered to be 'an attractive spot', he decided to build himself a farm. It was at this point that Thorvald realized that the region was not uninhabited after all. What at first had appeared to be three hillocks turned out to be three hide boats concealing three men beneath each one of them. Eight of these men Thorvald's crew seized and killed but the ninth escaped. When, as was probably inevitable, a vast throng of vengeful natives sailed up the fjord toward them, the Norsemen were forced into a makeshift defence from on board their ship, whilst arrows rained down on them. The wound that Thorvald received in the engagement proved to be fatal. His companions laid him to rest at his 'attractive spot', which they named Cross Point (*Krossanes*), and spent the remainder of the winter stowing grapes and grapevines on their boats and, without further adventure, returned to Greenland.

The infestation of Vinland and its regions by the *skraelings* that Thorvald's men doubtless reported to the Eastern Settlement did nothing to deter further attempts by others to establish a colony in the New World. But, as the settlers of Greenland were later to discover to their cost, the *skraelings* were a threat that could not easily be avoided or overcome. In all likelihood, these native people were the Mi'kmaq, a tribe that had occupied the territories surrounding the Gulf of St Lawrence for over five thousand years and whose population numbered in the region of thirty-five thousand. Nor were the Norsemen free to wander without threat further north across Labrador or Baffin Island, as there they would have encountered the Eskimos. Perhaps persuading the Norsemen to persist was the unusual and temporary absence of the Native American Indians from the region surrounding L'Anse aux Meadows.[22] Alternatively, it may well have been nothing more than blind determination.

The next effort at colonization was prompted by Gudrid, the widow of Thorstein, a third son of Eirik the Red, who had died in the Western Settlement having failed in his own effort to make the crossing to Vinland. Gudrid soon remarried but remained enthused by her late husband's desire to reach Vinland. Her new husband, the prosperous Icelander Thorfinn Karlsefni, was readily persuaded that a visit to Leif's Vinland could prove both profitable and prestigious. According to *The Saga of the Greenlanders*, they set out in a particularly large ship accommodating sixty crew, five women and an assortment of livestock, although *Eirik the Red's Saga* claims that Karlsefni equipped three ships and had a company of 160 men and women. The winter of their first settlement passed well enough but in the spring the natives came to investigate, only to be frightened off by the roaring of the colonizers' bull. Within a brief space, however, they had sufficiently recovered themselves to enter into trade with the Norsemen and for a while all was well. Then, in one trading encounter, a disagreement flared and one of Karlsefni's servants killed one of the natives, whom he believed was pilfering. Open warfare ensued. Massively outnumbered, Karlsefni's men could do little more than play on the superstitions of the natives and, so, temporarily deter them. Around the same time, Gudrid delivered Karlsefni a child who they named Snorri and who had the distinction of being the first European born in North America. With such paternal considerations in mind and appreciating that 'despite everything the land had to offer there, they would be under constant attack from its prior inhabitants',[23] Karlsefni loaded his ship with grapes, grapevines and furs and prepared to depart. According to *Eirik the Red's Saga*, a terrifying and bizarre encounter with a murderous uniped further up the coast eventually convinced Karlsefni that his future lay back in Greenland.

One more child of Eirik the Red had yet to try their hand in Vinland. In this case it was his daughter Freydis, and on the subject of her voyage the two sagas are sharply divided. *The Saga of the Greenlanders* describes how Freydis broke her agreement with her Icelandic partners, the brothers Helgi and Finnbogi, by, in the first place, carrying more men concealed on board her ship than had been agreed, and, in the second place, by refusing to allow the brothers and their men lodging at Leif's camp. Not satisfied with this, Freydis then alleged some insult from the brothers and succeeded in inciting her husband to seize and murder them. The women folk, who were also taken captive, Freydis herself axed to death. Her return to Greenland was, quite understandably, ignominious.

By contrast, *Eirik the Red's Saga* includes an account of Freydis's time in Vinland as part of the adventures of Karlsefni, and locates the climax of the attempted settlement far to the south at Hóp, which signifies 'a landlocked bay'. In this account, it is not Freydis's vicious character that leads to the abandonment of the settlement project but the violent reception that the Norsemen received from the various locals at every landing. During the course of the hostilities, we are told, Freydis played an heroic role as an Amazonian-style warrior, rallying the men and slapping her bare breasts with a sword, thus terrifying the native tribes into flight. It is simply not possible to say which of these sagas gets nearer the truth of the matter, although the account depicting Freydis as a mean-minded murderer is, on the surface of things, the more persuasive. In either case, it is with the descriptions of Freydis, villain or virago, that saga accounts of the colonization of North America come to an end.

The *Vinland Sagas* continue to be the best available evidence for where and when these voyages of colonization took place and, while much remains unclear, it is undeniable that colonization of North America's east coast was attempted by Norsemen in the early decades of the second millennium. Nevertheless, while colonization proved impossible, and the destination too remote to attract a substantial migration west from the Norse colonies, contact with the North American continent continued for centuries. The singular aim of seemingly all but one of the subsequent voyages was to gather the valuables that were there for the taking, not only grapes but also that commodity most needed by Greenlanders and Icelanders, timber. As late as 1347 a Greenlandic ship was blown off course into harbour in Iceland, her storage areas stacked with timber from Labrador. A record of the one exception to these mercantile forays was set down in the Icelandic annal for the year 1121, when the spirited Bishop Eirik of Gardar in the Eastern Settlement of Greenland set sail in missionary spirit in search of Vinland. It is not recorded that he ever returned.

These westward voyages of settlement and discovery provide the most flattering epitaph for the Viking Age. Those who sailed west did so irrespective of the perils that were involved. What apparently motivated them was a combination of the frontier spirit of self-governance and self-improvement, and sheer curiosity. Our perspective on them is like that which we might get from studying the vanishing point on a painting. At first, the view is wide, and in this scene the surge of settlement toward Iceland, in particular, stands out sharp and clear, its characters well defined and its history brilliant. Then, in the middle distance, there is the settlement of Greenland, rough drawn in broad sweeps of colour. In the foreground the shades are light and airy but, in the background, they are dark and sombre. Finally, in the remote distance is the attempt to colonize Vinland with the thin line of voyagers making the ultimate westward journey eventually fading from view. Crudely violent and uncongenial the Vikings may have been, as far as their European neighbours were concerned, but these voyages of discovery to the edge of the world reveal an indomitable spirit that it is hard not to admire. This last image of the Vikings is, quite justifiably, a romantic one.

# Appendix

## THE ORIGINS OF ROLLO

The name Rollo is a corrupt Latinate form of the Norse name Hrolf. Medieval French sources, following Dudo of St-Quentin, indicate a Danish origin, but this may not mean much and could be just shorthand for describing anyone who had originated from Scandinavia. All Scandinavian sources, none of which are contemporary and all of which are deeply reliant on oral traditions, present Rollo as Norwegian, in effect Hrolf the Walker (O.N. Göngu Hrólfr), so named because he was so large that no horse could carry him. This assignation is, to some extent, made plausible by reference to the name of Rollo's daughter in Frankish sources as Gerloc (O.N. Geirlaug), which is of Norwegian origin. The Scandinavian sources are all Icelandic and are presented in Snorri Sturluson's *Heimskringla*, the Icelandic *Book of Settlements* and in *The Saga of the Orkney Earls*. All these are also consistent in crediting Hrolf as being the founder of the Norman dynasty, but such consistency does not necessarily mean a common literary tradition. Set together, these sources state that Hrolf was the son of the Norwegian aristocrat Earl Røgnvald of Møre and that Hrolf was unable to take on the earldom of Orkney, which was in the earl's gift, because the Norwegian king, Harald Finehair, had exiled him for acts of piracy against royal property.

Hrolf's lineage is indicated otherwise by the historically closest comment on his genealogy given by the late tenth-century French historian Richer of Rheims, who says that Rollo's father was called Ketil (Catullus in Latin). No tradition supports this elsewhere and one may well wonder why not. If Ketil was Hrolf's father, he was most likely a person of influence and pedigree, as Viking warlords were typically from the aristocratic elite of the Scandinavian community. One tendentious speculation that could explain Richer's note on Hrolf's father is the possibility that Hrolf had at some point been fostered, something that could occur even in teenage years. This may also be consistent with hints in saga traditions of a rift between Hrolf, his father Røgnvald and his brothers.

Given the weight that should be attached to Richer's near-contemporary evidence, and that which can be attached only to a much more developed competing tradition from twelfth- and thirteenth-century Iceland, the origin of Hrolf is likely to remain a mystery, for none of the evidence from any of the sources is unproblematic. The Icelandic accounts of Hrolf's origins are persuasive, not least because in these the appropriate pedigree is indicated, along with a convincing profile of Hrolf's violent personality. Had Hrolf been someone other than this, it is surprising that no saga or history mentions it. The fact that there is a fourteenth-century Icelandic saga named after Hrolf (*Göngu-Hrólfs Saga*) does not advance matters, as it is entirely fictional and makes no mention of his success in Frankia, locating him, instead, as a founding king of Russia. By comparison with such fantasizing, Richer of Rheims's Ketil looms large. When all is taken into account, it is perhaps only a preference for the more detailed Icelandic accounts that has caused the majority of historians to see Rollo as an exiled Norwegian aristocrat, able to command a great fleet and show natural leadership, unable to perceive any betters, and eager to construct a career out of challenging the rights and seizing the property of his European peers. None of this convincingly places him as a Norwegian or a Dane, as married into the Frankish royal family or as anything but a Viking whose dynasty survived into more certain historical records.

# Notes

## Notes to Chapter 1: The Viking Age

1  Michael Swanton, ed. and trans., *The Anglo-Saxon Chronicles* (London: Phoenix Press, 2000), Peterborough, p. 71.

2  For these doubts about the Peterborough entry, see P.H. Sawyer, *The Age of the Vikings* (2nd edn, London: Edward Arnold, 1971), p. 20.

3  From Alfred's preface to his translation of Pope Gregory's *Pastoral Care* (*Regula Pastoralis*). See Simon Keynes and Michael Lapidge, trans., *Alfred the Great: Asser's Life of Alfred and Other Contemporary Sources* (London: Penguin, 1983), p. 125.

4  As Patrick Wormald memorably remarked, 'though the Vikings may not have been mad, they were probably bad, and certainly dangerous to know'. See C. Patrick Wormald, 'Viking Studies: Whence and Whither?', in R.T. Farrell, ed., *The Vikings* (London and Chichester: Phillimore, 1982), p. 148.

5  H.B. Dewing, trans., *Procopius* (London: Heinemann, 1914), iii, bk iv, c. xiv, p. 413.

6  This view is argued in P.H. Sawyer, *The Age of the Vikings*, see especially pp. 202–3.

7  The number of those executed is given in the *Royal Frankish Annals*. See Bernhard Walter Scholz, trans., *Carolingian Chronicles: Royal Frankish Annals and Nithard's Histories* (Ann Arbor, University of Michigan Press, 1970), p. 61.

8  Stephen Allott, trans., *Alcuin of York, c. AD 732 to 804: His Life and Letters* (York: William Sessions, 1974), letter 12, pp. 18–20.

9  For a discussion of this supposition, see Rory McTurk, *Saga-Book*, 23, 5 (1992), review, p. 381.

## Notes to Chapter 2: Society and Religion

1  All excerpts from the poem are from Carolyne Larrington, trans., *The Poetic Edda* (Oxford and New York: Oxford University Press, 1996), pp. 246–52.

2  The name Erna indicates the attribute of vigorousness.

3  Larrington translates the name as 'Kin', but here it is replaced with the Old Norse original 'Kon' in order to indicate the pun on 'king'.

4  H.M. Smyser, trans., 'Ibn Fadlan's Account of the Rus with Some Commentary and Some Allusions to *Beowulf*', in J. B. Bessinger and R. P. Creed, eds, *Medieval and Linguistic Studies in Honour of Francis Peabody Magoun Jr* (London: Allen and Unwin, 1965), p. 101.

5   Ibid., p. 94.

6   Ibid., p. 98.

7   Ibid., p. 100–1.

8   Francis J. Tschan, trans., *Adam of Bremen, History of the Archbishops of Hamburg-Bremen* (New York: Columbia University Press, 1959), p. 190.

9   See Christopher J. McDonough, ed. and trans., *Warner of Rouen: Moriuht. A Norman Latin Poem from the Early Eleventh Century* (Toronto: Pontifical Institute of Mediaeval Studies, 1995).

10   'Sirius' is Al-Tartushi's own supposition regarding the identity of the god being worshipped, but this deity is not otherwise known in connection with the Norse pantheon.

11   Gwyn Jones, *A History of the Vikings* (revised edn, Oxford and New York: Oxford University Press, 1984), pp. 176–77. Translated from Harris Birkeland, 'Nordens historie i middelalderen etter arabiske kilder', in *Skrifter utgitt av det Norske Videnskaps-Akademi I*, Oslo II, Hist-Filos. Klasse (Oslo, 1954), pp. 103–04.

12   Timothy Reuter, trans., *The Annals of Fulda*, Ninth-Century Histories, 2 (Manchester and New York: Manchester University Press, 1992), p. 70.

13   Tschan, trans., *Adam of Bremen*, pp. 207–8.

14   Eljas Orrman, 'Church and Society', in Knut Helle, ed., *The Cambridge History of Scandinavia*, i, *Prehistory to 1520* (Cambridge: Cambridge University Press, 2003), pp. 421–62. Translated from M. Cl. Gertz, ed., *Vitæ Sanctorum Danorum* (København, 1908–12), p. 83.

15   Larrington, trans., *The Poetic Edda*, p. 24.

*Notes to Chapter 3:  Battle on Land and at Sea*

1   Simon Keynes and Michael Lapidge, trans., *Alfred the Great: Asser's Life of King Alfred and Other Contemporary Sources* (Harmondsworth: Penguin, 1983), p. 86.

2   *The Saga of Harald Sigurtharson (Hardruler)*, in Lee M. Hollander, trans., *Snorri Sturluson: Heimskringla. History of the Kings of Norway* (Austin: University of Texas, 1964), p. 654.

3   *Saga of the Ynglings*, in Hollander, trans., *Snorri Sturluson: Heimskringla. History of the Kings of Norway*, p. 10.

4   *Saga of Harald Fairhair*, in Hollander, trans., *Snorri Sturluson: Heimskringla. History of the Kings of Norway*, p. 74. Haklang's death is recounted by the skald Hornklofi.

5   Hermann Pálsson and Paul Edward, trans., *Göngu-Hrolfs Saga* (Edinburgh: Canongate, 1980), pp. 99–100.

6   *Saint Óláfs Saga*, in Hollander, trans., *Snorri Sturluson: Heimskringla. History of the Kings of Norway*, p. 494.

7   Ibid., p. 502.

8   Michael Swanton, ed. and trans., *The Anglo-Saxon Chronicles* (London: Phoenix Press, 2000), Winchester, p. 70.

9   Seán Mac Airt and Gearóid Mac Niocaill, eds, *The Annals of Ulster (to AD 1131)*, i, *Text and Translation* (Dublin Institute for Advanced Studies, 1983), p. 369.

10  Translation in Paul B. du Chailu, *The Viking Age: The Early History, Manners, and Customs of the Ancestors of the English-Speaking Nations* (New York: AMS Press, 1970; reprinted from 1889), ii, p. 541.

11  *Sturlubók* recension of *Landnámabók*, in Jakob Benediktsson, ed., *Íslendingabók. Landnámabók*, Íslenzk fornrit, 1 (Reykjavík, 1968), p. 32.

12  Ibid., *Hauksbók* recension of *Landnámabók*, p. 33.

13  Alistair Campbell, ed., with supplementary notes by Simon Keynes, *Encomium Emmae Reginae* (Cambridge: Cambridge University Press, 1998), p. 19.

14  *The Saga of Harald Sigurtharson*, in Hollander, trans., *Snorri Sturluson: Heimskringla. History of the Kings of Norway*, pp. 623–24.

15  *The Saga of Magnús the Good*, in Hollander, trans., *Snorri Sturluson: Heimskringla. History of the Kings of Norway*, p. 556.

16  *The Saga of Óláf Tryggvason*, in Hollander, trans., *Snorri Sturluson: Heimskringla. History of the Kings of Norway*, pp. 239–40.

17  Ibid., p. 220.

*Notes to Chapter 4:  England, Ireland and Wales, 789–900*

1  Michael Swanton, ed. and trans., *The Anglo-Saxon Chronicles* (London: Phoenix Press, 2000), Peterborough, p. 55.

2  A. Campbell, ed., *The Chronicle of Æthelweard* (London, 1962), p. 27.

3  The evidence is from a Kentish charter of 792.

4  Swanton, ed. and trans., *The Anglo-Saxon Chronicles*, Winchester, pp. 54 and 56.

5  Stephen Allott, trans., *Alcuin of York, c. AD 732 to 804: His Life and Letters* (York: William Sessions, 1974), letter 26, pp. 36–38.

6  Ibid., letter 12, pp. 18–20.

7  Ibid., letter 29, pp. 39–40.

8  Ibid., letter 12, pp. 18–20.

9  Archaeological investigations have revealed fire damage at both Jarrow and Wearmouth that may well be the physical evidence of this attack. It has, however, been argued that this damage resulted from a raid led by Halfdan in 870. An alternative suggestion for the location of the attack is the mouth of the River Don in Yorkshire.

10  Allott, trans., *Alcuin of York, c. AD 732 to 804: His Life and Letters*, letter 29, pp. 39–40.

11  Joseph Stevenson, *The Church Historians of England*, iii, pt 2, *The Historical Works of Simeon of Durham* (London: Seeleys, 1855), *History of the Kings*, pp. 425–617, p. 457.

12  Seán Mac Airt and Gearóid Mac Niocaill, eds, *The Annals of Ulster (to AD 1131)*, i, *Text and Translation* (Dublin Institute for Advanced Studies, 1983), p. 251.

13  Máire Ní Mhaonaigh, 'The Vikings in Medieval Irish Literature', in Anne-Christine Larsen, ed., *The Vikings in Ireland* (Århus: The Viking Ship Museum, 2001), p. 99.

14  Swanton, ed. and trans., *The Anglo-Saxon Chronicles*, Peterborough, p. 65.

15  S.D. Keynes and M. Lapidge, trans., *Alfred the Great: Asser's Life of King Alfred and Other Contemporary Sources* (Harmondsworth: Penguin Books, 1983), p. 74.

16  Ubba and Halfdan are not included in the account given by Saxo Grammaticus.

17  Swanton, ed. and trans., *The Anglo-Saxon Chronicles*, Peterborough, p. 71.

18  The location of Meretun is unknown.

19  J.A. Giles, trans., *Roger of Wendover's Flowers of History*, i (London: Henry G. Bohn, 1849), pp. 191–92.

20  Swanton, ed. and trans., *The Anglo-Saxon Chronicles*, Peterborough, p. 73.

21  Mac Airt and Mac Niocaill, eds, *The Annals of Ulster*, p. 329.

22  See Martin Biddle and Birthe Kjølbye-Biddle, 'Repton and the "Great Heathen Army" 873–4', in James Graham-Campbell, Richard Hall, Judith Jesch and David N. Parsons, eds, *Vikings and the Danelaw: Select Papers from the Proceedings of the Thirteenth Viking Congress, Nottingham and York, 21–30 August 1997* (Oxford: Oxbow Books, 2001), p. 67.

23  Ibid., p. 67.

24  Ibid., p. 81.

25  Ibid., p. 82.

26  Ibid., p. 81.

27  Swanton, ed. and trans., *The Anglo-Saxon Chronicles*, Winchester, p. 74.

28  Ibid., p. 74.

29  S.D. Keynes and M. Lapidge, trans., *Alfred the Great: Asser's Life of King Alfred and Other Contemporary Sources*, p. 85.

30  Eric Christiansen, trans., *Dudo of St Quentin: History of the Normans* (Woodbridge: Boydell Press, 1998), p. 16.

31  Two of Hastein's sons were the godchildren of Alfred and Ealdorman Æthelred, which suggests that a deal involving Hastein's baptism had previously been struck.

32  Swanton, ed. and trans., *The Anglo-Saxon Chronicles*, Winchester, pp. 89–90.

33  J.H. Todd, ed., *The War of the Gaedhil with the Gaill* (London: Longmans, Green, Reader and Dyer, 1867), p. 15.

34  Cited in Alfred P. Smyth, *Scandinavian Kings in the British Isles, 850–880* (Oxford University Press, 1977), p. 115.

35  Mac Airt and Mac Niocaill, eds, *The Annals of Ulster*, p. 303.

36  Ibid., p. 353.

*Notes to Chapter 5: England, Wales and Ireland, 900–1070*

1  Michael Swanton, ed. and trans., *The Anglo-Saxon Chronicles* (London: Phoenix Press, 2000), Winchester, p. 92.

2  *Annals of St Neots*, cited in Swanton, ed. and trans., *The Anglo-Saxon Chronicles*, p. 92, n. 9.

3  Swanton, ed. and trans., *The Anglo-Saxon Chronicles*, Worcester, p. 97.

4  Ibid., Abingdon, p. 105.

5  Ibid., Winchester, p. 103.

6  Ibid., Winchester, p. 104.

7  Seán Mac Airt and Gearóid Mac Niocaill, eds, *The Annals of Ulster (to AD 1131)*, i, *Text and Translation* (Dublin Institute for Advanced Studies, 1983), p. 363.

8   Eadwulf (d. 913) was reeve at Bamborough in Northumbria. His sons were subject to Ragnald after his triumph at Corbridge.

9   Swanton, ed. and trans., *The Anglo-Saxon Chronicles*, Winchester, p. 104.

10  'The Battle of Brunanburh', in Richard Hamer, *A Choice of Anglo-Saxon Verse* (London and Boston: Faber and Faber, 1970), pp. 41–47, lines 1–4.

11  Ibid., lines 32–36.

12  See Bernard Scudder, trans., *Egils Saga*, in Örnólfr Thorsson, ed., *The Sagas of the Icelanders: A Selection* (London and New York; Allen Lane The Penguin Press, 2000), see ch. 59, pp. 107–8.

13  Swanton, ed. and trans., *The Anglo-Saxon Chronicles*, Worcester, p. 112.

14  J.A. Giles, trans., *Roger of Wendover's Flowers of History*, i (London: Henry G. Bohn, 1849), p. 256.

15  D.M. Hadley, *The Northern Danelaw: Its Social Structure, c. 800–1100* (London and New York: Leicester University Press, 2000), p. 300.

16  Archbishop Wulfstan's retrospective criticism is included in the *Chronicle* entry for 963. See Swanton, ed. and trans., *The Anglo-Saxon Chronicles*, Peterborough, p. 115.

17  Ibid., Peterborough, p. 114.

18  J.H. Todd, trans., *The War of the Gaedhil with the Gaill* (London: Longmans, Green, Reader and Dyer, 1867), pp. 159–60.

19  For an attempt to rehabilitate Æthelred's reputation, see Ian Howard, *Swein Forkbeard's Invasions and the Danish Conquest of England, 991–1017* (Woodbridge: The Boydell Press, 2003).

20  Swanton, ed. and trans., *The Anglo-Saxon Chronicles*, Abingdon, p.126.

21  Ibid., Canterbury, p. 128.

22  Ibid., Peterborough, p. 133.

23  Ibid., Peterborough, p. 133.

24  Ibid., Peterborough, p. 135 and n. 9.

25  Ibid., Peterborough, p. 141 (my italics).

26  Ibid., Peterborough, p. 142.

27  Ibid., Peterborough, p. 145.

28  Ibid., Worcester, p. 148.

29  Ibid., Peterborough, p. 152.

30  *The Saga of Harald Sigurtharson*, in Lee M. Hollander, trans., *Snorri Sturluson: Heimskringla. History of the Kings of Norway* (Austin: University of Texas, 1964), p. 653

31  Swanton, ed. and trans., *The Anglo-Saxon Chronicles*, p. 199.

32  *The Saga of Harald Sigurtharson*, p. 655.

## Notes to Chapter 6: Scotland and the Orkneys

1   *The Saga of Harald Finehair*, in Lee M. Hollander, trans., *Snorri Sturluson: Heimskringla. History of the Kings of Norway* (Austin: University of Texas, 1964), p. 76.

2   *Historia Norwegiae*. Cited in James Graham-Campbell and Colleen E. Batey, *Vikings in Scotland: An Archaeological Survey* (Edinburgh University Press, 1988), p. 5.

3   Barbara E. Crawford, ed., *Scandinavian Settlement in Northern Britain* (London and New York: Leicester University Press, 1995), p. 57.

4   Hermann Palsson and Paul Edwards, trans., *Orkneyinga Saga: The History of the Earls of Orkney* (Harmondsworth: Penguin, 1981), ch. 5, p. 28.

5   This may also have been the Viking known in French sources as Rollo, who founded the Norman dynasty. See Chapter 7 and Appendix for an account of Rollo's career and his origins.

6   Palsson and Edwards, trans., *Orkneyinga Saga: The History of the Earls of Orkney*, ch. 8, p. 33.

7   Seán Mac Airt and Gearóid Mac Niocaill, eds, *The Annals of Ulster (to AD 1131)*, i, *Text and Translation* (Dublin Institute for Advanced Studies, 1983). The annal entry for 987 gives the number of deaths as 'three score and three hundred', p. 421.

8   Pálsson and Edwards, trans., *Orkneyinga Saga: The History of the Earls of Orkney*, ch. 12, p. 37.

9   Magnus Magnusson and Hermann Pálsson, trans., *Njal's Saga* (Harmondsworth: Penguin, 1970), ch. 157 passim. This episode in the saga includes the eddic poem *Darraðarljóð*, or *The Lay of Dorrud*. Dorrud is said to be the man who witnessed the Valkyries at their morbid loom.

10   See Crawford, ed., *Scandinavian Settlement in Northern Britain*, pp. 71–72, for this argument. Others have argued the case for Malcolm II's grandson, Duncan. In *Orkneyinga Saga*, the antagonist is said on this occasion to be a certain Karl Hundison, probably an invented name meaning 'low born son of a dog'.

11   Pálsson and Edwards, trans., *Orkneyinga Saga: The History of the Earls of Orkney*, ch. 20, p. 54.

12   Ibid., ch. 20, p. 55.

13   *Saint Óláf's Saga*, in Hollander, trans., *Snorri Sturluson: Heimskringla. History of the Kings of Norway*, p. 515.

*Notes to Chapter 7: Western Europe*

1   Cited in Janet L. Nelson, 'The Frankish Empire', in Peter Sawyer, ed., *The Oxford Illustrated History of the Vikings* (Oxford and New York: Oxford University Press, 1997), p. 20.

2   Bernhard Walter Scholz, trans., *Carolingian Chronicles: Royal Frankish Annals and Nithard's Histories* (Ann Arbor, University of Michigan Press, 1970), p. 83.

3   Ibid., p. 108.

4   Ermentarius, *The Life and Miracles of Saint Philibert*, in David Herlihy, ed. and trans., *The History of Feudalism* (London: Macmillan, 1970), p. 11.

5   Janet L. Nelson, trans., *The Annals of St-Bertin*. Ninth-Century Histories, 1 (Manchester and New York: Manchester University Press, 1991), p. 30.

6   Ibid., p. 50.

7   Ibid., p. 56.

8   Ibid., p. 55.

9   Jón Stefánsson, 'The Vikings in Spain: From Arabic (Moorish) and Spanish Sources', in *Saga-Book of the Viking Club*, Society for Northern Research, 4 (London: Curtis and Beamish, 1908–9), pp. 33–34.

10   Nelson, trans., *The Annals of St-Bertin*, p. 62.

11   Ibid., p. 86.

12   Ibid., p. 86.

13   Ermentarius, *The Life and Miracles of Saint Philibert*, in David Herlihy, ed. and trans., *The History of Feudalism*, pp. 11–12.

14   Stefánsson, 'The Vikings in Spain: From Arabic (Moorish) and Spanish Sources', p. 40.

## Notes to Chapter 8:  Russia and the East

1   The term Varangian may well derive from Old Norse *várar* and so signify 'men of the pledge' or 'confederates'. This, in turn, could indicate those who struck bargains as merchants or, more probably, those who pledged themselves to the service of the Byzantine emperor. More generally, the term indicated the origin of Scandinavians in Russia. The Baltic was known as the Varangian Lake.

2   The origin of the term Rus is disputed. It may derive from the Finnish word for the Swedes *Ruotsi*, which in turn signifies 'rowers', or it may derive from *rusioi*, meaning 'blondes', the Greek word for the Scandinavian tribe the Heruli, who were active in the Eastern Roman Empire from the third to the sixth centuries. From written sources it is apparent that the term could be applied widely to signify any Scandinavian or Scando-Slav.

3   *Ynglinga Saga*, in Lee M. Hollander, trans., *Snorri Sturluson. Heimskringla. History of the Kings of Norway* (Austin: University of Texas, 1964), pp. 6–50, see chapters 32 and 43–44.

4   C.H. Robinson, trans., *Rimbert: Anskar the Apostle of the North, 801–65* (London: Lives of the Early Missionaries, 1931), p. 30.

5   Samuel Hazzard Cross and Olgerd P. Sherbowitz-Wetzor, trans. and ed., *The Russian Primary Chronicle: Laurentian Text* (Cambridge, Massachusetts: The Mediaeval Academy of America, 1953), pp. 59–60.

6   Cyril Mango, trans., *The Homilies of Photius, Patriarch of Constantinople*, Dumbarton Oaks Studies, 3 (Cambridge, Massachusetts, 1958), p. 74ff.

7   Cross and Sherbowitz-Wetzor, trans. and ed., *The Russian Primary Chronicle. Laurentian Text*, p. 60.

8   Cyril Mango, trans., *The Homilies of Photius, Patriarch of Constantinople*, p. 74ff.

9   Cross and Sherbowitz-Wetzor, trans. and ed., *The Russian Primary Chronicle: Laurentian Text*, p. 64.

10   Ibid., p. 65.

11   Ibid., p. 65.

12   This story is also given as the reason for the death of the hero of the Icelandic *Saga of Arrow Odd* and would seem to have been imported from Russia.

13   F.A. Wright, trans., *The Works of Liudprand of Cremona* (London: 1930), p. 185.

14   There is doubt as to whether Igor did, in fact, launch a second attack. It is possible that

the account of it is merely the *Chronicle*'s attempt to counterbalance Igor's humiliation in 941.

15 H.R. Ellis Davidson, *The Viking Road to Byzantium* (London: George Allen and Unwin, 1976), p. 134.

16 Cross and Sherbowitz-Wetzor, trans. and ed., *The Russian Primary Chronicle. Laurentian Text*, p. 78.

17 Ibid., p. 84.

18 R.J.H. Jenkins, trans., *Constantine VII Porphyrogenitus: De administrando imperio* (Washington: Dumbarton Oaks Texts, no. 1, 1967), ch. 9.

19 Cross and Sherbowitz-Wetzor, trans. and ed., *The Russian Primary Chronicle: Laurentian Text*, p. 84.

20 Ibid., p. 86.

21 George Vernadsky, *Kievan Russia* (New Haven and London: Yale University Press, 1948), p. 42.

22 *Yngvar's Saga*, in Hermann Palsson and Paul Edwards, trans., *Vikings in Russia* (Edinburgh: Polygon, 1990), pp. 44–68.

23 *Eymunds Saga*, in Palsson and Edwards, trans., *Vikings in Russia*, pp. 68–89.

24 *Saga of Harald Sigurtharson*, in Hollander, trans., *Snorri Sturluson: Heimskringla. History of the Kings of Norway*, pp. 577–663.

25 Davidson, *The Viking Road to Byzantium*, p. 209.

26 *Saga of Harald Sigurtharson*, in Hollander, trans., *Snorri Sturluson: Heimskringla. History of the Kings of Norway*, p. 596.

27 C.A. Macartney, *The Magyars in the Ninth Century* (Cambridge: 1930, reprinted 1968), p. 213–14.

*Notes to Chapter 9:  Atlantic Explorations and Settlements*

1 J.J. Tierney, ed. and trans., *Dicuili: liber de mensura orbis terrae* (Dublin: The Dublin Institute for Advanced Studies, 1967), p. 77.

2 Bernard Scudder, trans., *Egils Saga*, in Örnólfr Thorsson, ed., *The Sagas of the Icelanders: A Selection* (London and New York: Allen Lane, The Penguin Press, 2000), pp. 11–12.

3 Tierney, ed. and trans., *Dicuili: liber de mensura orbis terrae*, p. 75.

4 Gwyn Jones, trans., *The Book of the Settlements. Landnámabók*, in Gwyn Jones, *The Norse Atlantic Saga: Being the Norse Voyages of Discovery and Settlement to Iceland, Greenland, America* (London: Oxford University Press, 1964), p. 118.

5 Vésteinn Ólason, *Dialogues with the Viking Age: Narration and Representation in the Sagas of Icelanders*, Andrew Wawn, trans. (Reykjavík: Heimskringla, 1998), p. 9.

6 Keneva Kunz, trans., *Eirik the Red's Saga*, in Thorsson, ed., *The Sagas of the Icelanders: A Selection*, p. 654.

7 Tenth-century Icelanders may also have known of a land far away to the west as a result of the *hillingar* effect, an arctic mirage that causes the horizon to be extended far beyond the natural curvature of the earth. This phenomenon causes the coast of Greenland to become visible from the mountain tops in the west of Iceland.

8   The term Eskimo is now in common use, even among Eskimos. The name was probably given to them by Algonquin Indians and meant 'eaters of raw flesh' (*Esquimawes*). An alternative and less likely theory is that 'Eskimo' was a corruption of *Excomminquois*, a word thought to have been used by Jesuit missionaries in eastern Canada in the sixteenth century. Eskimos traditionally refer to themselves as Inuit, which means 'real people'.

9   Jones, *The Norse Atlantic Saga*, p. 61.

10  Henrik Rink, trans., *Tales and Traditions of the Eskimos* (London: C. Hurst and Co., 1974), pp. 320–21.

11  Jones, *The Norse Atlantic Saga*, p. 71.

12  Kunz, trans., *The Saga of the Greenlanders*, in Thorsson, ed., *The Sagas of the Icelanders: A Selection*, p. 637.

13  Ibid., p. 638.

14  Ibid., p. 638.

15  Ibid., p. 639.

16  Ibid., p. 639.

17  Ibid., p. 639.

18  Ibid., p. 640.

19  Ibid., p. 641.

20  Francis J. Tschan, trans., *Adam of Bremen: History of the Archbishops of Hamburg-Bremen* (New York: Columbia University Press, 1959), p. 38. The transmission confusion theory points out that *vínber* and *vínviður* (grapes and grapevines) could have been *vínber* and *viður* (grapes, as in berries, and timber).

21  This, however, is pure conjecture, as the sagas consistently refer to Leif's camp (*Leifsbuðir*) as being in Vinland.

22  See Birgitta Linderoth Wallace, 'L'Anse aux Meadows and Vinland: An Abandoned Experiment', in James H. Barrett, ed., *Contact, Continuity and Collapse: The Norse Colonisation of the North Atlantic* (Turnhout, Belgium: Brepols, 2003), pp. 207–38.

23  Kunz, trans., *Eirik the Red's Saga*, in Thorsson, ed., *The Sagas of the Icelanders: A Selection*, p. 671.

# Bibliography

Adams, Jonathan and Katherine Holman, eds, *Scandinavia and Europe 800–1350: Contact, Conflict, and Coexistence* (Turnhout, Belgium: Brepols Publishers, 2004).

Allott, Stephen, trans., *Alcuin of York, c. AD 732 to 804: His Life and Letters* (York: William Sessions, 1974).

Barrett, James H., ed., *Contact, Continuity, and Collapse: The Norse Colonization of the North Atlantic* (Turnhout, Belgium: Brepols Publishers, 2003).

Batey, Colleen E., Judith Jesch and Christopher D. Morris, *The Viking Age in Caithness, Orkney and the North Atlantic: Select Papers from the Proceedings of the Eleventh Viking Congress, Thurso and Kirkwall, 22 August–1 September 1989* (Edinburgh: Edinburgh University Press, 1993).

Benediktsson, Jakob, ed., *Íslendingabók. Landnámabók*, Íslenzk fornrit, 1 (Reykjavík, 1968).

Binns, Alan, *Viking Voyagers: Then and Now* (London: Heinemann, 1980).

Brøndsted, Johannes, *The Vikings* (Harmondsworth: Penguin Books, 1965).

Brown, R. Allen, *The Norman Conquest of England: Sources and Documents* (Woodbridge: The Boydell Press, 1984).

Byock, Jesse, *Viking Age Iceland* (Harmondsworth: Penguin Books, 2001).

Campbell, A., ed., with supplementary notes by S. D. Keynes, *Encomium Emmae Reginae* (Cambridge: Cambridge University Press, 1998).

Campbell, A., ed., *The Chronicle of Æthelweard* (London, 1962).

Christiansen, Eric, trans., *Dudo of St-Quentin: History of the Normans* (Woodbridge: Boydell Press, 1998).

Christiansen, Eric, *The Norsemen in the Viking Age* (Oxford: Blackwell, 2002).

Clarke, Helen and Björn Ambrosiana, *Towns in the Viking Age* (revised edn, London and New York: Leicester University Press, 1995).

Crawford, Barbara E., ed., *Scandinavian Settlement in Northern Britain* (London and New York: Leicester University Press, 1995).

Cross, Samuel Hazzard and Olgerd P. Sherbowitz-Wetzor, trans. and ed., *The Russian Primary Chronicle: Laurentian Text* (Cambridge, Massachusetts: The Mediaeval Academy of America, 1953).

Crouch, David, *The Normans: A History of a Dynasty* (London and New York: Hambledon and London, 2002).

Dewing, H.B., trans., *Procopius*, 3 (London: Heinemann, 1914).

du Chailu, Paul B., *The Viking Age: The Early History, Manners, and Customs of the Ancestors of the English-Speaking Nations*. 2 vols (New York: AMS Press, 1970; rpt from 1889).

Ellis Davidson, Hilda, *Gods and Myths of Northern Europe* (Harmondsworth: Penguin Books, 1990).

Ellis Davidson, Hilda, *Pagan Scandinavia* (London: Thames and Hudson, 1967).

Ellis Davidson, Hilda, *The Viking Road to Byzantium* (London: George Allen and Unwin, 1976)

Ellis Davidson, Hilda, ed., and Peter Fisher, trans., *Saxo Grammaticus: The History of the Danes, Books I–IX* (Cambridge: D.S. Brewer, 1996).

Farrell, R.T., ed., *The Vikings* (London and Chichester: Phillimore, 1982).

Faulkes, Anthony, ed. and trans., *Snorri Sturluson: Edda* (London: J.M. Dent, 1995).

Fell, Christine, Peter Foote, James Graham-Campbell, Robert Thomson, eds, *The Viking Age in the Isle of Man* (Gloucester: Alan Sutton Publishing Ltd: Viking Society for Northern Research, University College London, 1983).

Gibson, Michael, *The Vikings* (London: Wayland Documentary History Series, 1972).

Giles, J.A., trans., *Roger of Wendover's Flowers of History*. 2 vols (London: Henry G. Bohn, 1849).

Graham-Campbell, James and Colleen E. Batey, *Vikings in Scotland: An Archaeological Survey* (Edinburgh: Edinburgh University Press, 1988).

Graham-Campbell, James, Richard Hall, Judith Jesch and David N. Parsons, eds, *Vikings and the Danelaw: Select Papers from the Proceedings of the Thirteenth Viking Congress, Nottingham and York, 21–30 August 1997* (Oxford: Oxbow Books, 2001).

Griffith, Paddy, *The Viking Art of War* (London: Greenhill Books, 1995).

Hadley, D.M., *The Northern Danelaw: Its Social Structure, c. 800–1100* (London and New York: Leicester University Press, 2000).

Hall, Richard, *Viking Age York* (London: B.T. Batsford and English Heritage, 1994).

Hamer, Richard, *A Choice of Anglo-Saxon Verse* (London and Boston: Faber and Faber, 1970).

Harrison, Mark, *Viking Warrior* (Oxford: Osprey Publishing, 1993).

Haywood, John, *Encyclopedia of the Viking Age* (London: Thames and Hudson, 2000).

Haywood, John, *The Penguin Historical Atlas of the Vikings* (Harmondsworth: Penguin Books, 1995).

Helle, Knut, ed., *The Cambridge History of Scandinavia*, i, *Prehistory to 1520* (Cambridge: Cambridge University Press, 2003).

Herlihy, David, ed., *The History of Feudalism* (London: Macmillan, 1970).

Hines, John, Alan Lane and Mark Redknap, *Land, Sea and Home. Proceedings of a Conference on Viking-Period Settlement at Cardiff, July 2001* (Leeds: Maney Publishing, 2004).

Hollander, Lee M., trans., *Snorri Sturluson: Heimskringla. History of the Kings of Norway* (Austin: University of Texas, 1964).

Holtzmann, R., ed., *Theitmar of Merseburg: Merseburgensis Episcopi Chronicon* (Berlin: SSRG, 1935).

Howard, Ian, *Swein Forkbeard's Invasions and the Conquest of England, 991–1017* (Woodbridge: The Boydell Press, 2003).

Jenkins, R.J.H., trans., *Constantine VII Porphyrogenitus: De administrando imperio*. Dumbarton Oaks Texts, 1 (Washington: 1967).

Jesch, Judith, ed., *The Scandinavians from the Vendel Period to the Tenth Century: An Ethnographic Perspective* (Woodbridge: The Boydell Press, 2002).

Jesch, Judith, *Women in the Viking Age* (Woodbridge: The Boydell Press, 1991).

Jóhanesson, Jón, *A History of the Old Icelandic Commonwealth*, trans. Haraldur Bessason (University of Manitoba Press, 1974).

Jones, Gwyn, *A History of the Vikings* (revised edn, Oxford and New York: Oxford University Press, 1984).

Jones, Gwyn, *The Norse Atlantic Saga: Being the Norse Voyages of Discovery and Settlement to Iceland, Greenland, America* (London: Oxford University Press, 1964).

Keynes, S.D., and M. Lapidge, *Alfred the Great: Asser's Life of King Alfred and Other Contemporary Sources* (Harmondsworth: Penguin Books, 1983).

Larrington, Carolyne, trans., *The Poetic Edda* (Oxford and New York: Oxford University Press, 1996).

Larsen, Anne-Christine, ed., *The Vikings in Ireland* (Århus: The Viking Ship Museum, 2001).

Logan, F. Donald, *The Vikings in History* (London and New York: Routledge, 1991).

Mac Airt, Seán, and Gearóid Mac Niocaill, eds, *The Annals of Ulster (to AD 1131)*, i, *Text and Translation* (Dublin Institute for Advanced Studies, 1983).

Macartney, C.A., *The Magyars in the Ninth Century* (Cambridge University Press, 1930; reprinted 1978).

Magnusson, Magnus and Hermann Pálsson, trans., *Njal's Saga* (Harmondsworth: Penguin, 1970).

Mango, Cyril, trans., *The Homilies of Photius, Patriarch of Constantinople.*
  Dumbarton Oaks Studies, 3 (Cambridge, Massachusetts: 1958).
Marsden, John, *The Fury of the Northmen: Saints, Shrines and Sea-Raiders in
  the Viking Age, AD 793–878* (London: Kyle Cathie, 1994).
McDonough, Christopher J., ed. and trans., *Warner of Rouen: Moriuht. A
  Norman Latin Poem from the Early Eleventh Century* (Toronto: Pontifical
  Institute of Mediaeval Studies, 1995).
McDougall, David and Ian McDougall, ed. and trans., *Theodoricus Monachus:
  historia de antiquitate regum Norwagiensium. An Account of the Ancient
  History of the Norwegian Kings* (Viking Society for Northern Research,
  University College London, 1998).
McTurk, Rory, review of Donald Scragg, ed., *The Battle of Maldon, AD 991*
  (Oxford and Cambridge, Massachusetts: Blackwell, 1991), in *Saga-Book*, 23,
  5 (1992).
Nelson, Janet L., trans., *The Annals of St-Bertin*. Ninth-Century Histories
  (Manchester and New York: Manchester University Press, 1991).
Niles, John D and Mark Amodio, eds, *Anglo-Scandinavian England:
  Norse-English Relations in the Period before the Conquest* (Lanham, New
  York and London: University Press of America, 1989).
Norwich, John Julius, *Byzantium: The Apogee* (London and New York:
  Penguin Books, 1993).
Ólason, Vésteinn, *Dialogues with the Viking Age: Narration and Representation
  in the Sagas of Icelanders*, translated by Andrew Wawn (Reykjavík:
  Heimskringla, 1998).
Pálsson, Hermann and Paul Edwards, trans., *Eyrbyggja Saga*
  (Harmondsworth: Penguin Books, 1989).
Pálsson, Hermann and Paul Edward, trans., *Göngu-Hrolfs Saga* (Edinburgh:
  Canongate, 1980).
Pálsson, Hermann and Paul Edwards, trans., *Orkneyinga Saga: The History of
  the Earls of Orkney* (Harmondsworth: Penguin, 1981).
Pálsson, Hermann and Paul Edwards, trans., *Vikings in Russia: Yngvar's Saga
  and Eymund's Saga* (Edinburgh: Polygon, 1990).
Peirce, Ian G., *Swords of the Viking Age* (Woodbridge: The Boydell Press, 2002).
Poertner, Rudolf, *The Vikings: Rise and Fall of the Norse Sea Kings* (London:
  St James Press, 1975).
Price, Neil S., *The Vikings in Brittany*, Viking Society for Northern Research
  (University College London, 1989).
Pulsiano, Phillip, ed., *Medieval Scandinavia: An Encyclopedia* (New York and
  London: Garland Publishing, 1993).
Reuter, Timothy, trans., *The Annals of Fulda*. Ninth-Century Histories
  (Manchester and New York: Manchester University Press, 1992).

Richards, Julian D., *Viking Age England* (Stroud: Tempus, 2000).

Rink, Henrik, trans., *Tales and Traditions of the Eskimos* (London: C. Hurst, 1974).

Ritchie, Anna, *Viking Scotland* (London: B.T. Batsford, 1993).

Robinson, C.H., trans., *Rimbert: Anskar the Apostle of the North, 801–65* (London: Lives of the Early Missionaries, 1931).

Roesdahl, Else, *The Vikings* (Harmondsworth: Penguin Books, 1987).

Rumble, Alexander R., *The Reign of Cnut, King of England, Denmark and Norway* (London and New York: Leicester University Press, 1994).

Sawyer, Birgit and Peter Sawyer, *Medieval Scandinavia: From Conversion to Reformation, circa 800–1500* (Minneapolis and London: University of Minnesota Press, 1993).

Sawyer, P.H., *Kings and Vikings: Scandinavia and Europe, AD 700–1100* (London and New York: Routledge, 1989).

Sawyer, P.H., *The Age of the Vikings* (2nd edn, London: Edward Arnold, 1971).

Sawyer, Peter, ed., *The Oxford Illustrated History of the Vikings* (Oxford and New York: Oxford University Press, 1997).

Scholz, Bernhard Walter, trans., *Carolingian Chronicles: Royal Frankish Annals and Nithard's Histories* (Ann Arbor, University of Michigan Press, 1970).

Siddorn, J. Kim, *Viking Weapons and Warfare* (Stroud: Tempus; and Charleson, SC: Arcadia, 2000).

Simpson, Jacqueline, *Everyday Life in the Viking Age* (London: B.T. Batsford; New York: G.P. Putnam, 1967).

Smyser, H.M., trans., 'Ibn Fadlan's Account of the Rus with Some Commentary and Some Allusions to *Beowulf*', in J. B. Bessinger and R. P. Creed, eds, *Medieval and Linguistic Studies in Honour of Francis Peabody Magoun Jr* (London: Allen and Unwin, 1965).

Smyth, Alfred P., *King Alfred the Great* (Oxford: Oxford University Press, 1995).

Smyth, Alfred P., *Scandinavian Kings in the British Isles, 850–880* (Oxford University Press, 1977).

Smyth, Alfred P., *Scandinavian York and Dublin: The History and Archaeology of Two Related Viking Kingdoms* (Dublin: Irish Academic Press, 1987).

Stefánsson, Jón, "The Vikings in Spain: From Arabic (Moorish) and Spanish Sources', in *Saga-Book of the Viking Club*, Society for Northern Research, 4 (London: Curtis and Beamish, 1908–9).

Stenton, F.M., *Anglo-Saxon England* (3rd edn, Oxford: Oxford University Press, 1971).

Stevenson, Joseph, *The Church Historians of England*, iii, pt 2, *The Historical Works of Simeon of Durham* (London: Seeleys, 1855).

Swanton, Michael, ed. and trans., *The Anglo-Saxon Chronicles* (London: Phoenix Press, 2000).

Thorsson, Örnólfr, ed., *The Sagas of the Icelanders: A Selection* (Harmondsworth and New York: Allen Lane, 2000).

Tierney, J.J., ed and trans., *Dicuili: Liber de Mensura Orbis Terrae* (Dublin: The Dublin Institute for Advanced Studies, 1967).

Todd, J.H., trans., *The War of the Gaedhil with the Gaill* (London: Longmans, Green, Reader and Dyer, 1867).

Tschan, Francis J., trans., *Adam of Bremen, History of the Archbishops of Hamburg-Bremen* (New York: Columbia University Press, 1959).

Wahlgren, Erik, *The Vikings and America* (London: Thames and Hudson, 1986).

Wallace-Hadrill, J.M., *The Vikings in Francia* (University of Reading, 1975).

Wawn, Andrew, and Þórunn Sigurðardóttir, eds, *Approaches to Vínland: Proceedings of Conference at the Nordic House, Reykjavík, 9–11 August, 1999* (Reykjavík: Sigurður Nordal Institute, 2001).

Wilson, David M., *The Vikings and their Origins: Scandinavia and the First Millennium* (London: Thames and Hudson, 1970).

Wormald, C. Patrick, 'Viking Studies: Whence and Whither?', in R.T. Farrell, ed., *The Vikings* (London and Chichester: Phillimore, 1982).

Wright, F.A., trans., *The Works of Liudprand of Cremona* (London: 1930).

Vernadsky, George, *Kievan Russia* (New Haven and London: Yale University Press, 1948).

# Index